THE ANNOTATED MIXTAPE

ALSO BY JOSHUA HARMON

Quinnehtukqut
Scape
Le Spleen de Poughkeepsie
History of Cold Seasons

THE ANNOTATED MIXTAPE

JOSHUA HARMON

Dzanc Books
5220 Dexter Ann Arbor Road
Ann Arbor, MI 48103
dzancbooks.org

ISBN 978-1-936873-24-1
Cover design by Steven Seighman
Cover photograph by James Gehrt

Grateful acknowledgment is made to the publications in which these essays were originally published, sometimes in slightly different form: *AGNI, The Believer, Black Warrior Review, Cincinnati Review, Cloud Rodeo, Coldfront, DIAGRAM, Five Points, Florida Review, Gulf Coast, Hobart, MAKE, New England Review, New England Review Digital, The Normal School, Open Letters Monthly, Quarterly West, The Rumpus,* and *Salt Hill.*

The author is especially grateful to Carolyn Kuebler, Stephen Donadio, and Katy Henriksen for publishing many of these essays, and for editorial advice that has improved them immeasurably.

Library of Congress Cataloging-in-Publication Data

Harmon, Joshua, 1971–
The annotated mixtape / Joshua Harmon. — First edition.
pages cm
ISBN 978-1-936873-24-1 (pbk.)
1. Harmon, Joshua, 1971– —Knowledge—Music. 2. Sound recordings—Collectors and collecting—Biography. 3. Music—Biography. I. Title.
PS3608.A7485Z46 2014
814'.6–dc23
[B]
2014037078

Printed in the United States of America
FIRST EDITION

To my parents, for my first stereo; to Sue and Steve Price, for early lessons in listening; to Ben Reid, Mikey Thaller, Will Pritchard, Hua Hsu, and Jed Mayer, for the mutual enabling; and to Sarah Goldstein, for her patience—

CONTENTS

But if I hear a tune with understanding, doesn't something special go on in me—which does not go on if I hear it without understanding? And *what?*

—Ludwig Wittgenstein, *Zettel*
(translated by G.E.M. Anscombe)

What the gramophone listener actually wants to hear is himself, and the artist merely offers him a substitute for the sounding image of his own person, which he would like to safeguard as a possession. The only reason that he accords the record such value is because he himself could also be just as well preserved. Most of the time records are virtual photographs of their owners, flattering photographs—ideologies.

—Theodor Adorno, *Essays on Music*
(translated by Thomas Y. Levin)

C-90

"I'd give anything to know whether she likes me for my personality or for my comic-book collection," Charlie Brown broods in a thought bubble above the bubble of his own oversized head. Because I have more than four thousand vinyl records in my living room, I understand well this sort of nagging introspection. Charles Schulz sketched the panel in 1953, but the intricate, implicated relationships we have with our possessions continue to generate such age-old questions, and such unanswerable ones.

Do I like myself—do I want to be liked—for my personality, or for my record collection? Or: does she like me—do I want her to like me—for my personality, or for my record collection? Are such collections—and attendant anxieties about being liked—purely the province of those who, like Charlie Brown, remain fixed at a particular age, who refuse in some way to mature? Or, worse:

amid a burgeoning body of literature in which every possible cultural artifact or phenomenon appears as an aide-mémoire, who wants to be the dude staying up too late, rattling his keyboard to describe the fundamental effect some crappy pop song had on his teenage self-understanding?

Still, Charlie Brown—and Charles Schulz—might be disappointed to learn that few music fans continue to collect in the way that word has usually been understood. For well over a decade, our music has existed primarily in digital form on our hard drives. More recently, a number of on-demand, cloud-based services have revised the meaning of—or the need for—even incorporeal collections, and rendered the act of listening simply a question of bandwidth. Music has become so readily accessible that we have little need to store it, or even to own it: whenever we want to hear a particular song, we can almost always satisfy that urge, no matter how obscure the music, via some online stream in no more time than it takes to type a title—or even less time, with auto-complete. For listeners who grew up after the file-sharing era began—and for listeners for whom music functions as background noise, something to accompany other, more primary activities—this situation is unremarkable. For many decades, music has entered our homes and our cars via the airwaves. But I have been a record collector ever since the day in 1982 when I pedaled my ten-speed to some long-gone record store in Tatnuck Square, handed over a few damp, crumpled bills for a shrinkwrapped copy of Duran Duran's *Rio* LP, and then, in the privacy of my bedroom, felt moved as much by the music as the blurry nighttime cityscape on the back cover, or what seemed the weird poetry of the lyrics printed on the inner sleeve ("Must be lucky weather when you find the kind of wind that you need"). My ever-evolving record collection still often feels like a reference to my personality, or vice versa, and the collection's physical bulk sometimes seems reassuring evidence of my history.

In any case, those of us who do still collect music might more accurately be said to select: we don't—most of us—collect *anything*; collecting *everything* is impossible, short of a Smithsonian-sized space, budget, and mission. No, we collect in part to preserve and recall—and exclude—small memories, I might argue: the record an ex-girlfriend or -boyfriend owned, the song that was playing when..., the LP I should have (and so easily *could* have) bought five or fifteen years ago because..., and so on. If we didn't desire to relive chosen bits of our lives via music, we wouldn't bother stockpiling recordings. We wouldn't need to: we'd simply let our endless soundstreams' random, present-tense moments stir whatever feelings and associations they might. In an age when the imperative *share* appears throughout our cross-networked social media apps, owning music—or letting it own us—seems almost deliberately perverse.

▶

During high school, my friends and I saw swapping music as a type of homework far more important than geometric proofs and term papers about *The Merchant of Venice*. Our medium was the ninety-minute cassette—"C-90," in industry parlance—often re-recorded so many times the tape warbled. Our bedroom stereos allowed us the privacy for intense, studious retreat, and we filtered our lives into sequences of songs to match our moods. In an unconscious erotics of analog machinery, I'd finger the buttons on my tapedeck, rewinding and pausing; lightly touch stylus to spinning vinyl; then press play + record to try to fill every millimeter of tape with sound, cramming the end of a side with short songs and hoping the last song's fadeout didn't run onto the leader tape. I'd always crank up the line-level adjustment to flirt with 0 dB—where the bars turned from blue to red—so that the mixtapes I made sounded as loud as possible when played back.

While burning a CD or uploading a playlist takes no more than a moment, making tapes devoured more than real time. A ninety-minute cassette involved hours of effort: gathering the chosen records, determining a sequence, dubbing each song to tape, re-recording mistakes, erasing a few songs when the order seemed wrong, writing out the tracklist, and drawing or collaging cover art. "*Making* tapes," we called this activity, to emphasize the personally constructed, labor-intensive process: the cassettes we used may have been shoddy, mass-produced throwaways, but our attention and care transformed each one into something singular—and, of course, we found pleasure in the production as much as in giving each other the tapes. And while certain music apps will publicize your listening choices from your home computer to the newsfeeds of your nine hundred friends, mixtapes were made, and usually listened to, in private: no one could mock your music, or add a comment that they loved a song, too. The mixtape was an intimate, one-off object, made by one person for a very specific audience of one other person, and the burden of figuring out a band or a song—never mind the possible significance behind the gift—was yours alone.

Our high school mixtapes were educational—as much as that word applies to the mutually uninformed—especially since few of us in my provincial city knew much about the bands whose records we bought, beyond what we could deduce from LP covers and liner notes, record-store-guy lore, outdated issues of *NME* or *The Catalogue,* a barely caught MTV News update, or someone's brother's Xeroxed 'zine. For that reason—and others having mostly to do with teenage buying power and the drinking age at the clubs where bands played—chronology wasn't crucial; in a sense, everything we heard seemed new, everything coexisted, and our mixtapes reflected that fact. We were enthusiasts, not experts. Wildly dissimilar bands suffered each other's presences on the same ribbons of tape because our tastes were less exclusive than accommodating as we taught ourselves and each other what we liked. The principles of our selections were rarely powered by a thesis more particular than *I want you to hear this*—or, at times, *I want you to know that I know more obscure music than you do.* But when we made mixtapes out of our romantic yearnings, then our selections were informed by the infinite variations of desire.

More than our other tentative gestures at sartorial, political, and philosophical deviation, these cassettes we compiled reassured us that our evolving tastes were worth remarking (and celebrating), and helped convince us, rightly or wrongly, of our difference from the other kids we knew. We tested ourselves through music, since the tests we took in school offered only rote reminders that we were being socialized—even if we didn't always recognize it—for lives of nine-to-five drudgery. The music that mattered most was the music that evaded our expectations, that came to us not from WAAF's "Top Five at Five" or MTV's rotation but from a shopworn import LP with a strange cover in one of the bins at Al Bum's. When our music seemed to question cultural forces that indicated the limits of decorum or beauty or value, of course we started doing the same. (At sixteen, I thought John Lydon sounded bracing as he ranted, "Fat pig priest / Sanctimonious smiles / He takes the money / You take the lies!" Now, not so much.)

▸

I made my earliest home recordings live, direct-to-tape. In a ritual common to my generation, but which now must seem unfathomably absurd to anyone under the age of thirty, I'd press my portable cassette recorder to the speaker of a portable radio and record the songs the DJ played. While some friends captured huge swaths of a DJ's set, letting the tape run until it was full, I preferred to edit, waiting patiently for a specific song, then hurriedly pressing buttons and hoping the DJ didn't talk over too much of the song's introduction or fade its ending into another song's beginning—especially one I didn't like, since that combination would become part of my own version of the song, in the same way, hearing a song today that someone once recorded for me on a mixtape, I also hear ghost sequences of the songs that followed it. Fidelity was irrelevant, given the fuzziness of the FM signal and the cheapness of my recording devices: what mattered to me as I taped music from the airwaves was what I might learn from these songs I preserved—about music as pop-cultural entry point and schoolyard currency, and about myself as auditor.

On a shelf in my closet, along with other vestiges of former lives, I still keep several shrinkwrapped Maxell cassette tapes that I've held onto through at least six moves. In 2003, I bought a CD-R recorder and connected it to my stereo system—and while it coexisted with my old tapedeck for a while, I eventually ran out of rack space, boxed up the tapedeck, and carried it down to the basement. I used to buy cassettes in ten-pack bricks for convenience, since I'd routinely send friends several mixtapes at a time: these last reminders of my taping days seem too valuable simply to throw away.

For a few years, my friend Will and I allowed media self-consciousness to creep into our tape-swapping, wondering aloud which tape we made for the other would be the last. On November 20, 2001 (I delete old e-mail as often as I throw away old cassettes), a message from Will notes the arrival of my latest "tapes...[which] will provide the soundtrack for our drive to and from the San Juans over the holiday," but continues in a more ominous vein: "And I am working on a CD for you." By February of 2002, Will referenced his "CD-R[,]... a Philips. It hasn't gotten much use this year, partly because it was malfunctioning, and partly because my G4 at work has a CD burner in it. The iTunes software makes it pretty fun and easy to design and burn CDs. The problem is, you have to get the music *into* the computer first." In 2004, Will gave me *Mix Tape: The Art of Cassette Culture,* an anthology of various musicians' ruminations on mixtapes come and gone, with reproductions of doodled-on J-cards listing hipster songs of the 1970s and '80s, though at that point the gift was, like the anthology itself, mostly an act of nostalgia. When Will came to visit me a few years ago, he brought his laptop and ripped a stack of my CDs into his own iTunes library. A few weeks later he wrote to say how much he was enjoying some of the songs, as if I'd had anything to do with his enjoyment.

▶

For years after high school, I continued to make mixtapes: for friends, for potential (or actual) girlfriends, for people I'd just met, and sometimes for myself; later, for strangers with whom I exchanged tapes in the mail, or for a few of my students. I jotted possible tracklists on scraps of paper or in notebooks the same way I jotted down ideas for stories or poems. A half-unspooled mixtape might stay in my tapedeck for weeks while I finished it. I don't mean to romanticize this sort of activity—I didn't romanticize it then; it was simply habit. Then one day I connected a CD recorder to my stereo and started digitizing my vinyl; I began using iTunes; no one had tapedecks anymore, or had one only in an older car until that, too, was replaced. For a while, I made CD mixes, if without the same ardor, but at a certain point I just started e-mailing friends a bunch of links to YouTube videos.

Recently I received news of the unexpected and much-too-young death of a friend I hadn't seen in the twenty years since high school graduation: we'd met in homeroom on the first day of junior high, and for much of that year carried on an argument involving the merits of the Beatles—he in favor, I opposed. Later, our tastes converged on post-punk and hardcore. I recalled—correctly, it turned out—that this friend had properly used semi-colons when he'd inscribed my high school yearbook, and I felt the need to reread what he'd written, which, I discovered, included this clause: "thanks for making tapes." I couldn't help flipping other pages. "That Joy Division tape you made me," another old friend had noted, "is starting to grow on me."

▶

When I was seventeen, my grandmother mailed me a card in which she'd enclosed a $50 gift certificate to Rockit Records in Nashua, New Hampshire, where she lived. Every time we went to her house, I'd pester my mom to take me to Rockit on our drive back. On the card, my grandmother had written, simply, "Come see me, too." That last word shamed me then, and shames me now: did I need such a reminder to visit her as well as Rockit's superb selection of UK imports? Did she see herself as mere afterthought to my real passion? I'm similarly shamed to note that I still remember specific records I bought in that store—the *U2 Three* 12"; *Chairs Missing*—more than I remember specific visits with her from that time. But even if the often-mopey music I listened to then had trained me to see myself as overlooked and insignificant, I'm no longer surprised that my grandmother had noticed how important music was to me: I'm not sure I ever entered her house without hearing the radio playing from her enormous walnut console stereo.

My grandmother sent the card not long after I'd acquired my

own car, which had previously been hers. Although records then seemed the primary way I might make sense of the world, or make the world more bearable, they taught me little about how to treat the people I knew. Still, I treasured my grandmother's gift—the knowledge that she deemed me interesting enough to come see her by myself: *she* liked me for my personality, and my record collection had no bearing on her opinion of me—even if my records were, then, increasingly how I defined myself.

THE RECORDS

I met my mailman, Barney, an affable fellow with white hair and tinted glasses, the day I moved into my rental house in Rhode Island, May 2001. He stopped his USPS Jeep beside the twenty-foot Penske truck that my wife, Sarah, and I had rented, and leaned out the window to shake our hands and pass us some mail that had already found us here. He drove away and I wiped sweat from my face with my shirtsleeve. Our friend Will had brought a dozen donuts and a gallon of water and come to help Sarah and me unload the truck. By the time Barney arrived, we'd been moving furniture and boxes from their piles in the truck to new piles in the house for an hour or two; we'd worked our way to the front of the trailer, where, the previous afternoon, in Pennsylvania, we'd stacked all the heaviest boxes—most of which were either boxes of books or boxes of LPs, with a few boxes of CDs mixed in.

"How many more boxes of books?" Will gasped, and I remembered him telling me, months earlier, about a comment a hired mover had once made to him: "I hate moving smart people." Sitting in front of the box fan we'd plugged in, swigging water from the plastic jug, I wondered how the mover would have felt about moving music-obsessed people.

I talked to Barney many times after that first afternoon. Because we then lived on a rural route, Barney drove down our road, stopping only to reach out to slip mail in mailboxes, collect outgoing envelopes, and lower red metal flags. But since a large percentage of the mail I received didn't fit inside my box, Barney instead leaned on his horn for a good three seconds as he approached my box. The first time he did this, I opened the front door to see what was going on outside, and he waved me over. "I've got a package for you," he said, handing me a few envelopes along with a cardboard LP mailer. I quickly learned that a blast from Barney's horn was intended—despite the neighbors—only for me, and he quickly learned my addiction: "You're a record collector, eh?" he asked about the third or fourth time he handed me a box of records. "Yeah. How'd you guess?" I answered, lamely.

But Barney and I never had much to say to each other, mostly because I often felt somewhat ashamed when I saw him—ashamed that I was almost always home when he arrived with the mail; ashamed that he served as witness to and bearer of my consumption, which otherwise would have been largely inconspicuous. When I wasn't home to fetch my packages, Barney—a veteran with a slow gait—had to climb out of the truck and leave them by my door, and that too shamed me.

I felt an odd codependency with Barney in these facts: that I worried about what my mailman thought as he delivered my mail, and that I believed he might actually be thinking about me and my mail rather than last night's Red Sox game or what he'd eat for lunch or an itch on his heel; that I wondered if he were angry about having to deliver—even though his job required it—so many packages to my door, and also wondered whether I should feel guilty about this potential anger; and that I envisioned that, because of his horn-blowing, my neighbors peered from behind curtains, shaking their heads or clucking their tongues as I walked out to Barney's truck to receive my near-daily ration of records.

As for my addiction, I received a credit card bill that summer tallying one month's reckless spending: of the $846.39 total, over 70 percent went toward record purchases. I mention this figure—which is, let me hasten to add, not at all typical—not so that you may share the shock I felt, or feel the same disapproval I imagined my neighbors felt, but to illustrate this point: most of my transactions that summer involved one to four records at a time, at an average cost of probably $7 to $10 per record, and since they occurred over a thirty-day period, you get some idea of the number of packages Barney loaded into his truck, the number of times he had to beep me out of the house.

▶

It seemed appropriate that Will helped me carry all those boxes of LPs into my new house the day I met Barney. More than anyone else I know, Will suffers from the same affliction I do, or at least shows signs of having been afflicted, since his buying has slowed down. ("There's not much that I'm still looking for," he recently confessed.) His collection of rock, pop, new wave, soul, R&B, disco, country, jazz, folk, and other LPs still dwarfs mine. My binge record-buying may suggest my insecurity about the size of my own collection, my anxieties about losing touch with my own past, the pathetic comfort I find in material things, a frequent desire to escape "boredom," or all of the above. I've always, since preadolescence, bought a lot of records, but it's only become more excessive over the years. I can relate to the claim Tim Gane of the British band Stereolab once made to a BBC interviewer: "I've probably spent a year of my life in record shops and I don't think this much of an exaggeration. Since I was thirteen there has hardly been a week where I haven't bought a record."

Will once told me—circa 1999—that he thought my collection was the "right size," that he admired it—and by extension, perhaps, what he falsely imagined as my restraint—for still maintaining what he called "a semblance of control." But I exercise little control when Will and I shop together: we resemble two alcoholics on a bender, staggering from record store to record store, blinking at the daylight as we emerge from each one, and bearing increasing burdens as we go. An ex-girlfriend once told me, not long after we met, that she loved shopping for records but hated going to record stores with her friends, who sighed and rolled their eyes at how much time she spent browsing. (After perhaps the second or third time my ex-girlfriend and I went to a record store together, she sighed and rolled her eyes at how much time *I* spent browsing.) When Will and I shop, neither of us sighs or rolls his eyes. We don't speak much, but we do pull albums that the other might find interesting, given our somewhat different tastes in music. After an hour, one of us will linger by the door, studying taped-up flyers for shows at local teen centers and bands seeking drummers, pretending to be almost ready to leave, while the other one continues flipping through the last few unflipped bins. Soon whoever wanted to move on is searching again too—now, perhaps, inspecting the soundtracks section, or the exotica/lounge section, or even the unsorted, unalphabetized LPs below the regular bins—and it takes us a good ten or fifteen minutes of this back-and-forth before we're finally freed of the store's gravitational pull. In fact, looking at my credit card statement, I can retrace the steps Will and I took in and around Harvard Square one afternoon that summer—Other Music, In Your Ear, Planet Records, Mojo Music.

Will and I met in rural Pennsylvania at an isolated university that had hired us both as visiting professors. The only place to buy vinyl was the local flea market—lots of Herb Alpert and the Tijuana Brass, or *Sing Along with Mitch,* but not much else; still, I pawed through mildewy stacks of LPs most weekends, and did manage to spend some money: Walter Carlos's *Switched-On Bach,* the Byrds' *Turn! Turn! Turn!* in mono, an original pressing of Al Green's *Let's Stay Together.*

Despite my weakness for pop hooks, I've always let my vanity about my own singular tastes lead me toward the obscure—if obscurity, post-Google, post-YouTube, still means anything—so even when I've lived in towns with record stores, I've still bought much of my music through the mail. For a long time, this meant writing letters and sending an SASE to an independent record label's headquarters, which was also often someone's mom's house. In return, I'd receive a tiny, photocopied catalog—at most, a sheet of 8½ × 14-inch paper—often with only a dozen releases listed, no reproductions of cover art, and only the briefest descriptions of the music. I'll quote a 1992 TeenBeat catalog as an example: "EGGS 'Bruiser' CD: Eggs, America's new favorite indie-rock band, hit in the eye but still coming up with the goods. Some serious shit. Put a cold steak on it boys. Includes 'Spaceman' & a new recording of 'Ocelot.' CD $10." I'd write a list of the records I wanted—not always certain what prompted my desire, given the oblique descriptions—and send a check or some cash wrapped inside several sheets of paper. In all, it might take a month to get a few records.

Before the secure server's shopping cart standardized the transaction, mail order seemed to admit me into an appealing and esoteric community—a circle of strangers who, I felt, knew far more about music than I ever would: joining this community required at least the small effort of writing a note and buying a stamp. Although based on commerce, my exchanges with them seemed a strange blend of the intensely personal and the utterly anonymous. I never met the people who ran these labels—often members of the bands whose records I bought—but they became odd pen pals, my purchases of music a declaration of our shared passion. These curators of some musical sub-genre or other were also often college kids like me, and they scribbled goofy replies and enclosed pieces of candy with my records.

▸

I am walking, music spurring my steps: down snow-packed South Flagg Street late on a midwinter night, accompanied by Wire's "Outdoor Miner" on my Walkman; or following surf lapping the fogged-in beach at Eastham, Massachusetts, while listening to a taped copy of Section 25's *Always Now* LP; or stepping out of the Haymarket Café with a friend, both of us reciting one of Ann Magnuson's monologues from Bongwater's *The Power of Pussy*.

I learn of my grandfather's death at nearly the same time I've discovered R.E.M.'s brand-new "South Central Rain," linking the two forever. Another friend remarks, as I drive him around in my old Mercury Bobcat, that the song playing on the tape-deck—Throwing Muses' "And a She-Wolf After the War," one of my favorites at the time—is "soundtrack music." And though I don't realize it then, my friend is right: here is another song in the soundtrack to all the incidental memories that measure my life.

One afternoon, after a few hours of Nerf football with my friends on a practice field at the local state college, I walked into the student center for hot chocolate. I might have been twelve. I no longer recall whose idea this was, or how we knew we'd find hot chocolate inside, but remember my curiosity and my desire to make even the smallest claim on this territory so clearly not our own. As we entered that cavernous room—nearly empty at four o'clock on a weekday afternoon—I heard the Who's "Baba O'Riley" roaring from the speakers hanging among the exposed rafters and ductwork. At that moment, for whatever odd and muddled reasons—I'd heard the song before this—I felt the first inkling of what being a teenager might involve, might require of me, the first stirrings of adolescent self-consciousness. Or perhaps in that moment I foresaw that music would be my means of self-definition in adolescence, the thing that would see me safely through it.

All of this music seems inseparable from these recollections, or at least from certain moments; the records themselves seem almost the physical forms of memories, accessible by dropping a stylus onto grooved vinyl or tracing a disc's code with laser. I'd long since have forgotten such everyday insignificances, except for the fact that when I replay certain songs, my unconscious mind summons these constellations of associations.

But records can also sometimes inspire imaginary nostalgia, faked memories. Years ago, I knew someone who deliberately scuffed and scratched his brand-new copy of Echo and the Bunnymen's first LP in order to make it seem worn through years of playings, as if he'd been hip enough to have heard that group before they became popular. I doubt that anyone cared when this kid first heard Echo and the Bunnymen, and I doubt that anyone running a background check on his indie cred would have thought to study the condition of his vinyl. In any case, a true collector would never have damaged the record, but would have claimed that he kept it pristine through careful application of Discwasher every time he played it, that he took such loving care of it because of its importance to him.

▶

Speaking of Bongwater's *The Power of Pussy:* in 1994, I sold all of my Bongwater records to Main Street Records in Northampton, Massachusetts. The clerk, who moments before had been loudly discussing the Red Krayola with his co-worker, tried to persuade me not to do it. At the time, I probably smirked at his inferior musical tastes. Mine had advanced far beyond the world of Bongwater, a duo as antic and surreal as their *nom de musique* suggested. Whatever bands I was listening to in 1994 seemed to me incompatible with Bongwater; thus, I had to purge my collection.

Similar urges have befallen me over the years. Not long after the release of *The Joshua Tree,* I sold my entire U2 collection, some fifteen or twenty records, including their first few import singles, to a girl in my high school for $50. It took me only a half-dozen years to realize how serious an error this was, or for nostalgia to take effect—and though the two are not the same thing, I'll probably never be able to distinguish them. Records, as with any commodity traded, have wildly fluctuating values, both financially and emotionally. Now that I've realized this, after years of selling off records I thought I'd outgrown, my collection has become less exclusive—roomy enough, even, for some of the classic rock the kids in my high school argued over (that eternal ninth-grade debate: "Who's a better guitarist? Jimmy Page, Jimi Hendrix, or Eddie Van Halen?") and which for years I despised in comparison to the post-punk and new wave I grew up on. It took years before I could imagine owning a copy of the Rolling Stones' *Let It Bleed,* or *Led Zeppelin I.* But classic rock has a firm place in the soundtrack to my memories of childhood, and maybe I needed to reach a certain age before even those aspects of my childhood I would once have passed over as junk appeared valuable.

By graduate school, when I subsisted largely on Annie's Macaroni and Cheese, I sold off many older records which had, like U2 and Bongwater, come to seem obsolete given the directions my taste in music was taking. Old Factory Records singles, the first Chameleons LP, three of Sonic Youth's early LPs, the first 7″ by Codeine, and countless others all brought me the money to buy the then-new records by Broadcast, Fridge, Prefuse 73, and Novak. I doubt I'll again find certain of the old records I sold, but the prospect of not having bought, say, the debut album by Movietone seems equally preposterous—I cannot imagine my old apartment on Tompkins Street in Ithaca without simultaneously hearing, in my memory, the delicately finger-picked guitars and mumbled vocals of Movietone's "Late July." But if I see music as memory given physical and aural form, then the revision of my music collection must also be the revision of myself—as if certain albums represent aspects of me or my past I'd like to forget, or to retrieve. Since few people ever give more than a passing look to my record collection, the person most often casting judgment over these unwelcome remnants of my identity is me. To browse the racks of records in my living room reminds me of leafing through an old diary, albeit one from which I have torn certain pages, or tipped in new ones.

I could download "Miss Moonlight" by Stockholm Monsters—sold off during graduate school, the one record I'd most like to recover—or pay $61 for the 12″ single on eBay, as someone recently did, but listening to an MP3 of "Miss Moonlight" coming from my iBook's single speaker would not only sound terrible, but, as an experience, could never match sitting crosslegged on the floor before my stereo, holding the Cultural Revolution–inspired sleeve in my hand, and watching the record revolve on my Thorens turntable.

▶

I've always been a collector. In the early days my collections consisted of dinosaur books, Legos, and Star Wars action figures; other kids spent their allowances on candy bars, while I hoarded my money for a trip to the toy store. I don't know if my habit of collecting arose from a childhood where money was sometimes scarce, but until fairly recently I did consciously prefer to spend my money on actual objects rather than consumables—sometimes I'd even think of a four-dollar pint of beer as a four-dollar 7″ I could have bought instead, no matter how much fun I'd had at the bar. I began buying records and books at a young age, and to this day a persistent problem in my house is the need for a new bookcase or record bin.

Some of my best friends are compulsive collectors as well—not only Will and his records, but Mikey, who owns scores of vintage Catalin radios, many of which he has repaired (he built his own laboratory and taught himself how to make Catalin-replica plastics, in order to replace missing knobs and handles); or Andrew, who has amassed a near-museum of toys and dolls from the 1960s and '70s (his molded plastic figures of the Mamas and the Papas are my favorites); or Natalie, who combs flea markets and junk stores for old agricultural paraphernalia—photos of tractors, tin road signs, and the paper labels from vegetable and fruit crates; or Jordan, who collects antique photos and memorabilia of pit bulls. None of us has ever asked each other, as far as I know, *why* we collect whatever we collect—I think we all understand, even if we can't articulate a reason. It may be a simple comfort to us that there are other people we know whose homes and apartments are also turning into archives.

▶

Book collectors use a terminology of deterioration: closed tears, foxed endpapers, sunned or price-clipped dustjackets, soiled paper wraps, remainder marks, bumped corners. (Without getting too defensive about it, I'll point out that the *Oxford English Dictionary* contains an entry for bibliomania—"an extreme passion for collecting and possessing books"—but no corresponding entry for those who suffer an extreme passion for collecting and possessing records. Bibliophilia and bibliomania are sanctioned passions; a bibliophile is seen as a scholar, while a vinylphile is seen as indulging in an extended adolescence.) The argot of record collectors is similarly concerned with decay—split sleeves, skips and scratches, missing inserts, ringwear, spindle marks, paper scuffs, cutouts, and sticker tears, though the grading system for records is less standardized than that for books. (Although *Goldmine,* a long-running magazine for record collectors, has an "official" grading system, it's widely altered, misunderstood, or ignored.) Most sellers locate both vinyl and sleeve on a spectrum from M (mint) to P (poor), but exactly what constitutes an NM (near mint) or a VG++ (two increments better than very good) is a matter often left to approximation or opinion, as well as to the inflated economy for anything possibly collectible.

Such obsessive cataloging of and concern for the integrity—even sanctity—of the physical artifact seems a sort of nostalgia which seeks to recreate rather than simply recall the past. The object itself is most desirable when it is found in a condition most closely approximating its original state. Two Usenet newsgroups for vinyl collectors define mint condition in this way:

> A mint record should look like it has just left the manufacturer, with NO flaws whatsoever. It should look as though it had never been handled.... We should actually use the term PERFECT rather than the term MINT.... PERFECT is to say that man [*sic*] (who is not perfect) can produce a perfect item.

The real concern in buying used records, however, is not perfection. Relying on a bit of diamond dragged through a groove on a stamped vinyl platter to transmit sound is not a perfect method of sound reproduction; many of the new, sealed records I buy pop once or twice the first time I play them.

We can recall or imagine the past by playing a reissue of *The Velvet Underground and Nico.* But, despite finding a mint, original copy of this same LP today, we cannot recreate the experience of coming home from the record shop in 1967 to peel the banana sticker from the Warhol sleeve, or the experience of hearing the seven jagged, nihilistic minutes of "Heroin" in the context of "Incense and Peppermints," "Daydream Believer," or "I Think We're Alone Now," to cite a few of 1967's top forty hits—unless, that is, we owned the record in 1967 and already had those experiences. The search for the untouched, unsullied object—which, because of its perfection, has no human mark upon it, and thus no real history, no accompanying narrative—attempts to deny the passage of time, to wish oneself back to an earlier era, to impose one's own history on an object's blank slate. If the record is mint, one can pretend to have bought it when it was released—one can recreate one's past, reconstruct one's own identity, as the kid who scratched up his Echo and the Bunnymen LP attempted to do.

An LP from my own collection: crackling as it spins, its vinyl scuffed because, over the years, I carelessly and repeatedly slid it in and out of its paper sleeve; the occasional hairs of my old dog or cat, both long dead, stuck to the grooves of a record I haven't played in a while; a sleeve split during one of my many moves—all of these remind me of my own history, the LP revealing them as conspicuously as rings on a tree trunk.

▸

As the steady stream of cardboard mailers addressed to me arrived in Barney's truck, I'd carefully slice them open with a Swiss Army knife. Maybe the mailer contained a few 7″s, an LP, and a CD. I might have played one of the records immediately, usually first choosing a 7″ because it was short and required the least initial investment of energy and attention.

I might also have gone to the kitchen to make a sandwich, or, even more likely, to sit in front of the computer to search for other records to buy. The records began to pile up. There was no longer enough room in the 12″ bins, so I leaned arriving LPs against one wall in a neat row. I stashed the new 7″s—which, until I'd given them a few listens, I didn't want to vanish into the long racks of other 7″s—in the space between the stereo stand and the nearest rack, and, when that space was filled, against the fronts of some racks. Some hundred or hundred and twenty records, many still unplayed, occupied various postures on the living room floor, and I came to recognize the dangers of combining an adult's income with an adolescent's self-control. (My wife's application for sainthood is pending.) I was buying music at such a rate—I continue buying it at such a rate—that I didn't have time to listen to it all, or to get well acquainted with what I did listen to, a situation that Jacques Attali notes in his 1977 book, *Noise: The Political Economy of Music:*

> Music remains a very unique commodity; to take on meaning, it requires an incompressible lapse of time, that of its own duration. Thus the gramophone, conceived as a recorder to stockpile time, became instead its principal user.... *People must devote their time to producing the means to buy recordings of other people's time,* losing in the process not only the use of their own time, but also the time required to use other people's time. Stockpiling then becomes a substitute, not a preliminary condition, for use. *People buy more records than they can listen to. They stockpile what they want to find the time to hear.*

Whenever I've determined that I want a record, I usually bend my will toward finding it; however, by the time it's found and in my house, I'm already searching for another half-dozen records which have, in the interim, come to seem even more necessary. In his essay "Finding," Guy Davenport, discussing his weekly hunts for Native American arrowheads with his father, describes the special skills of observation he developed, and the satisfaction he felt at using these skills to locate, for example, "the splendidest of tomahawks." He also notes that "once we had found our Indian things, we put them in a big box and rarely looked at them.... Our understanding was that the search was the thing, the pleasure of looking." Lately, I've realized, I don't listen to music as much as I'd like to because I spend so much time searching for it. The greater my collection becomes, the less intimate are my experiences with each record in it. David Shields records a similar phenomenon in one of the several essays titled "Desire" in his book *Remote:* a desired object "attained this one quality: it was outside my consciousness. The moment I held it, my mind experienced it, so I no longer wanted it."

In 1996, when I was a graduate student, Stereolab released a limited-edition, UK-tour-only, blue-vinyl split 7″ with the band Tortoise—both bands were then at the height of their collectability, and the record fetched upwards of $50 when it was offered for sale. I loved Stereolab, and owned nearly every one of their records, so obviously I needed this one as well. I attempted to buy the 7″ several times unsuccessfully—some other collector always outbidding me—until, after a few months, I finally tracked down a copy online at a small British shop for £25: a good deal, I believed (the exchange rate was more favorable then). I purchased an international money order from the post office, sent it overseas, and waited.

During the weeks since I'd first learned of the record's existence, I'd imagined everything about it—what its sleeve might look like, what the song would sound like, and so on. I'd read various comments—vague but laudatory, boastfully triumphant—posted to a fan website by the lucky few who owned copies. The Stereolab song was titled "Speedy Car," and even these words suggested distinct possibilities to me.

When the package finally turned up in my mailbox, I ran up to my third floor apartment and ripped it open. The copper-colored sleeve bore the close-up image of a signal-path schematic: even then, a trite and uninspired choice of artwork. The song, as I cued it and sat back on my Salvation Army couch to listen, featured some chimes, a repeating horn blat, a two-note keyboard riff, a measure of blurry bass notes, and contrapuntal vocals. I disliked it almost instantly. The production sounded congested and thin, and the music itself seemed to me a dead-end free-jazz experiment.

Maybe—after all my hoping and hunting and waiting—the record was doomed to disappoint my expectations. My desire for the record had increased in direct proportion to its elusiveness, but once I managed to consummate that desire, I saw how baseless it was. Buyer's remorse? No. Even today, "Speedy Car" is my least favorite song in Stereolab's vast catalog, and the 7″ worth far less, but the collector in me is still pleased to own the record.

Buying music, for me, almost always requires a certain leap of faith, and for years, even using a downloaded MP3 to help winnow my purchasing options seemed unsporting. The simple question—*will I like this?*—hangs over many of my purchases, and I can rarely answer it without first turning on the stereo. If I remove this element of uncertainty, I deny myself the opportunity to be pleasantly surprised—or astounded—by a record I've just bought.

In junior high and high school, I had limited funds for purchasing new music: my allowance, or, later, the earnings from my first few jobs, some of which also had to be earmarked toward car repairs, gas, coffee, and the other expenses of a teenage existence. If I had $10 to spend on an import LP at Al Bum's, and unwisely bought an album by the Bolshoi instead of one by the Razorcuts, well, that was my tough luck; I'd find out how tough only after the Razorcuts LP shortly went out of print while the Bolshoi's LP mocked me for years whenever I searched the bargain bins.

Still, such purchasing decisions—even though I later donated many albums to my younger sister or sold them back to Al Bum's at a loss—forced me to cohabit with certain records more than I otherwise might have, and more than I do now. Having invested in them, I was not content to play the one song I knew, but waded through the duds, toss-offs, experiments, and occasional moments of stupendous beauty. I know certain albums from early in my collecting career backward and forward, even after not playing them for years. I can't imagine what my collection would look like had I been able to endlessly sample music before deciding to commit to it; if I'd heard excerpts from A Certain Ratio's *To Each...* or Swell Maps' *A Trip to Marineville* before buying them, maybe I would never have opened my wallet, but then neither would I count these two LPs among my favorites.

▶

I sometimes feel depressed when I contemplate the amount of money represented by the racks of vinyl that occupy a large corner of the living room. It is terrible to feel in thrall to one's things, and yet I keep bringing things into the house, each one making me more fearful of some potential loss.

When I sold my "Miss Moonlight" 12″ in graduate school, the buyer was a man who'd once possessed every release from the influential British label Factory Records. I too had collected records from this label, if not to such an extent, and sold him a few that had come to seem dispensable. He told me he was trying to reassemble his collection, bit by bit, because his house had burned down, taking with it everything he owned. In the abstract, the idea horrified me, but until recently I think I failed to understand this idea in more than an abstract way. Now I wonder: was I conducting a fire sale of my own, selling off these scraps of my past, believing that I valued the object less than the memories it held for me? Or, if one has escaped such catastrophe, how and why do records still matter?

▶

An old friend once gave me a small, spine-cracked novelty book called *The IN and OUT Book*. Robert Benton and Harvey Schmidt, the book's authors, illustrate with copious examples the distinctions between "in" and "out" circa 1957:

> There are two kinds of people in this world: IN and OUT. A thing can be IN for three reasons: a. Because it is so classic and great. Example: the Plaza Hotel. b. Because it is so obscure. Example: Veda Ann Borg movies. c. Because it is so far OUT even the OUT people won't touch it. Example: Tchaikovsky. Some OUT people try to get IN by saying they like IN things but since OUT people can never be IN, they can only manage to ruin some good IN things. Everything that is not IN is OUT.

A detailed list follows this taxonomy. Many music collectors make similar classifications, in just as codified a way—and, as in *The IN and OUT Book,* the codes are always changing: to Benton's and Schmidt's assertion that "making your own preserves and jellies is going OUT fast (unless you live west of the Alleghenies)," or "It's OUT to own small individual Modern Library editions of *Remembrance of Things Past* but it's IN to own the big showy expensive edition," I might counter that owning the original vinyl LPs by My Bloody Valentine is IN, but saying you're still waiting for Kevin Shields, the band's chief songwriter, to finish their next album—famously delayed since 1992—is OUT. (This statement was IN c. 2001, when I originally wrote it, and was perhaps still tenuously IN in 2004, when this essay was first published, but after My Bloody Valentine's 2009 reunion tour, and the 2013 release of their *mbv* LP, it is indisputably OUT.)

Benton's and Schmidt's three-part definition of how a thing gets to be IN applies perfectly to music as well—which is cool because it's classic and great (*Odessey and Oracle, Forever Changes, Radio City,*

King Tubbys Meets Rockers Uptown, Marquee Moon, It Takes a Nation of Millions to Hold Us Back), cool because it's obscure (the Electric Eels, Little Ann, Naffi, Chrome, the Bush Tetras), cool because it's so uncool (the Shaggs, the Beau Brummels, Esquivel, the Cure). And because everything's IN status is constantly in flux, a patient record collector can do well either by buying duplicates of records about to become IN in order to trade them for other rare records, or by waiting until a good record is OUT before buying it.

But such speculation is difficult. Over the years I've foolishly ignored all manner of music, much of which many people raved about, because of some misguided principle, a reluctance to try to hear the band's music through the noise of hype, or a song that misrepresented the band's larger oeuvre: the Pixies' album *Doolittle,* which I deemed too commercial upon its release (OUT); the noisy pop from New Zealand's incestuous music scene, which for years I couldn't be bothered to untangle (so IN that it was OUT); the post-1987-or-so releases by Sonic Youth (ruined by OUT people trying to be IN).

Also, in retrospect, some bands seem to have gained importance—in my own musical landscape as well as in the wider world—so that while I originally passed on buying their work, now I feel it should find a place in my collection on the basis of how classic and great it has turned out to be. Am I OUT if I base my purchases on external forces, or am I trying too hard to be IN if I refuse to buy a band's older records simply because they've become more popular in the interim?

As *The IN and OUT Book* demonstrates—as does Pierre Bourdieu's *Distinction,* in a slightly more elaborate manner—possessions and culture become mere proxies for our identities. My belief that my record collection will reveal aspects of my personality to others reveals more about me than the records themselves ever could.

▶

Listening to music is by nature a fleeting, temporal experience, which we cannot simultaneously suspend and hear, the way we can isolate a single frame from a film on a VCR, or stare at a painting or a sentence in a book as long as we like—and even though the record is a way to recreate that experience endlessly (as I memorably discovered at a young age, playing "I Get Around" from one of my mother's old Beach Boys records over and over, lifting the needle only to cue the song again, until, her voice tinged with hysteria, she screamed down the stairs for me to stop), pressing the pause button on a CD player brings us only silence, not a single sustained note.

Though I enjoy returning to the pages of certain books, I usually reread magazines only if I want to teach an article from one of them; too few films reward multiple viewings. Music is the only form of popular art which we tend to replay over and over—at least until we've "worn out" a song or an album. Is this because music is inherently nostalgic, or because its pleasure is so elusive, so transient, that we try to capture it through repetition?

▶

Late in 2001, I mailed Will a draft of this essay, along with two tapes I'd made for him. He responded, in part:

> Your self-diagnosis made me aware of the ways in which my "affliction" differs from yours. For one thing, I have always been cheap. Lots of my records were purchased because they cost less than other records which I actually wanted more.... Of course, I do recognize many of the symptoms you identify: buying music and failing to listen to it, fusing music with events contemporaneous with its purchase (e.g., Steely Dan's *Katy Lied* and the 1986 ALCS), selling and later regretting having sold, shopping with impatient women, the pleasure of "finding." One thing you didn't mention...is the excruciating moment at which one has "found" too many LPs or CDs and has to put a few back before proceeding to checkout. For me, that moment of self-denial is important to my sense of myself as someone who is Not Out Of Control.

One morning when I was fifteen years old, my friend Ben and I skipped school to catch an early Boston-bound Peter Pan bus. Once there, I gladly squandered my pocketful of cash at the record stores in the Back Bay and Kenmore Square. We snarfled an ice-cream lunch at Emack and Bolio's on Newbury Street before we decided, sometime in midafternoon, that it was time to head home. We took the T to South Station and walked into the bus terminal, only to discover that between us remained six of the ten or eleven dollars necessary for our return fares.

At this time the ATM was not the ubiquitous part of the landscape it has since become, and neither of us had bank cards anyway. We went into a vast marble bank lobby, thinking perhaps that we could withdraw money from the savings accounts we both had, failing to understand that having money in one bank does not mean that the money is accessible at another. The bank building we walked into was a large corporate office, not a branch, and a receptionist—likely noticing our skulking, uncertain, adolescent presences—asked us what we needed.

"Is there any way we can take out money from our accounts here, even if this isn't our bank?" we blurted. When she realized that we needed four dollars to get home, she opened her purse and handed us a few bills from her own wallet. She refused to give us her name so that we could repay her later.

If it's ever been important to me to see myself as in control of my record-buying habits, the memory of this day makes me think otherwise. To be sure, the moment Will describes is "excruciating," but what I've found even more excruciating over the years is to have held a record in my hands and then decided to put it back—perhaps thinking that I'll return and buy it in a day or two—only to find, on returning, that it's vanished from the bins. According to the Vinyl Tourist website, "It's axiomatic that the only purchase you'll ever regret is the one you didn't make when the opportunity presented itself."

▶

Some years back, while searching the messages posted to a vinyl-collecting forum, I discovered the following definition:

> Vinyl Junkie: A record collector [who] has the collecting fever so bad that nothing else really matters. He/she plans his/her vacations around looking for records. He/she spends his/her weekends going to the usual swap meets, garage sales and record meets. He/she spends hours on the phone and internet with fellow record collectors.

"The collecting fever": who knew I was simply infected? Thankfully, my record-buying binge of summer 2001 has—like other unsustainable practices of those years—since slowed, and I can say with certainty, or at least hopefulness, that this definition does not characterize me. I did recently find a flea market with bins and bins crammed with old records—perhaps a thousand or more. But these bins were mostly covered up with other junk—old throw pillows, wicker baskets, a lamp, a spool of fishing line, a dusty VCR—or inaccessible because of the junk on the floor in front of them, and I didn't fuss much, didn't even bother to flip through the Peter Frampton and Diana Ross and Herb Alpert and Ray Conniff in search of something better.

Once summer ended and I started teaching again, I was rarely home to feel ashamed when Barney delivered the mail—although, heading to class one day, I passed him a half-mile down the road from my house. I waved hello, but his wave in return was more frantic. I stopped the car beside his truck and rolled down the window, and he said, "Hi, Josh, I've got a package for you." He rummaged around the cab of the truck for a moment, and then reached his arm through the window, holding a cardboard LP mailer out to me.

"Here you go," he said, smiling.

THE ANNOTATED MIXTAPE

SALOON, "Shopping"
(b/w "Song for Hugo" 7″, Amberley Records, 2000)

In seventh grade, unused to choosing my own classes—unused, in fact, to the concept of taking multiple classes rather than sitting in one classroom all day with twenty other students, listening to the steam radiator clank, breathing the bitter scent of chalk dust, and watching the flicker of fluorescence—I enrolled in Spanish 1 instead of French 1, a choice that, to this day, I regret. In many ways, being thirteen felt perpetually like being a foreigner; the introduction of foreign-language classes to the curriculum merely emphasized my struggles to comprehend the strange territory in which I found myself.

Spanish, my mother pointed out, was the more practical choice. I practiced the words I learned but which only a few of us in that classroom could properly pronounce by drafting letters to my patient Mexican grandmother, who simplified her vocabulary in the responses she wrote on pastel stationery. Along with the other kids tongue-testing a *«¿Cómo se llama?»* less eagerly than the Bartles & Jaymes wine coolers we sneaked into the high school football games, my face would blush when I was called upon to speak, though I showed no shame in joking about our teacher's clothes. Mr. Nicholas's fashion sense—paisleys and checks in a palette ranging from mustard and orange to brown, sport coats with sleeves no longer reaching his wrists, lapels and ties both too wide—reinforced what I saw as my own poor decision.

One afternoon early in the year, the boy at the desk in front of mine turned in his seat, pointing to a page near the end of our textbook: this page, titled *Preguntas,* showed a suggestive, soft-focus photo of a young woman with downcast gaze. "She's pregnant," my classmate insisted, eyes darting behind his glasses, cheeks suddenly flushed at this scandalous yet exciting possibility. Though we did later learn to define *pregunta* on a vocabulary quiz, our class stumbled so slowly through the textbook that even by the pollen-perfumed days of spring we had not reached that tantalizing page, and I like to imagine that my classmate spent his summer wondering about that young woman. What, indeed, were her questions?

The kids in French classes seemed perpetually, mysteriously other: their small numbers alone marked them as special. Even then I doubt I could have pinned down the nature of that specialness, or described its outward signs; now, I've mislaid such details, along with the other minor secrets of those days. In junior high, even certain homerooms seemed more prestigious than my own. Because I determined positive qualities such as prestige mainly by their absences in my life, I imagined that the kids taking French were free from the anxieties I felt about everything from girls to algebra. Did their French textbook contain references to teen pregnancy? I was certain it did not. I'm no Francophile, and though the rolled *r*'s and soft rising inflections did seduce me, I think I was seduced less by the language than by the kids who studied it, less by the kids than by the fact that they studied it, which underscored the disparity between them and me: they had chosen, impractically, a different course than the rest of us, and though at the age of thirteen I would not have expressed it this way, I have always admired refusals to yield to the practical. It took the presence of a native Castilian *se llamaban* Susana to redeem Spanish somewhat for me.

My wife, Sarah, a Canadian who practiced her school-mandated French during college in Montreal, claims that knowledge conferred no benefit: the Québécois shopkeepers would, when she attempted her French on them, stubbornly continue the conversation in English. Four years in Montreal left her with no romance for the French language, though of course some would argue that the French spoken in Quebec bears as much resemblance to the French spoken in Paris as the Spanish spoken in the dusty classrooms of Forest Grove Junior High School bore to the Spanish that Susana pronounced with a breezy lisp.

By the end of high school, my five years of Spanish classes were already fading—a vestigial memory, no different than orthodontics, after-school track meets, and lost locker combinations.

▶

It's easy to fetishize a language one does not speak, easy to lift that language from the culture—or to lift the culture from the language—and imagine it as some sort of romantic ideal. It's similarly easy to fetishize a vinyl 7″ record in these last days of vinyl, when the factories that press it grow nearly as few in number as the members of the Doherty Memorial High School French Honor Society (three, according to the photo in my yearbook, by which point they had, in my estimation, renounced all claim to mystery and allure and proven themselves no less dorky than the seven kids in the Spanish Honor Society). If a band releases a record on both vinyl and digital formats, I always choose the former, if only for the fact that, in the twenty-first century, vinyl appears invariably in a limited edition, the sort of thing that by virtue of its production run alone becomes sought-after, prestigious, special.

After a few home-released records, the Reading, UK band Saloon debuted in 2000 with their single "Shopping," which was not available on CD, thus making it even more ideal for vinyl fetishists like myself. The sleeve's artwork seemed a nod in the direction of the famous Factory Records label—itself famously fetishist (a 1981 label-defining LP was issued in a heavy matchbook-style jacket that unfolded to reveal an interior printed with a marbled paper design under license from the French firm Ste. Keller-Dorian Papiers)—and the song too seemed an homage of sorts to the Factory Records sound: the nervous tick-tick-tick-tick of the ride cymbal; the shimmery wash of minor-key guitar chords; the droning analog synthesizers; the swooning and lovely and, yes, French female vocals. After the record had stayed on my turntable for a week, I asked Sarah to translate the lyrics for me: I felt some combination of the seventh-grader's fear of being excluded and the familiar regret at not understanding what the singer was making sound so beautifully wistful; over the years I've picked up a vague reading knowledge of French, but remain tone-deaf to the spoken version. To my ears, the voice in "Shopping" conjured—well, maybe a wind-damaged dandelion, or the view through a wavy-glass windowpane to a rainswept street, or the feeling of walking home from the post office at which you've just mailed a letter to some distant and much-missed friend. Such foolish, sentimental imagery seemed, in this case, okay, in part because it occurred in the context of a pop song, in part because of the gauzy effect of the French.

This is how Sarah rendered the song's opening lines into English:

> I would like to buy a chair, sir
> I would prefer the blue one
> I saw it in the shop window the other day...

So even the most insipid and pedestrian thoughts, sung in French, attained a certain beauty. Did they seem beautiful only because I didn't know their meaning, or because of the nostalgic connotations this language has for me? Or because I was—as if returned to a preliterate, prelinguistic state—reveling solely in the sound of that voice?

The sleeve of "Shopping," in true Factory Records tradition, offered no information about Saloon's members—not even their names—so it was not until later that I laughed upon learning that the *chanteuse* who so captivated me *se llama* Amanda Gomez, a surname from the "wrong" side of the Pyrenees. When I bought the band's next record, I was similarly amused to see that one song was titled "Sueño Escolar"—appropriately, I thought, given how often those of us in Mr. Nicholas's Spanish 1 class nodded off on our laminated desktops, unconcerned with the distinction between the preterite and the imperfect, between *por y para,* scholars of nothing linguistic at all. Our scholarship involved recalling the last time Mr. Nicholas had worn his lemon yellow blazer, re-enacting dialogue from *Saturday Night Live* skits, and debating endlessly the comparative merits of various exegeses over who had dumped whom in a particular relationship. We scribbled our dissertations on lined notebook paper folded into duodecimos and distributed in the corridors during passing time or flipped from desk to desk when Mr. Nicholas turned to scrape his chalk stub across the blackboard. Junior high school operated under the tacit specifics of the hegemony we inherited (few among us questioned the supremacy of Nike sneakers and Levi's jeans), so I doubt that my inquiry into the nature of French 1's difference would have roused much critical interest, though I never allowed my admittedly weak hypothesis to be peer-reviewed. The French 1 kids were cool in a way that the Spanish 1 kids could not hope to be. I left it at that, and in those days that was enough for me.

But now I wonder what those kids in French class daydreamed about those of us taking Spanish—about our own myriad mysteries—while their teachers explained the distinction between *l'accent aigu et l'accent grave.* The accidental nature of my selection—the unbearable lightness of choosing—underscored the insignificance, for my adolescent self, in the difference between French and Spanish. Each language offered me the myth of access, but it would be another half-dozen years before, having worked after high school to save up for a Continental tour, I stood on European soil, struggling to understand and to make myself understood. In the meantime, I was untroubled by the complexities of the choice, aware of French and Spanish only as abstract indicators of junior-high cool, living a life free of any pressures to see myself as *un extranjero.* In seventh grade, using a discarded Harman-Kardon turntable, an old pair of speakers, and a new Sony receiver, I cobbled together my first stereo system, and, ever since, music has been my lingua franca.

SCUD MOUNTAIN BOYS, "Massachusetts" (*Massachusetts* LP, Sub Pop, 1996)

"I could never leave you, Massachusetts," Joe Pernice sings over a few slow bass notes, a softly strummed acoustic guitar, and a lap steel's lonesome sigh: this apostrophe to my—our—native state is a thought I've often seconded, though his voice itself—a near-whisper, a hushed breath about to crack, a mumble too sweet to suggest exhaustion, and so it registers for me as regret—conveys a certain amount of ambivalence toward the words it proclaims, and maybe it's this ambivalence that draws me into the song.

Joe Pernice is one of the few rock vocalists who can imbue even the phrase "your pretty white ass" with a boundless and convincing melancholy. Imagine, then, what he might do with the sibilant syllables of "Massachusetts." Is his vision the one I want to consult for sentiment regarding my native soil when my own sentiments about that soil are so conflicted? Pernice's songwriting—whether in the Scud Mountain Boys or his later band, the Pernice Brothers—allows such words as "ruinous," "eclipsed," "trauma," and "indentured." (Pernice earned an M.F.A. in creative writing.) He can take a line such as "this fascination with the moribund," deliver it in a wistful croon, and marry it to both swelling violins and the sort of sunny, chiming guitar chords that filled the AM radio airwaves of my early childhood.

Such covert duplicity is the marrow of Massachusetts. I have followed a country road through apple-orchard hills to its sudden end in a sooty brick ghost town where the storefront windows contain only the faint circular swipes of dried soap and illegible scraps of newsprint blow along weedy sidewalks to catch in chain-link fences. My neighbors in upstate New York chuckled forlornly about the timing of an April Fool's Day storm that offered us an inch or two of snow a few years back, but I can recall from my Massachusetts boyhood an afternoon in the midst of a glorious May when skies sunny an hour before began to swirl down clots of snow, crushing lilac and apple blossoms in my backyard. Over a foot fell in my hometown that day.

▸

> Massachusetts herself, despite her welter of intellectual improvement, remained curiously provincial.
>
> —Henry F. Howe, *Massachusetts: There She Is—Behold Her*

During the years I lived in upstate New York and rural Pennsylvania—years to which I referred only half-jokingly as "exile," though New England remained no more than a few hours' drive away—a fellow Massachusetts native once told me I was romanticizing our home state: "What about all those kids you couldn't stand in your high school?" he asked, by way of example. "What about the drivers?"

He didn't understand, or I failed to make clear, that by the word *Massachusetts* I really meant the familiar. I wanted to gather within this single word the countless evocative fragments of the place it indicated—fragments profound to me yet ultimately meaningless to anyone else. In this sense, "Massachusetts" means a collapsing stone wall deep in leaf-littered woods; it means Routes 9 and 122 and 31; it means the signs throughout my home city showing a red heart hollowed out and pierced by a pointing arrow, and, in small block lettering below this, the word DOWNTOWN; it means the sound of rain on the roof mingled with the early morning rush of water through the pipes in my bedroom wall as my father showered before work; it means the spray-painted graffiti I inadvertently memorized—NUCLEAR POWER MEANS CANCER FOR OUR CHILDREN—from an overpass on I-290; it means the smell of woodsmoke on an evening not long after the end of Daylight Savings time, when the sun has set but a band of its yellow light along the horizon still specifies exactly the bare branches of trees against the sky. Or perhaps it is the strange possessiveness I feel toward these banal and homely things that I mean when I say "Massachusetts."

But my Massachusetts is a selective fiction: to me, Massachusetts has nothing to do with clam chowder and lobster, with parking a car in Harvard Yard, with Kennedys or Puritans, with bus riots and racism.

In my exile, I sometimes called the state where I lived Pennsylslovakia, after the liner notes on the Swirlies' EP *Brokedick Car*—a shorthand way to underscore for myself the foreignness of even small-town streets laid out in a grid and named by numbers; of a town with more churches than bars; of a cuisine in which waffles are topped with chicken and gravy, and "scrapple" is eaten for breakfast. And even though my friend misunderstood me, I would have taken every one of those kids with whom I coexisted uneasily in high school—their expansive anger, their narrow imaginations—over the peaceful Mennonites who, bonnets and handmade dresses flapping, pedaled their bicycles along the roads outside of my Pennsylvania town.

"You're livin' in your own private Idaho," Fred Schneider of the B-52's declared in a 1980 song, and though "your own private Massachusetts" doesn't fit the line's meter, I'd nod my head to the substitution. My own private Massachusetts: perhaps this is all I'd ever want, these hills and woods and beaches, the only somewhat sullied acres of my youth, and no need to share.

▸

> But when an attempt is made to describe scenery, and that of so enchanting a spot as [western Massachusetts], the mind almost shrinks from the task. Accordingly, the only end of this effort will be a simple setting forth of the facts, and, very possibly, inciting in the mind of the reader a desire to visit the localities mentioned, so that these beauties of nature may be most fully appreciated.
>
> — Josiah Gilbert Holland, *History of Western Massachusetts*

I swear I've seen this spot, this road—telephone wires stretched so thin they seem to disappear against an inscrutable and overcast sky; the end-of-winter's sand striping the asphalt's edges; a wood-bumpered car parked on the grass, its rear window stickered with the names of forgotten local politicians—pictured on the back sleeve of the Scud Mountain Boys' album *Massachusetts.* The road is probably one of those that crisscross the Pioneer Valley of western Massachusetts—perhaps Rt. 116 north of Amherst, or Rt. 63 in Montague—but what matters most about the photo to me is how its various components seem to capture so much of how I might characterize Massachusetts, so much of what Massachusetts means to me: the lovely poverty of the intimate, the impositions of weather, the reliance on self-reliance, the making-do, the resignation to circumstance, everything the slightest bit canted, off-kilter, not plumb. The album is a triumph, yet this photograph conveys an overwhelming sense of some very recent failure.

By contrast, the photograph on the front of the sleeve—single-story suburban homes beneath a faint arc of rainbow—may have been taken in Massachusetts, or it may have been taken anywhere else. The houses and rainbow and landscape do not signify anything so particular as an actual place, and for that reason have nothing to do, for me, with Massachusetts. But the idea that Massachusetts could contain such anonymity is also why Massachusetts, for me, no longer has much to do with itself.

▶

> Northampton, perhaps, will impress us with its beauty next, seeming so delightful for a home or a summer residence, its

> streets so beautifully shaded with grand elms, and the whole village environed with green meadows and forest trees. Then the carpet of nature's own coloring, in the meadows of Northampton and Hadley. . . almost impress[es] us with the belief that we are fairies, ourselves, and inhabitants of an enchanted land.
>
> —Holland, *History of Western Massachusetts*

> The grandchildren of the old West consider the word "culture" a byword somehow synonymous with Boston. They still come back to Massachusetts in droves, either to study or to imbibe, as tourists, some faint relic of the enchantment with which Massachusetts culture held their grandsires spellbound.
>
> —Howe, *Massachusetts: There She Is—Behold Her*

I lived in Northampton, Massachusetts, during 1994 and 1995, when a local—if not provincial—band suddenly rode a crest of enthusiasm toward a national recording deal and a brief moment of wider recognition. The Scud Mountain Boys. At the time, the name itself struck me as ridiculous, unpleasant to the ear, a faux-hillbilly retroism, reason enough to ignore the music. "Scud" too deliberately recalled the missiles flung from Iraq during the first Gulf War; the Scud Mountain Boys evolved from an earlier band, the Scuds—another name which suggested to me a suspect aesthetic. "Mountain" itself was fine; I'd just been living on one in Vermont. But "Boys"? I didn't want to hear music made by boys or by men who called themselves boys. And I've always been distrustful of hyped bands—preferring to listen, if at all, only when that hype has quieted enough that I might hear the actual songs. So I didn't show up at any of the Scud Mountain Boys' many in-town shows; I didn't imbibe what I've since come to see as the considerable enchantments of their music. Friends described their music as "country," and I had no interest in acoustic country music in 1994 and 1995—especially, I felt certain, if it was "recorded live with one microphone in the kitchen at the Woodmont Hotel, Northampton, MA, when it was cold," as the note on the back of their first LP attests.

I had no idea that I was missing some of the best music recorded during these years, that I was refusing the opportunity to see one of the era's most interesting bands refine its talents in small venues a short walk from my own door. But any Massachusetts native knows all about spite, all about hasty judgment and absolute conviction, all about the willful denial of pleasure.

> Who are you to tell me?
> Who are you to tell me?
> Who are you to try and lead me from a place you never
> even came?

So Joe Pernice, in the chorus of "Massachusetts," wants to know. Who, indeed.

This music might have been the perfect soundtrack to my aimless drives through the Pioneer Valley and the Hilltowns—all the towns I'm even now unwilling to name, to keep their few remaining secrets my own—had I listened.

▶

> The charter of Massachusets [sic] was not so great a boon.
> —Thomas Hutchinson, *The History of the Colony of Massachuset's Bay*

After fifteen years, my exile ended, and I returned to my home state. And yet this return has allowed me to see what I missed from further away. My Massachusetts has rapidly vanished into a state too much like every other: the same franchise restaurants and parking-lot-girdled megastores, the same overcrowded highways (the fact that so much of my own Massachusetts involves the automobile notwithstanding), the same suburban spec houses encroaching on the little land left. According to the *Boston Globe,* a 2003 report by the Massachusetts Audubon Society has found that "40 acres of Massachusetts forest, farmland, and open space are being developed every day, about 90 percent of which is being used to build new homes." Further, "the report...paints a picture of increasing sprawl where Massachusetts residents live in large suburban houses and commute long distances to work, and a state where affordable housing remains in short supply."

Each day, as I too join the commute to work in Massachusetts, the landscape reminds me of the bleak vision of America John Cheever depicted in his 1982 novel *Oh What a Paradise It Seems:*

> Seven seventy-four was now a length in that highway of merchandising that reaches across the continent. It would be absurd to regret the obsolescence of the small dairy farm, but the ruined villages were for Sears a melancholy spectacle, as if a truly adventurous people had made a wrong turning and stumbled into a gypsy

> culture. Here were the most fleeting commitments and the most massive household gods. Beside a porn drive-in movie were two furniture stores whose items needed the strength of two or three men to be moved. He thought it a landscape, a people—and he counted himself among them—who had lost the sense of a harvest.

Cheever dubbed such a culture "nomadism," and another of the novel's characters feels about his transient world as I do about Massachusetts: "He seemed to be searching for the memory of some place, some evidence of the fact that he had once been able to put himself into a supremely creative touch with his world and his kind. He longed for this as if it were some country which he had been forced to leave." Could a visitor from out of state now draw the same distinctions I once drew between Pennsylvania and Massachusetts? Can I?

▶

> I describe [Boston] in terms of the old because I want to show her as one would show a fine old canvas from which the smoke and oil-deposit and soilure of a viscous atmosphere have been removed.
>
> —David McCord, *About Boston: Sight, Sound, Flavor and Inflection*

The 1980s slogan "Make It in Massachusetts" was crafted by the administration of Governor Ed King to counteract the nickname "Taxachusetts," and to attempt to lure business to the state—the same corporate dollars that helped taint my Massachusetts. I suppose the lovely ambiguity of that "it" is the only reason why any of us remember this phrase. I would pay good money, now, for a T-shirt with that slogan and its concurrent emblem: a fist with upraised thumb, a hand ready to hitchhike to this state of plenty.

The new state slogan suggests precisely everything wrong with Massachusetts, the primary reason why I sometimes feel my home state's ruined: "Massachusetts...Make It Yours." This slogan makes explicit an act of imagination that I have long believed only I was entitled to perform—only I was knowledgeable and discriminating enough to perform—and my vision of Massachusetts cannot suffer competitors. This slogan recognizes that Massachusetts is dynamic rather than static, that a process begun when the Abenaki and Wampanoag and Nipmuc burned parcels of forest to plant corn, when the pilgrims offered to this rugged coastline—safe haven, fearful wilderness, paradise—the English names they'd abandoned, is ongoing.

How wrong-headed is my Massachuscentrism, this Massachusetts of my mind? With any discovery—and I certainly discovered a previously unknown Massachusetts during the various years I've lived here—coexists the desire to tame, to define, to leave one's stamp. The frustration of my own colonial desires vexes me, partly because I believe that others view as irrelevant those aspects of Massachusetts that I treasure, partly because of the visible and mutually exclusive ways others have marked my home state. Why have I thought for so long that this tiny crooked state and its one grasping arm contain some immeasurable secrets unobtainable elsewhere—or that one could indeed make it here?

In the Pernice Brothers' song "She Heightened Everything"—the one in which Joe Pernice rhymes "mortal wound" to "moribund"—he sings, "It fills me with regret / I can't believe in love, but I want to believe." Can one be both pragmatic and romantic? Some part of me hopes to rekindle my love for Massachusetts while the rest of me knows this is impossible, as I drive its moribund strips of cinderblock malls, its glass-gleaming office parks rising from mortally wounded woodlands. We know each other too well by now, Massachusetts and I; there are so few secrets left, and too much history.

▶

Two excerpts from the liner notes on the Scud Mountain Boys' first LP:

> I was out for a walk with Mr. Fiddler the other night, when he turned to me and said, "This is the time of year when this region is at peace with itself."
>
> ...searching for some sign of human residence here beneath the justifiably uncelebrated Massachusetts sky.

▶

Sometime in my elementary school years—when I was old enough to know the meaning of the word "impregnable" and the power of poetic inversion, but still young enough to enjoy playing with toy guns, or bark-stripped sticks that served as toy guns—a friend and I found a spot near his house that we named "the fortress impregnable." His house, like mine—and many others in my hometown—was built on the steep shoulder of a hill; his street dead-ended in a narrow band of woods. Here kids had worn tracks in the earth with their feet, and my friend and I dug pits and trenches we covered with elaborately woven branches heaped with dead leaves; we bent back young birches and lashed their tops to the ground; we tried to make tripwires. In the woods, time passed at a rate entirely unrelated to that of the outside world, and we might spend what seemed days in a stick swordfight beneath the leaf-sifted sun—tumbling over rocky dirt, splintering our weapons against each other's, proclaiming our imagined injuries, choking out dying breaths and looking our last at this world of swaying shadow among maple trunks—to find that, when we returned to his house for Fritos or cookies, a mere hour had elapsed. I doubt anyone much passed through that narrow strip of woods—other kids and perhaps an occasional dog-walker—but we still considered them ours, and our traps were intended to discourage trespassers. Across the street from his house, another house was perched high on the slope, requiring a long set of nearly switchbacked concrete steps to reach its front door. At one of the bends in this stairway was a landing, surrounded on all sides by short concrete retaining walls and further reinforced by some low bushes: we named this spot the fortress impregnable, where we would hunker down, our fractured swords now rifles, waiting for the other kids we played with to cross the street below or emerge from the woods.

I had thought my Massachusetts impregnable, infinitely defensible from those forces that would make of it something other than what I believed it was, something other than what I wanted it to be. But the bulldozers have come for the trees, and from newly cleared circles in the woods rise house frames sheathed, at least temporarily, in Tyvek HomeWrap rather than weathered shingles or narrow clapboards. My Massachusetts is safe, intact, unblemished only in the sense that Daniel Webster once proclaimed it: "I shall enter on no encomium upon Massachusetts; she needs none. There she is. Behold her, and judge for yourselves. There is her history; the world knows it by heart. The past, at least, is secure."

The past is secure as well in the deliberately old-fashioned songs of the Scud Mountain Boys, which today sound almost like hymns to a vanished era. Though Pernice eventually dissolved the band to form the Pernice Brothers, and though that band uses keyboards and programmed drums rather than mandolin and lap steel, his music and lyrics still traffic in nostalgia, if for a different era and of a different kind. Maybe this is why I like the Pernice Brothers' records almost as much as those by the Scud Mountain Boys. Either way, I know that I am in the company of a vigorous and choosy memory—just as I am in my Massachusetts, though its memorials are being slowly, irrevocably effaced. My own tracks through and across this state remain as vivid in my recollections as the blue paint of the Freedom Trail as it winds through the Boston streets.

I cue *Yours, Mine & Ours,* the 2003 record by native son Joe Pernice, and hear him begin one song with the words "Sometimes, it's better not to know / Holding onto something when you should just let go." In the chorus of another song, he repeats these lines: "So familiar that it feels too strange / Give a name to this terrifying change."

THE MODERN LOVERS: "Roadrunner"

(*The Modern Lovers* LP, Beserkely Records, 1976)

Nowhere felt further from Massachusetts than a sorry, post-industrial Hudson Valley city with a boarded-up downtown, racially segregated neighborhoods, an urban deer herd, and high-rise projects overlooking a PCB-clogged river—not because I'd never found these things in my Massachusetts, but because they felt so familiar I could itemize every slight difference and vex myself with it. The me-against-the-world vibe and enthusiastic declarations of "Roadrunner" offered some solace those first few months I found myself dislocated, as did its Farfisa organ and bass chug. "I'm in love with Massachusetts," Jonathan Richman proclaims, and though my feelings about that state remained bewildering, maybe this song did "[help] me from being lonely late at night," a little. Still, Massachusetts is, crucially, only one beloved thing among many beloved things that Richman cites: "the neon when it's cold outside," "the highway when it's late at night," "modern moonlight," "[Route] 128 when it's dark outside," "the radio on," "rock and roll," and all the other passions that allow youth to think it's "got the world." (The power one feels when one's world exists solely as private property!) Listening at a distance, I couldn't help but hear these lines through the locus of my longing, but also couldn't help thinking about all the sensible conditions to these loves—not just neon, but neon *when it's cold outside.* Desire is endlessly specific, and endlessly inexplicable: so much so that, when fortune posed us the option, Sarah and I packed our house and returned to the particulars of the Massachusetts we imagined rather than remain amid the particulars of the Poughkeepsie we endured. "Bye bye!" Richman drawls at the end of the song. Like the Modern Lovers, we escaped via car, under night's anonymity, to some new frontier of "suburban trees, suburban speed."

THE CAPTAIN AND TENNILLE: "Love Will Keep Us Together" (*Love Will Keep Us Together* LP, A&M Records, 1975)

Why are the songs that I listened to only circumstantially—or, rather, *heard* only circumstantially: mostly because they happened to be on the radio—also the songs that are bound up most intimately with my vague-but-compelling, inarticulable and semi-formed memories of childhood? Dispossessed of all agency and stuck in the back seat of my parents' old Jeep—or allowed to lie on a musty blanket in the way back—while we drove from our house to someplace I had no say in whether I did or did not go, the AM-only radio turned on, fenceposts and trees and telephone wires, overpasses and streetlights and signs, houses and hillsides flicking past the rear window at however-many miles per hour: in this way I unwittingly consumed the pop music of the early and mid-1970s. These songs became the soundtrack to my primordial memories not because I liked them, not because my parents necessarily liked them, but simply because one of my parents had turned on the radio while we drove. I became a self-aware person to the sounds of Orleans' "Dance with Me," Elton John's "Bennie and the Jets," 10cc's "I'm Not in Love," Neil Sedaka's "Laughter in the Rain," Roberta Flack's "Feel Like Makin' Love," Wings' "Band on the Run," Jim Croce's "Time in a Bottle," Joni Mitchell's "Help Me," Stevie Wonder's "Sir Duke," Seals and Croft's "Summer Breeze," Carole King, Anne Murray, Barry Manilow...and the Captain and Tennille.

Who listens to such songs out of choice, out of a desire to hear them at a specific moment? I didn't, not then, and not later when I was defining and redefining my musical preferences—which, it is not unreasonable to suggest, were consciously shaped out of a reaction against the songs I heard on 1970s AM radio and what I felt they represented. I have always self-identified much more with Joy Division's "Love Will Tear Us Apart" than the Captain and Tennille's sunnier sentiment, and yet my preferences are still informed, somewhat less consciously, by an abiding, guilty-pleasure fondness for the structures and sounds of 1970s pop.

Except for quasi-ironic, decade-in-review nostalgia television and YouTube's ongoing cultural recovery project, these songs have faded into the past along with all the other forgotten background noise of my own early life. To recall 1975 in music now is, for me, to recall the year the Ramones signed to Sire Records, the year Patti Smith confessed that "Jesus died for somebody's sins, but not" hers, the year Brian Eno recorded and released *Another Green World,* the year Augustus Pablo's "King Tubby Meets the Rockers Uptown" forever defined dub, the year Van McCoy and the Soul

City Symphony's "The Hustle" continued to bring disco out of clubs and into living rooms, the year David Bowie sang the "phoniest R&B [he'd] ever heard," the year the Sex Pistols had the plug pulled twenty minutes into their first gig. Certainly other music fans would recall it differently—but I wonder how many would now recall it as the year of the Captain and Tennille.

Pop songs are, and always have been, constructed to restate clichés in an immediately familiar way; to be so catchy and compelling that we can't ignore them, that we find ourselves humming or singing along, even in the music's absence; and to withstand constant broadcast on the radio, at least for a brief time, until we tire of them—and yet these songs are also meant as throwaways, to be replaceable by other, often similar songs on next week's Top 40. Endless replay and of-the-moment sonic particulars instantly fossilized 1970s pop songs in their moments, as those moments came and went. Still, these songs never left me. Neurologist Oliver Sacks has proposed that "there are attributes of musical imagery and musical memory that have no equivalents in the visual sphere, [perhaps]...because we have to *construct* a visual world for ourselves, and a selective and personal character therefore infuses our visual memories from the start—whereas we are given pieces of music already constructed[,]...[and] the recall of a musical piece has to be close to the original." Sacks's hypothesis offers a testament to the violence done by radio. For the past thirty-some years, I have, whenever I've re-encountered some 1970s pop hit, recognized—anticipated—its every lyric, its every melody and harmony, its every drumbeat and synthesizer squiggle. Love kept us together far less than the brutality of broadcast.

▶

"You, you belong to me now / ain't gonna set you free now," sings Toni Tennille—all huge, predatory eyes and toothy smile—and it's true: I do belong to her, to this song, the #1 song of 1975 on the *Billboard* Top 100, and Grammy Award winner for Record of the Year. But until I finally submitted and salvaged the LP from a dollar bin a few years back, I had never heard this song except by chance, despite which it simultaneously signifies for me childhood and the 1970s more than any other three and a half minutes I know.

And, disregarding the song's dowdy opening bars and its cheerful pop insistence, the odd textures and flourishes of Daryl Dragon's Mini-Moog synthesizer and his bizarre synth solo, when I listen to "Love Will Keep Us Together" now, I notice its peculiarities and darker corners. What I at first hear as a celebration of marriage, or at least commitment—a seemingly conservative gesture in the post–Free Love years of no-fault divorce laws and singles bars, though perhaps not to Toni Tennille and Daryl Dragon, who were married in 1975, and who remained married for nearly forty years, before finally announcing their divorce in 2014—is instead, I quickly realize, the entreaty of a woman begging her husband not to stray. There's a sad desperation in how she keeps imagining "some sweet-talkin' girl" he will encounter, or "those girls…hangin' around," and in how she obliviously fulfills the nagging wife stereotype in the line "I've said it before and I'll say it again": and an equal desperation in the background harmonies that, during the chorus, increase in pitch to a near-screech as they plead, "stop! st-op! really love you! / stop! st-op! thinking of you!"

and chant "love, love, love, love, love!" like some deranged mantra. Unlike the other songs on the record that feature Toni Tennille's sisters as backup singers, "Love Will Keep Us Together" includes harmonies overdubbed by Toni herself—making the singer seem intent on preserving control over a position she feels is threatened. The song promotes not sexual liberty (as does Donna Summer's 1975 hit "Love to Love You Baby") but old-fashioned love, not independence (as does Helen Reddy's 1972 hit "I Am Woman") but mutual dependence, and, in the social and political context of its time—the Equal Rights Amendment, the Billie Jean King vs. Bobby Riggs "Battle of the Sexes" tennis match, Phyllis Schlafly, *Ms.* magazine, *All in the Family,* the *Laurel's Kitchen* cookbook—it seems a tame throwback. It doesn't advance or elaborate the basic forms of the chart hit, which is probably why I remember it at least as well in terms of its historical moment as in terms of its music.

When the Captain and Tennille performed the song live at the Grammy Awards show, Toni Tennille introduced it by fixing her gaze at the camera and saying, "We're so grateful to the American people for the way they've received our record that we've asked a few of 'em to sing along with us tonight." As they performed, an accompanying video montage of people-on-the-street mumbling and occasionally crooning phrases from the song might have suggested individual empowerment, the consumer adapting the song for her or his own purposes, but Toni Tennille's word "received," and the shy self-consciousness of most of these singers—unwilling to trespass on the phrases her powerful voice had animated from their radios all summer—told us all we needed to know about how this song reached us, and how much say we had in it. In my case, I received it while literally strapped tight to a padded vinyl seat.

▸

The world I passed through as my parents drove seemed complicated, huge—not because I was smaller then, but because I could not discern its workings, and because I felt, and was, so powerless to effect any outcome in my own life. To be a child often means one is unable to effect outcomes. We can say the same about being a radio listener, despite the call-in vote for the top five at five, or the request line, or the long-distance dedication: none of these participatory gestures will be acknowledged unless they concede to both current demand and a station's specific format (and, except for the fact they they help popularize radio stations, and thus increase advertising revenue, they would not exist). The commercial radio of the 1970s, like that of today, was as predictable in its structures as the songs it broadcast—a short set of music, a commercial bumper or station ID, a long set of advertisements, maybe a brief traffic or weather update, another commercial bumper, some allegedly personal blather from the DJ, another short set of music—and offered us only the narrowest slices of all possible experiences, repeated hourly, even as we hoped to hear some minor variations in that routine. Radio is a form of manufactured and unreciprocated desire that convinces us the one song we really want to hear is "coming up," and then deliberately delays that moment. And radio infantilizes us with its devotion to popularity and hits and countdowns, its admonitions—*don't touch that dial!*—and its sound effects, its drive-time gags and its shock jocks. For decades it has been an increasingly dehumanized medium, its playlists determined by industry or algorithm. It gives us nothing except on its own terms, which are the terms of the market: as Jacques Attali noted in 1977, "It appears increasingly to be the case that a radio station has an audience only if it broadcasts records that sell.... Radio has become the showcase, the publicity flier of the record industry."

In an era in which at least the illusion of consumer choice is sacred—even if such choices generally involve the products of one corporation pitted against those of another—it's unsurprising that many people now listen to the radio a lot less than they once did. Most of us prefer to shut out that huge and complicated world in favor of creating our own soundscapes to usher us through it, and rely on radio only when we're offered no better options. The radio we do listen to is often, as with Last.fm and Pandora ("It's a new kind of radio—stations that play only music you like"), personally tailored to the point of absurdity. I typed the name of the band Josef K into Pandora's search function and was told that the songs played by the resulting "station" would feature "electric rock instrumentation, punk influences, a subtle use of vocal harmony, repetitive melodic phrasing, and major key tonality"; when I gave one of those resulting songs a thumbs-down, the software apologized so profusely—"Sorry about that—we'll try something else, and we'll never play that song again on this station"—I felt guilty.

Such wisdom-of-the-crowd, data-mined programming seems its own form of brutalism. I don't want my music parsed so finely (and who's to say what is or isn't a "punk influence"? a "subtle" vocal harmony?), don't want the mysteries of my taste anatomized or predicted based on what some other listener has liked or disliked, listened to or skipped: the reasons *I* like Josef K have nothing to do with the explanations Pandora cited for me, and despite the fact that I am talking about the products of mass popular culture, I want to pretend that my relationships with them are unique, unpredictable. Record collecting has been my way, however meager, of refusing radio's calculated randomness, and after a few years in which I filled cheap cassettes with songs taped from the radio (a form of proto-collecting), my records supplanted radio entirely for me. Listening to my iPod shuffling through its 1970s playlist, I like that "Where Is the Love" has segued to "Drug-Stabbing Time," "The True Wheel" to "African Descendants," "Granny Scratch Scratch" to "Gimme Danger" or—a few months ago, in one of the most sublime pairings ever—"We've Only Just Begun" to "Ghost Rider": such randomness is not beholden to market ratings or FCC regulations, but only to my own approval.

I plug my iPod into my car stereo if I'm taking a drive longer than fifteen minutes—and, after buying *Love Will Keep Us Together* on vinyl, I digitized the title track so that now, driving my own car to destinations of my own choosing, I can, if I want, hear it once again:

"When the others turn you off, who'll be turnin' you on?

"I will! I will! I will!"

DEF LEPPARD: "Photograph"
(*Pyromania* LP, Mercury / PolyGram, 1983)
A FLOCK OF SEAGULLS: "Wishing (If I Had a Photograph of You)"
(*Listen* LP, Jive, 1983)

In 1983, in seventh grade, a friend detailed his plan to attract the attention of a girl he liked: he'd cue his *Pyromania* cassette to the moment in "Photograph" when the music drops out for a measure and the lead singer growls, "I wanna touch you!" Then he'd crank call the girl, holding the phone to his stereo as he played a few inches of tape before hanging up—leaving her wondering, presumably, just *who* wanted to touch her (and resonating unintentionally with the advertising campaign Ma Bell had introduced in 1979: "Reach out and touch someone"). Even still, my friend's approach seemed too direct an admission of desire. At that age, I preferred to simply imagine any potential romantic encounters, so they'd have no chance of failure.

▶

In the video, the lead singer wears a sleeveless Union Jack T-shirt, a white scarf, and leather pants cinched with a set of handcuffs. Singing in a rough, impassioned falsetto, he prances, shakes shaggy hair out of his eyes, pumps his fist, clutches the microphone stand, stares at the camera, writhes with legs spread wide, thrusts his pelvis, leaps through the air nearly touching his toes, leans against the lead guitarist, points at the camera, and finally contorts his face as he howls and grimaces. Along the side of the soundstage where he struts, heavily made-up women with teased hair and torn clothes lounge and shimmy inside their cages, snarling along with the music. The lead singer's name is Joe Elliott, and he performs a distressed ardor using classic lead singer gestures and poses: his performance is learned from other performances, acutely aware of its audience (even though there is no audience here except director and crew) and its reception.

The song Elliott sings concerns the inability of a representation to satisfy his longing: the presences of so many representations—every time he dreams, on every page of every magazine—haunt him. He wishes only for the intimate presence of the real; he needs to touch the object of his desire to escape her many confounding images. To underscore Elliott's postmodern dilemma, the video's director cuts from shots of the band playing to black-and-white, would-be film noir scenes of a Marilyn Monroe impersonator in trenchcoat, or lying facedown in a chalk outline, or—most hauntingly of all—posing for photographs in front of other photographs of herself. The reproductions proliferate. Everyone looks at the lens; we see everyone through the viewfinder. We learn the agony of desire when a Polaroid of a wailing Elliott is crushed beneath a single spiked heel.

▶

An early lesson on the male gaze and the slippages of language: Sunday afternoon at my grandparents' house. Parents, sisters, grandparents, aunts, uncles, cousins, and my fuzzy suspicions that I must be some foundling these people took in. One older cousin wears a pair of Chic brand designer jeans. Perhaps to make evident the increasing awkwardness I feel, perhaps because I have nothing else to contribute, I point to the Chic logo stitched in gold thread on the back pocket of her jeans and pronounce the word: "Chick."

My aunt's boyfriend, one of a number of embarrassing men she's dated since her husband's early death, grabs my hand. "Whoa," he says. "You can't call women that. That's male chauvinism." I blush—I am, maybe, ten—because although I know not to compare a girl to a baby bird, I have no idea why speaking a brand name is wrong. My aunt appears not to hear him—no one else does, thankfully—so he adds, "You have to be respectful," and turns away. At the next family gathering, or the one after that, my aunt arrives alone.

▶

In the video, four men with blowtorches and goggles attempt to repair their spaceship, but shake their heads sadly at the futility of the effort. (The *Millennium Falcon*'s malfunctioning hyperdrive had been a major plot point two years earlier.) The lead singer's name—Mike Score—also seems cribbed from a sci-fi movie's script, as does his pale hair, which is sculpted into a shape resembling a pair of wings with a long tail between them to cover one eye. But this video has little action: Score strolls the spaceship, hands in pockets, peering out at deep space, or wandering into different rooms to hold railings and sway in time to the music. His outfit is black, with zippers and tassels and a stiff collar, as futuristic as anything one would have found at a suburban shopping mall in the early '80s. There may be a stowaway on board—we catch quick glimpses of a woman's eyes, or see her silhouetted against the spaceship's bright lights; later, her form appears to dance in space as the ship passes through interstellar clouds—but she may also be only some absent presence, the ghost Score wishes to see. (Susan Sontag: "A photograph is both a pseudo-presence and a token of absence.... The sense of the unattainable that can be evoked by photographs feeds directly into the erotic feelings of those for whom desirability is enhanced by distance.")

The song Score sings catalogs his desire for this missing other, but only through the negation of reasons—he desires her not for the way she looks or smiles, not for the way she wears her hair, not for her makeup, not for how she dances. He can come no closer to explaining his desire than to note that he appreciates the way her "eyes are laughing as they glance across the great divide": his feelings are those of a Romantic poet encountering the sublime. Actions and words are insignificant: "Well, there must be something more," he confesses. Most of all, he wants a photograph of his beloved; he believes that this representation will supplant the real, so he won't "spend [his] life just wishing." At one of the spaceship's computer terminals, he watches a photograph of a woman's face take digital shape, then prints out this image on pinholed, continuous-feed computer paper, but, disillusioned, tears it in half. Score performs a studied melancholy we might trace back to nineteenth-century Parisian *flâneurs;* although the song yearns, the great divide of space and time has rendered him unable to muster enthusiasm for even the thing he claims to want most. The four members of the band take turns staring into a video console where they play their instruments with robotic precision. The spaceship, glowing blue, hurtles from a bright galaxy of stars into darkness, and the Earth's clouded orb—photographs of which forever changed our sense of the planet—spins and diminishes behind it.

▶

Or Guy Debord: "Everything that was directly lived has receded into a representation.... The spectacle is not a collection of images; it is a social relation between people that is mediated by images.... Real life is materially invaded by the contemplation of the spectacle, and ends up absorbing it and aligning itself with it.... The alienation of the spectator...works like this: The more he contemplates, the less he lives; the more he identifies with the dominant images of need, the less he understands his own life and his own desires."

Or Jean Baudrillard: "It is the fantasy of seizing reality live that continues—ever since Narcissus bent over his spring. Surprising the real in order to immobilize it, suspending the real in the expiration of its double."

▶

Def Leppard's "Photograph" and A Flock of Seagulls' "Wishing (If I Had a Photograph of You)" were both recorded in 1982 and released on LPs in the first months of 1983. Both are exquisitely overproduced, catchy, cynical pop songs that borrow enough tropes from other genres (heavy metal and new wave, respectively) to pass; both present a lonely narrator, separated from the object of his desire. Since both bands' videos appeared regularly on MTV during that network's early years, it is unsurprising that these two songs foreground visual representation.

In the '80s, we knew Def Leppard and A Flock of Seagulls as much from their videos as from their songs' radio play, and the visible signifiers of their style allowed us to differentiate them more than their layered, multi-tracked pop songs did: a shirtless drummer wearing Union Jack shorts and sweatband, and banging away at a full kit, conveyed virility; a balding drummer wearing a black vest and awkwardly bashing two Rototoms did not. These two videos shaped how we received the songs, of course: Def Leppard's video, with caged women, a spectral switchblade, and a lead guitarist apparently orgasming during his solo, pleased creepy kids with designs on sexual harassment; A Flock of Seagulls' video, with a guy moping around a nearly empty spaceship, pleased creepy kids who felt too shy for real human contact and just wanted to be left alone.

In 1983, seeking that solitude, I retired to my bedroom and my stereo, and began forging relationships with things as much as with people. I preferred the Flock of Seagulls song—it's marginally subtler than Def Leppard's song, and its repetitions and the way Mike Score implicitly curses his life's longueurs spoke to my own adolescent ennui—but I also preferred it because we who collect embrace mediated experience: otherwise, we wouldn't selectively hoard objects. The photograph fixing a person's likeness at some specific moment is perfect in a way the person can never be; photographs, like recordings, collapse distance and time, and enable fantasies of owning some enduring, always-available past. Joe Elliott's desire for contact is the same urge that brings music fans to concerts in search of an "experience," itself mediated, commodified, and existing primarily in our imaginations. I used to expect the real to correspond to its representation—at least on the concert stage—and was inevitably disappointed by the great divide between sloppy live musical performances and the records I'd idealized through repeated listening.

Though I probably wouldn't have admitted it to anyone, I liked the Def Leppard song, too. No matter how expansive my record collection, then or now; no matter the ardency of my desire for a certain record; no matter how much time I might spend listening to records; in the words of Joe Elliott, "It's not enough." John Berger has claimed that "photography is the process of rendering observation self-conscious." Once collecting records progresses from keeping a few favorites around the house to alphabetizing shelves one hopes one's friends won't touch, it is the process of rendering listening self-conscious.

▶

We understood desire as it was fabricated and promoted daily on our newly cabled TV sets and the networks that were developed to fill those channels. We were told we wanted our MTV, and soon enough we did want it. We slumped into our couches and stared, and spoke to each other mostly on vacant phone calls from our bedrooms, our walls screened with posters and glossy magazine clippings and photo collages we'd hung there to reflect ourselves to ourselves. We were always observed, always observing. We knew the crucial question—*How do I look?*—even if the answer eluded us. We learned how to gaze pensively into middle distance and how to clench a fist and pout at the mirror, learned the values of legwarmers and jelly bracelets and strategically deployed bandanas and Adidas trackpants and leather jackets and earrings in one ear and Swatch watches and giant T-shirts emblazoned with what Frankie said. We spiked and dyed and rat-tailed and crimped and shaved our hair, Moonwalked and pegged our jeans and practiced curled-lip sneers, wished our bedrooms were halls of mirrors outfitted with fog machines. We walked into stores and saw ourselves reproduced on monitors overhead. We failed to see the store managers watching us from behind one-way glass because we watched ourselves in that same surface. So many of the videos we viewed—"Borderline," "Billie Jean," "Don't You Want Me"—showed their subjects being photographed or filmed, and revealed the format as artifice even as they hoped we'd believe the stories they told. We did believe. We wanted to pose for our own photos and videos and invent our own stories, too—and we would, as soon as we looked perfect.

SECTION 25: "Trident"
("The Beast" 12″, Factory Records, 1982)

> Yet in spite of the immeasurable importance of nuclear weapons, the world has declined, on the whole, to think about them very much. We have thus far failed to fashion, or to discover within ourselves, an emotional or intellectual or political response to them. This peculiar failure of response...has itself been such a striking phenomenon that it has to be regarded as an extremely important part of the nuclear predicament.
>
> —Jonathan Schell, *The Fate of the Earth* (1982)

February 19, 1982: at Danceteria in New York City, Section 25—an obscure-and-growing-obscurer band from seedy seaside resort Blackpool, England—began their set with the four-and-a-half-minute instrumental "Trident." Little more than a single searing, oscillating synthesizer note, flanged drums bashing a martial rhythm, and a doomy, throbbing bassline playing an octave interval from which it climbed and descended, the song was "never performed in more dramatic style," according to the liner notes of *Live in America & Europe 1982,* a posthumously issued document of two brief tours Section 25 undertook that year. "Trident," like much of Section 25's output, is some of the most ominous, hypnotic, vaguely danceable music recorded in that era.

June 21, 1981: the Electric Boat Division of the General Dynamics Corporation announced "a very successful [test] run" of the USS *Ohio*—the United States's first Trident nuclear-powered submarine, a $1.2 billion, eighteen-thousand-ton vessel armed with Trident nuclear missiles, still considered "the world's deadliest weapon"—and promised to deliver it, two years behind schedule, to the Bangor Naval Submarine Base in Puget Sound later that year. Designed to patrol the seas, submerged for months at a time and following random courses to avoid detection, the Trident offered mobile deterrence to the USSR's more numerous land-based strategic nuclear arsenal, and was considered provocative in part because its missiles could be fired underwater from points near the Soviet coastlines, thus decreasing warning time. At the *Ohio*'s commissioning ceremonies, on Veterans Day, 1981, Secretary of the Navy John F. Lehman, Jr., told an audience of eight thousand that "our Trident submarines are deterrence personified." A month before Section 25 played at Danceteria, the Air Force Space and Missile Test Center announced that the *Ohio* had successfully test-fired its first Trident missile.

In England, meanwhile, Prime Minister Margaret Thatcher awaited a supply of Trident missiles she had requested for British NATO forces. Thatcher had approved memos written by Britain's Ministry of Defence in 1978, the year before she was elected, stating that Trident missiles should replace the 1960s-era Polaris nuclear missiles then arming British submarines. In its report on these memos, the *Manchester Guardian* noted that

> the British government opted for the Trident nuclear weapons system because it estimated it could kill up to 10 million Russians and inflict "unacceptable dam-

> age" on the former Soviet Union.... The breakdown of [Moscow or St. Petersburg] as a functioning community could be accomplished by inflicting "severe structural damage" on buildings across 40% of a city, the document argued. If the bombs were detonated in the air, this would be likely to kill at least 40% of the inhabitants instantly. But the document pointed out that up to 30% of city populations could be evacuated to a network of underground bunkers. These would protect people against bombs exploded in the air, it argued, but not against those detonated at ground level.

Between 1979 and 1981, police arrested over four hundred protesters at the General Dynamics shipyard in Groton, Connecticut. Activist Peter DeMott repeatedly drove a van into the rudder of the USS *Florida,* a Trident submarine under construction, during another launch ceremony; Navy Shore Patrol had to smash the van's windshield and pull DeMott out to get him to stop. Others hammered missile hatches and splashed blood on submarines, or simply chained themselves together to block the shipyard's entrance. A quarter of a million people marched through central London as part of a Campaign for Nuclear Disarmament rally to protest nuclear missile bases in the UK; a few months later, two or three times as many people gathered in New York's Central Park to support a nuclear freeze. Activists at Bangor regularly cut fences and planted gardens inside the base to protest the Trident program. When the USS *Ohio* finally arrived there—in August 1982, after voyaging from Groton through the Panama Canal and up the west coast—forty-six protesters defied its Coast Guard escort in an unsuccessful attempt at a blockade.

But by then, the *Ohio*'s twenty-four Trident I C-4 missiles—each of them, according to London's International Institute for Strategic Studies, with a range of over four thousand miles and bearing eight 100-kiloton, multiple independently targetable reentry vehicle (MIRV) warheads—were already on the path to obsolescence: the *New York Times* had reported in July 1982 that the United States Navy was "accelerating development" of the even more powerful Trident II missile. Not only would the Trident II D-5 be capable of destroying hardened installations, it would be accurate to within a hundred yards, and could achieve a top speed of nearly four miles per second—equivalent to more than 13,500 mph. (It was deployed in 1990.)

Soviet-American détente collapsed with the December 1979 Soviet invasion of Afghanistan and President Jimmy Carter's declaration of a grain embargo, as well as NATO's decision that same month to place US Pershing II missiles in Western Europe to counter Soviet SS-20s. Carter's 1980 boycott of the Moscow Olympics further damaged diplomacy—as did that year's presidential election in the United States, which included the pledge in the Republican National Convention platform "to achieve overall military and technological superiority over the Soviet Union." Ronald Reagan believed, as he said in a 1982 speech to British Parliament, that "the emergency is upon us," and oversaw the most extensive peacetime military buildup in American history. The nuclear arms race he relaunched in the initial months of his presidency would eventually cost the United States, during his administration, $34 million per *hour.* "An NBC/Associated Press survey in mid-December 1981 found that seventy-six percent of the public believed that nuclear war was 'likely' within a few years," according to Ronald E. Powaski's book *March to Armageddon.* "One defense expert after another warned that a nuclear war was inevitable if not imminent. Stated George Kennan: 'Never in my thirty-five years of public service have I been so afraid of nuclear war.' Said Admiral Hyman Rickover, creator of America's nuclear Navy: 'I think we will probably destroy ourselves.'"

▶

I learned the acronym ICBM—intercontintental ballistic missile—playing *Missile Command* on a friend's Atari 2600 around age ten. In that game, adapted from the arcade version, missile contrails a single pixel wide, fired by an unknown—but, at the dawn of the 1980s, implicitly Soviet—aggressor fell from the sky toward silhouetted cities our anti-ballistic missile batteries defended. When a missile struck, a small mushroom cloud expanded and buildings crumbled. We could intercept the incoming warheads, exploding them in digitized fireballs that rained no debris. But our own missiles, unlike those cascading upon us, were finite in number, and ultimately there was no real defense: the missiles came faster and in greater numbers—even as MIRVs—as the game progressed, until, inevitably, all six cities were annihilated.

If Cold War technologies now seem both fearsome and retro-futurist, provisional and yet enduring—the neutron bomb, the U-2 reconnaissance plane, Project Excelsior's open-air gondola—then the Atari 2600 console itself was an ideal object from the late Cold War: its hard, grooved black plastic (with a slot to shove the game cartridges into, a few metal switches, and a joystick with a single red button—and in the early 1980s, we all knew what having one's finger on the button meant) was accented with a fake woodgrain veneer strip along its front, as if to signify both homely appeal and mid-century modernist elegance. The Atari hooked up to the family television set: the tools of our warfare were both unimaginable and strangely familiar.

ICBM conjures a larger lexicon of historical anxiety—bomb shelter, missile silo, proliferation, first strike, NORAD, nuclear winter, mutual assured destruction, electromagnetic pulse—that we have updated to reflect contemporary anxieties: orange threat level, dirty bomb, WMD, anthrax, Homeland Security, pilotless drone, extraordinary rendition, sleeper cells, no-fly list, first responder, Patriot Act. The acronym ICBM depersonalizes weaponry we once knew by its often-mythic names—Atlas, Jupiter, Titan, Poseidon, Nike—but at the cusp of the 1980s we were all, willing or not, experts in military acronyms and terminology.

▶

Section 25, in 1982, barely remained a band. Brothers Larry and Vin Cassidy had fired guitarist Paul Wiggin, in part because of his refusal to fly to gigs. Wiggin's rasping, echoey textures defined the band's first two albums, and without him the Cassidys had to discard most of their repertoire. The first record, *Always Now,* had sold well, but, because of its expensive, elaborate packaging—a heavy, matchbook-style sleeve, the marbleized interior of which was reproduced under a special license—the band had seen little income from it. The self-produced second LP, *The Key of Dreams,* had been edited from hours of recorded studio improvisation, and their label, Factory Records, offloaded it to its subsidiary Factory Benelux imprint.

The British music press had long mocked Section 25 for their perceived seriousness and lack of humor: "Although the music is rolling, the vocals are harsh and packed with false anger," Mick Middles declared in *Sounds.* "The overall effect is unattractive and abrasive." *NME:* "Section 25, a drab three-piece. The small, austere bass player orated doomed and distant vocals over angular riffs and thrashing guitar chords." And in a review of *The Key of Dreams, Vinyl* offered a series of backhanded compliments:

> The strength of these very ordinary gloomy songs lies in their ability to convey subtleties of feeling with as few means as possible.... The only apparent structure in the music is effected by frugal but syncopated drum-beats. Bass guitar and guitar provide mainly atmospheric smears of sound... and the vocalist mouths his lyrics with every appearance of disgust. Provided that you are absolutely knackered or smashed this record will make an oppressive but lasting impression on you.

At Danceteria, the Cassidy brothers were joined by percussionist Lee Shallcross, and, as a three-piece, Section 25 played mainly repetitive, droning dirges, with taped backing tracks to fill out the meager instrumentation of some songs. Larry Cassidy either mumbled or shouted his minimal vocals. The applause following each song evidences a similar scarcity. Not long after the brief American tour, Section 25 retreated to the studio. "When we came back after that tour we did a few gigs in England, but we just were really pissed off at the way things were, and we took a year off to re-think things. Didn't do anything for a year but write songs," Vin Cassidy told an interviewer in 1985. "The fact that Paul, the old guitarist, was such a big part of the band when he left—well, it seemed a farce to try and continue doing some of those songs."

▶

The yellow-and-black fallout shelter symbols affixed to buildings were large enough to see from the car as we drove by, and I saw them everywhere in my hometown: on the granite-and-limestone Memorial Auditorium, on churches, on the courthouse, on brick tenements. Nearly everywhere I went, these rusting, three-triangle signs, hung in the decade before I was born, afforded inescapable reminders of the unthinkable. Replicas can now be purchased at Amazon.com for $19.99: "Rugged and Distressed for Vintage Look." "Create your own refuge with this Fallout Shelter Sign. Perfect for game rooms, garages, dens, and bars."

May Street School, which I attended from kindergarten through sixth grade, had been designated a fallout shelter. (Like every child raised in the postwar era, I had to apprehend, simultaneously, the myriad complexities of my life and the world, as well as the fact that it all could be obliterated in a flash of light, and I received these various educations at the same site. Did I know then the folly of believing my neighbors and I could survive a nuclear attack huddled in a basement lunchroom?) In those high-ceilinged classrooms, we hung our coats in cubbies, sat at wooden desks that still had inkwells, and opened the tall, multi-paned windows using poles tipped with brass hooks. We ended each school day with military efficiency, lining up double-file in the dark central hallway to form two patrol lines, each led by a student patrol leader wearing a fluorescent orange belt. Mr. Rowland, who taught sixth grade and supervised dismissal, would not release us until we'd satisfied him we were quiet—someone would always whisper, "Just shut up so we can go"—at which point our patrol lines marched out the north and south doors into the daylight to head home. At 10:00 A.M. every Tuesday, a nearby civil defense siren was tested, and its low wail, even repeated regularly, refused to harmonize with the other school sounds we knew so well: creaking floorboards, hissing radiators, the passing traffic on May Street, Ms. Nadolski's tapping chalk.

▶

The photograph covers the record's front sleeve: a steep slate slope in the Snowdonia region of Wales; the hilltop vanished in fog; a series of multicolored poles planted on this rugged terrain, starting from the foreground to shape a precise ninety-degree angle on the land's irregular contours. A thin gray banner, nearly as invisible as the hilltop, overlays this image: on it, in all-caps sans-serif type, appear the spaced words SECTION 25 FROM THE HIP FACT

90 FACTORY COMMUNICATIONS LTD. The back cover of the album is entirely pale blue but for a similar banner, on which have been reproduced vertical bars the colors of the poles from the front, spaced in 2-D the way the poles appeared in 3-D perspective on the front, with the numbers "25" and "90" inserted between two sets of these vertical bars.

I plucked this cryptic LP from a bin at Al Bum's—another site of much of my primary education—in 1987. Its cover image combined the pastoral and the postmodern in what felt a direct appeal to my young sensibilities: the natural was, as I experienced it, often obscured by the artificial—irreparably ruined, yet still somehow beautiful. ("This is the region you were born in," Larry Cassidy mutters in the downbeat "Regions" from *The Key of Dreams,* acknowledging that whatever world any of us has been born into is always already imperfect.) I knew the Factory label well enough to know I should buy the record; I knew that "FACT 90" was the record's catalog number; and I knew that if the music on the record was half as cool as the cover art, I would love it.

I did love the LP, eight songs of synthesizers both lush and brutal, crystalline and phantom, pinned down by crisp programmed drums and humanized by Jenny Ross's sweet, demure voice. I didn't yet know that this LP was borne of crisis and a year of sequestration, nor that it marked a huge stylistic shift for the band. I didn't realize that Section 25 had, by the time I found them, already disintegrated a second time, after *From the Hip* failed to earn the band a living. I only knew that I wanted to buy their other records as quickly as I could find them—first, at Al Bum's, the *Love & Hate* LP and the "Bad News Week" 12″—and then, at the old Planet Records shop in Boston's Kenmore Square, the *Always Now* LP and most of the early singles. From Newbury Comics, the "Looking from a Hilltop" 12″, discounted to $1.99. A friend's father's graduate student dubbed *The Key of Dreams* onto a cassette for me, and I wore that tape out before finding my own copy of the album. For years I headed straight to the "S" bin of every used record store I entered. What British music journalists had, a few years earlier, heard as derivative, dull, and earnest, I found bracing: mid-'80s corporate music insulted me with party-boy hair-band excess, hip-hop braggadocio, syrupy teen pop, and airbrushed has-beens, all so obviously focus-tested and target-marketed. I refused to be a target. Section 25's music and self-presentation were minimal—everything about the band signified a rigor and an indifference mostly absent in the era's mass culture. If I was intended to consume the easy and the approachable, my refusals began with my valuation of the difficult and the inaccessible.

My friend Ben and I had, those high school years, encoded the phrase "Nova Scotia" to indicate not only what we imagined a perfectly remote place, but also the idea of retreat from an at-times overwhelming world—"Such a Nova Scotia day," he'd mutter to me as we passed in the hall, or simply "Nova Scotia"—and Section 25's music connoted similar feelings. Both Section 25 and Nova Scotia seemed so far off the map of what mattered to everyone but me that I burdened them with whatever meanings I liked. Maybe in 1981 too much morose austerity infected pop music, but by 1987 I drowned in celebratory Reaganesque fake cheer. Like every teenager—though possibly to a greater extent than most—I walked through rainstorms until my sneakers squished, photographed the smokestacks and spires of my city at dusk, discovered the bottomless cup of coffee, wore out the horizon with watching. The relentless dissonance of "Trident" merely reinforced my worldview. How could I have failed to relate to a song titled "Bad News Week" that begins with the proclamation, "It's good news week: someone's dropped a bomb somewhere / contaminating atmosphere and blackening the sky"? A quarter century removed from my teenaged self, I still sometimes find solace in this music. Teen angst may never have found a more suitable set of reasons, a more potent real-world context, than the Cold War.

▶

Always Now begins with the propulsive track "Friendly Fires," in which the sole melodic notes are achieved by Larry Cassidy's flat, out-of-tune voice. The song is otherwise all insistent drumming, a three-note bassline, and a wash of distorted, screeching jet-engine guitar:

> Flying so high
> flying so high
> you can't hear them
> you can't see them
> they're on their way
> they're on their way
> over
> to you

No one can escape
this kind of war
40,000 feet above the floor
and the little children
have nowhere to run
they don't even know
what's going on

Flying so high
flying so high
you can't hear them
you can't see them
they're on their way
they're on their way
over
to you

As an introduction to Section 25, "Friendly Fires" sets forth not only the self-imposed, anxious constraints of the band's early sound, but also the dominant theme of much of their music: we are helpless against military power. The early records treat this topic with numbed despair; eventually, as the music became more melodic and sensual, war became something to resist with optimism, however naïve that optimism might seem. Still, it would be 1984 before Larry Cassidy could admit to an interviewer from the *Lancashire Evening Post* that "you're not as likely to feel suicidal when you hear us now."

If "Friendly Fires" puts the listener in the position of the

Vietnamese and Cambodians being carpet-bombed by B-52s cruising the stratosphere—and it is nearly impossible to hear the song without also recalling Nick Ut's photograph of Kim Phúc and other children fleeing a napalm strike—and if "Trident" distills the terror of nuclear warheads into a furious, wordless distress signal, Section 25's subsequent work refined and articulated such emotions. We regard our potential annihilation everywhere in the band's music, particularly in song titles—"Warhead," "Be Brave," "No Abiding Place," "The Last Man in Europe," "God's Playground," "Beneath the Blade"—and in so many lyrics about bombs going off, "blow[ing] it all to bits," "drop[ping] the bloody bomb," and on and on. On side two of *From the Hip,* the overbearing synthetic tensions of "Program for Light" resolve only in the sound of a massive explosion that leads straight into the acoustic lament "Desert"—a sequence of sounds and titles that does not seem accidental. But these prominent references never reduce the songs to agitprop or easy opportunism. Rather, they seem fundamental to Section 25's poetics—representing in music a particular dread and despair that afflicted the late 1970s and early 1980s. Countless bands have recorded an anti-nuclear song or two: but Section 25 differed from most in the depth of their sincerity—and, presumably, their terror—about the issue, and their inability to stop making music about our nuclear peril.

Haunted, melancholy soundscapes persisted on the band's late records, though they became gentler elegies—even featuring a recorder and acoustic guitar in 1985's B-side "The Guitar Waltz": "Just want to fry in the white light / With all my friends becoming bright / They glow for days, their fears unknown / And we don't hear a single moan." Section 25's music responded to the late Cold War as much as did *Missile Command*—it insisted that, in the atomic age, there isn't much else worth worrying about, no matter how much we may wish to deny the potential for nuclear apocalypse. But just before their 1983 hiatus, Section 25 realized an answer to these anxieties in the ethos not of punk but of hippie culture, and two songs recorded and released in the wake of the US tour document this changing view: "You say you want the truth? / You say you need the truth? / You need to feel the truth? / The truth is love, you know," Larry Cassidy moans in "The Beast." "I want to live and love / without fear," he admits in "Hold Me": "Without love / we are nothing." Transcribed, these lyrics seem like schoolboy flower-power clichés: trust me that the context of Section 25's music—especially since these were two of the band's first songs to feature prominently the warmth of analog synthesizers—transforms them. To counter the fear of annihilation with candid hopefulness aligned Section 25 with the anti-nuclear Plowshares activists—themselves an outgrowth of the 1960s—who used hardware-store hammers to batter missiles and submarines. We might consider Section 25's music some of the most secular-humanist post-punk ever recorded.

▸

A chronology of certain events in 1983:

> Having concluded correctly that they could no longer remain 'punks,' but rejecting a change of name, the

> Cassidy brothers recruited Larry's wife Jenny Ross to play keyboards and sing...new, lighter material....They unveiled a spiked synthetic pop outfit of considerable sophistication.... The new-look Section 25 premiered an embryonic electro set at the Hacienda, Manchester, on 3 February 1983....While by no means disastrous, the date was poorly attended, and...the quartet promptly cancelled further live work to concentrate on further refining their new musical direction.... Between February and August 1983 the core quartet of Larry, Vin, Lee and Jenny worked tirelessly on new material for their make-or-break third album.... In August, the band recorded what became *From the Hip* at Rockfield Studios in Wales. (James Nice, liner notes to Section 25, *Deus ex Machina: Archive Recordings 1983–1985* CD.)

The cover of *TIME* magazine's January 31 issue depicted a Pershing II missile lifting into a clouded sky. "NUCLEAR POKER: The Stakes Get Higher And Higher," read the caption. Strobe Talbott's lengthy cover story dubbed 1983 "The Year of the Missile," because of the ongoing dispute about intermediate-range Soviet SS-20 missiles aimed at Western Europe, and the scheduled deployment of intermediate-range US Pershing II missiles in West Germany to counter them; the Pershing II, launched from a mobile carrier and accurate to within fifty meters, could reach targets in the Soviet Union in four to six minutes—leaving the USSR almost no time for a retaliatory strike. "The sense of urgency is intense, the diplomatic activity frenzied," Talbott wrote. "The Pershing IIs would arc-up to the edge of space and unleash earth-penetrating warheads that can destroy concrete-reinforced bunkers 100 ft. underground," he noted, adding that "the West Europeans [fear] that their countries might be the battlefield" for the "limited" nuclear exchange Reagan's administration believed possible.

The Soviets' covert activities were similarly frenzied. Throughout the early 1980s, the USSR operated the largest-ever peacetime "intelligence program, . . . to scrutinize the United States and NATO for evidence of immediate preparations for nuclear war," former CIA officer Peter Vincent Pry writes in his book *War Scare: Russia and America on the Nuclear Brink*. "It was funded and manned at a wartime level, on the assumption that nuclear war was imminent," and its documents "make crystal clear the Soviet Union's virtual obsession during the 1980s with the immediate threat of a US nuclear surprise attack." On February 17, 1983, the KGB cabled its operatives that the program had "acquired an especial degree of urgency" because of NATO's scheduled deployment of the Pershing II.

Reagan, speaking at the National Association of Evangelicals convention in Florida on March 8, named the USSR an "evil empire." Two weeks later, in a nationally televised prime-time speech, Reagan announced his Strategic Defense Initiative (or SDI; the next day, Senator Ted Kennedy criticized the plan as "reckless Star Wars schemes," and the insult stuck):

> It took one kind of military force to deter an attack when we had far more nuclear weapons than any other power; it takes another kind now that the Soviets, for

> example, have enough accurate and powerful nuclear weapons to destroy virtually all of our missiles on the ground. Now, this is not to say that the Soviet Union is planning to make war on us. Nor do I believe a war is inevitable—quite the contrary. But what must be recognized is that our security is based on being prepared to meet all threats....
>
> Let me share with you a vision of the future which offers hope. It is that we embark on a program to counter the awesome Soviet missile threat with measures that are defensive....
>
> What if free people could live secure in the knowledge that their security did not rest upon the threat of instant US retaliation to deter a Soviet attack, that we could intercept and destroy strategic ballistic missiles before they reached our own soil or that of our allies?
>
> ...Isn't it worth every investment necessary to free the world from the threat of nuclear war? We know it is.

The nuclear-scare movie *WarGames* premiered on June 6, 1983. Twelve years old, I saw it that summer, perhaps because it seemed, with high school–age characters, a movie aimed at kids—especially kids, like me, who'd dabbled with computers. In the film's opening sequence, one member of an American missile silo crew draws a pistol on his superior, who is unwilling to follow protocol and "kill twenty million people" during a launch exercise that neither man knows is only a test. "Twenty-three minutes from warning to impact," an assistant says in a meeting at North American Defense Command (NORAD) after the failed test. "Six minutes if it's sub-launched." She speaks these specifics in a weary, almost blasé tone—and because her words delineated how little I knew about the details of nuclear war, they suggested, as I sat in the theater's darkness, how suddenly and terribly our ends might come. "I wish I didn't know about any of this," Matthew Broderick's character complains, late in the movie, when he thinks that the simulated nuclear war he started on a computer will, within hours, incite a real one. "I wish I was like everybody else in the world and tomorrow it would just be over."

We see two primary sets in *WarGames*—the rumpled suburban bedroom of a computer nerd, and NORAD's war room beneath Cheyenne Mountain. The computer terminal and the cathode-ray tube screen link these two rooms; in each room, characters initiate and observe nuclear war simulations. As the film clarifies, the bedroom *is* a war room in a nuclear conflict: civilians and cities are primary targets, as are airstrips, silos, and radar installations. The film offers optics not unlike those of my friend's Atari running *Missile Command,* though on the cinema's wide screen: as NORAD's computer cycles through various possible causes and strategies under which nuclear war might be waged, the flickering graphics of missile flight paths and strikes play over the characters in the film and the audience in the theater, all of us rapt at the prospects our technologies have wrought.

If the idea that a computer could start World War III seemed no more than a chilling fiction in the summer of 1983, consider Ronald E. Powaski's assertion that

> in an eighteen-month period that ended June 30, 1980,...NORAD experienced 147 false alarms that were serious enough to require an assessment of whether they constituted a Soviet attack. In November 1979 fighters were scrambled after a NORAD computer falsely indicated that a Soviet attack was in progress. Twice in June 1980 a computer falsely warned that the Soviets had launched submarine- and land-based missiles at the United States. It was discovered that a computer chip costing forty-six cents was responsible for the false alarms. No one could say how many computer failures and accidents the Soviets [had] experienced. Ultimately, and ironically, America's security had come to depend as much on the efficiency of Soviet computers as on its own.

Korean Air Lines Flight 007—a Boeing 747 traveling from New York to Seoul with a layover to refuel in Anchorage, Alaska—strayed unaware into Soviet airspace in the early morning hours of September 1, 1983. A Soviet Sukhoi Su-15 intercepted Flight 007 over the Sea of Okhotsk and Sakhalin Island before firing two missiles that brought down the airliner. The crew and passengers—269 people, including Larry McDonald, a congressman from Georgia—were all killed.

Several months earlier, shortly after Reagan's announcement of SDI, the US Pacific Fleet had conducted its largest maneuvers since World War II. "During the three-week exercise, Navy warplanes...directly overflew Soviet military installations on the Kurile Islands, just north of Japan," Seymour Hersh writes in his book *"The Target Is Destroyed."* And on the night of August 31 to September 1, Hersh reports, a US RC-135 reconnaissance aircraft—a modified Boeing 707—had flown figure-eights off the Kamchatka peninsula in advance of a suspected Soviet missile test; KAL 007 flew into the airspace the RC-135 had just vacated. In *War Scare,* Pry—citing a KGB double agent—claims that "the Soviets may have shot down KAL 007 because they mistook the airliner for an RC-135....Their hysteria about an anticipated US surprise attack led them to overreact," and concludes that

> the United States and its NATO allies have never shot down even a Soviet or Russian intelligence aircraft, let alone a civilian airliner, in retaliation for airspace violations, because the threat posed by such intrusions does not justify so draconian a response. The Soviet destruction of KAL 007 makes sense militarily and politically only if the Soviets believed an attack on their territory was imminent.

As US and Japanese intelligence assembled intercepted Soviet communications and determined that the airliner had been shot down, Hersh recounts, "some senior Air Force and Navy officers in the Pacific...'got emotional,' as one officer recalled, and began formulating actions 'that could have started World War III.'" US officials began a propaganda war—through the press, on the floor of the United Nations, and during previously scheduled arms talks in Geneva—with their Soviet counterparts over incompletely interpreted and translated intelligence. The US stoked public anger over what Reagan called a deliberate "massacre"; Soviet General Secretary Yuri Andropov claimed the flyover was a premeditated provocation and accused the Reagan administration of "imperial ambitions," "extreme adventurism," and "hypocritical preaching about morality and humanism."

If the shootdown of KAL 007 was "a function," as Hersh writes, "both of poor command-and-control and a 'spastic response' by Soviet Air Defense officials," then the actions of Soviet Lieutenant Colonel Stanislav Petrov a few weeks later were anything but. Petrov commanded an early warning bunker outside Moscow on September 26, when, as he recalled in a 1998 interview with the *Daily Mail,* the "system suddenly showed the launch of five ballistic nuclear missiles within three minutes from a base on the Atlantic coast of America. It was showing a full nuclear attack. I felt as if I'd been punched in my nervous system." But the nuclear first strike is designed to overwhelm an opponent's offensive and defensive capabilities and neutralize retaliatory capabilities; five missiles could not do so. After ground-based radar failed to confirm incoming ICBMs, Petrov surmised that the system had malfunctioned, and didn't forward the alert up the chain of command.

The *Washington Post,* describing the incident in 1999, reported that

> Petrov...recalled making the tense decision under enormous stress—electronic maps and consoles were flashing as he held a phone in one hand and juggled an

> intercom in the other, trying to take in all the information at once. Another officer at the early-warning facility was shouting into the phone to him to remain calm and do his job.
>
> "I had a funny feeling in my gut," Petrov said. "I didn't want to make a mistake. I made a decision, and that was it."

Petrov was substituting for another officer who should have been on duty that night. The radar glitch was, according to the *Post,* "traced to [a] satellite, which picked up the sun's reflection off the tops of clouds and mistook it for a missile launch. The computer program that was supposed to filter out such information was rewritten." "After it was over," Petrov said, "I drank half a liter of vodka as if it were only a glass, and slept for 28 hours."

"What was probably the single most dangerous incident of the early 1980s," according to Pry in *War Scare,*

> occurred during a NATO military exercise known as ABLE ARCHER–83, held on November 2–11, 1983.... It was nothing less than a rehearsal for World War III, with US nuclear forces based in Europe practicing nuclear-release procedures and going through the steps for making a nuclear strike. The Soviets were leery of NATO military exercises, because Soviet military doctrine warned that an enemy might use training to conceal preparations for an actual attack.

Don Oberdorfer, in *From the Cold War to a New Era,* confirms this danger, writing that, as NATO intelligence monitored transmissions during ABLE ARCHER–83, "an unusually sharp increase in the volume and urgency of the Warsaw Pact traffic was noted. More ominously, Moscow placed on higher alert status about a dozen nuclear-capable Soviet fighter aircraft stationed in forward bases in East Germany and Poland."

A front-page article in the *New York Times* on November 4 noted that a nuclear-powered Soviet attack submarine had surfaced fewer than five hundred miles off the South Carolina coast. Within a day the *Times* reported that the submarine might have been disabled by a US destroyer towing a sonar device—with which it was hunting Soviet subs. This submarine, "designed to kill US ballistic missile submarines," as Pry writes, was loitering not far from US "anchorages at Charleston and King's Bay, Georgia.... Its presence...off Charleston at this particular moment, in the middle of ABLE ARCHER–83...might have been coincidence, but probably it was not." (Soviet ships, trailed by US reconnaissance aircraft, towed the submarine to Cuba for repair.)

"The United States and NATO remained in the dark about the danger while ABLE ARCHER–83 was going on. It is inconceivable," Pry argues, "that the president, Joint Chiefs, and NATO allies would allow the war game to continue in the face of clear evidence the exercise could provoke a Soviet nuclear strike."

I watched *The Day After*—a made-for-TV movie depicting a thermonuclear attack and its aftermath, a movie about which I've retained few memories save images of people being vaporized—

with my parents, who had participated in duck-and-cover drills when they were students. A hundred million people in the United States tuned into ABC's broadcast on November 20; those of us in school had been prepared in class for the movie and instructed not to watch it alone. Counselors waited on toll-free hotlines. Secretary of State George Shultz gave an uneasy televised performance following the broadcast; even eternal optimist Ronald Reagan confided in his diary that the advance screening he saw "left [him] greatly depressed." My experience of the movie was one of utter dread, a dread that the ensuing weeks failed to diminish. I understood little of global politics, and nothing of conflicting US-Soviet ideologies beyond the inherited schoolyard insult "commie," but I understood all too well a vague-but-intense terror of nuclear war that the movie's sanitized details—"The catastrophic effects you have just witnessed are, in all likelihood, less severe than the destruction that would occur," a statement at the end of the film warned us—still magnified.

"The movie did not exaggerate," wrote Anthony Lewis in the *New York Times,* the morning after it aired. "Nor did it really tell us anything new; as one of the characters in it remarked, we have known the truth about nuclear weapons for nearly 40 years.... What the film did was to make our abstract knowledge of nuclear devastation concrete: personal, individual, and therefore terrible. It made us aware of reality."

The previous day, in his own first strike, *Times* television critic John Corry had asserted that "'The Day After' engenders a feeling of hopelessness, and to be without hope is to be passive. It is to believe that nothing will avail. Psychologically, this is to want to disarm, to throw down weapons rather than take them up." Corry presented a different awareness of reality:

> The Soviet Union has 5,000 ICBM warheads; the United States has 1,054 missile silos. The Soviet Union could target two ICBM warheads to each American silo, leaving it 3,000 warheads; 500 of these could be used to destroy American airfields, and another 500 could be used to wipe out military communications centers. This would still leave the Soviet Union with 2,000 warheads with which it could erase our cities.
>
> American Trident submarines would still be at sea, but the submarines do not have the ability to fire their missiles with the accuracy necessary to eliminate the second-strike Soviet missiles. If an American President declined to surrender after the first Soviet strike and ordered the Trident submarines to launch their missiles, he would be condemning our cities to their deaths.

This stark, simple, unnerving distillation of the "limited nuclear war" doctrine—in the newspaper of record, in the context not of political or military reporting but a review of a made-for-TV-movie—may have persuaded some readers of the virtues of deterrence and Reagan's arms buildup. (Limited nuclear war assumes "that nuclear hostilities can be halted at some new equilibrium in the balance of forces, before all-out attacks have been launched," writes Jonathan Schell in *The Fate of the Earth,* describing Corry's scenario as one "argued recently by nuclear theorists." In such a scenario, "rather than initiate the annihilation of both societies" following the Soviet strikes, "American leaders might acquiesce." Further, while the term "nuclear winter" was coined a month after Corry's article, its effects had been known for a decade. The hypothetical detonation of three thousand nuclear warheads in North America would have made retaliation pointless, because the resulting global cooling and ozone depletion would have condemned any surviving cities anyway.)

In a roundtable discussion ABC hosted after the movie, Carl Sagan presented another way of imagining deterrence: "Imagine a room, awash in gasoline. And there are two implacable enemies in that room. One of them has 9,000 matches. The other has 7,000 matches. Each of them is concerned about who's ahead, who's stronger.... If it weren't so tragic, it would be laughable."

On November 24, the first Pershing II missiles arrived at a US airbase in West Germany—fewer than twenty-four hours after West Germany's parliament voted in favor of their deployment.

Martin Walker, summing up the events of 1983, writes in *The Cold War: A History* that "US intelligence analyses of the great panic about an imminent US nuclear strike which had hit Moscow in the autumn of 1983, between the shooting down of the Korean airliner and the NATO Able Archer exercise, had sobered President Reagan. 'I don't see how [the Soviets] could believe that, but it's something to think about,' Reagan told his National Security Adviser, Robert McFarlane."

As for me, in February 1983 I graduated from cheap plastic boombox to receiver, turntable, and tapedeck, and spent much of that year in the bunker of my bedroom on Havelock Road. My windows screened by spruce branches, I listened intently on huge headphones to all the records I hoped might provide me the intelligence to decipher even the smallest fragments of the precarious, provisional nature of what I was experiencing.

▶

Section 25, if they were remembered at all in the years before the *Pitchfork* generation rediscovered Factory Records, were remembered for the modest club hit "megamix" of "Looking from a Hilltop," the second track on *From the Hip.* James Nice, in his 1997 biographical liner notes, argues that this track presents one possible genesis of acid house, because, performed live, it

> featured hard sequencer patterns and the piercing Roland TR-303 sound later typical of acid house. Vin Cassidy had stumbled across the remarkable effect by accident early in 1983, employing it to good effect on the unreleased 12″ remix of "Beating Heart," and in live performance the following year. While it might seem unlikely that audience members in Chicago or Detroit were inspired by Section 25 to further refine house and techno, the fact remains that a full year before these sounds reached Europe, a band from Blackpool had toured it across most of the major cities in the United States.

Music critic Sasha Frere-Jones, writing in the December 2001 issue of *The Wire,* indirectly supports this thesis with his reminiscence about seeing a 1984 Section 25 show in New York:

> I'd never heard drum machines through a PA and had no idea how punishing they could be. I couldn't hear a single word but I couldn't get their weird sound out of my head. The next day I bought the only Section 25 12″ I could find, 'Looking from a Hilltop (Megamix).' Backwards drum machines flew out like sparks, but crazy funky like someone here had programmed them, not some… foreigner. Then there was a blast of tape-mangled whiteboy guitar noise and some mopey chords and what was that girl saying? The whole thing floated in the fjord between the icy Factory scene in England and uptempo NYC edit tracks by Big Apple Productions and the Latin Rascals. Charging and droning, blowing my tiny mind, 'Hilltop' still sounds like music of no country.

Musicologically, such facts offer one ready reason for Section 25's posthumous reputation. Still, for years I felt surprised whenever I stumbled upon a reference to some Factory band other than Joy Division or New Order—especially Section 25, a band Ben and I considered our personal Nova Scotia. But in the wake of 9/11—whether because of renewed postmillennial anxieties, or simply because enough time had passed for the obligatory nostalgia-induced revival: or both, as in the case of Frere-Jones's reverie—post-punk regained cultural currency, spawned a bunch of admiring plagiarists, and Section 25's albums were reissued on CD a second time, along with rare, live, and archival recordings.

The informed dread and misplaced optimism of Section 25's work still seem to me the only viable options for maintaining one's sanity and one's humanity in the post–Cold War, ongoing War on Terror era—which may be another reason this band's music continues to speak to us so profoundly. Our anxieties may no longer be nuclear ones, though we still feel keenly the precariousness of our lives, whether via terrorism, environmental catastrophe, or economic crisis. Frere-Jones is correct in noting the apparent national exile of Section 25: missiles that can hurtle thousands of miles in minutes and bombers that can be refueled in flight to reach the opposite side of the earth without stopping render meaningless the idea of borders.

▶

Jenny Ross died of cancer in November 2004, after aborted attempts in the preceding years to resume playing music with Larry and Vin Cassidy. After her death, and nearly two decades after *Love & Hate,* the brothers did release two albums of new material, the second of which included Larry and Jenny's daughter on vocals. A third album, featuring re-recorded and reinterpreted versions of some of the band's 1980s tracks, was being prepared for a fall 2010 release when Larry Cassidy was found in his home, dead from an apparent blood clot.

The desk at which I sit is under the flight path of C-5 Galaxy transport airplanes from nearby Westover Air Reserve Base—which, during the Cold War, was a Strategic Air Command base, and thus a primary target of the USSR. Eight nuclear-armed B-52 bombers stood on twenty-four-hour alert at Westover, and could, within fifteen minutes of an alarm, be airborne, en route to the Soviet Union via the North Pole. Many afternoons the whining drone of a C-5's engines disrupts the quiet as the huge planes, big-bellied and low-flying, pass overhead.

In the line of hills I can see from my desk when the leaves are down, the former Strategic Air Command bunker, now owned by Amherst College, serves as a library depository and houses over eight miles of books. According to the *Boston Globe,* the bunker once held "food and water for a staff of 350 to survive for 35 days," and was designed to withstand the Soviet nuclear strike that would have incinerated Westover's B-52s and much of western Massachusetts. Its thinnest concrete walls are allegedly seven feet thick.

In 1983, the United States was estimated to possess more than 23,000 nuclear weapons—on submarines, in missile silos, on bombers, and in stockpiles. The Soviet Union was estimated to possess nearly 36,000 nuclear weapons that same year. (The two superpowers' combined total of warheads would peak at 64,000 in 1986.) As of February, 2011, the Federation of American Scientists reports that the United States and Russia each maintain an operational arsenal of approximately 1,900 warheads on high alert; the two countries combined still possess a "total inventory" of nearly

20,000 nuclear weapons; France, the United Kingdom, China, Israel, India, Pakistan, and North Korea are now estimated to possess more than 2,500 nuclear weapons among them.

The USS *Ohio,* originally scheduled for retirement in 2002, was—along with three more of the United States' eighteen Trident submarines—modified to transport guided missiles instead of ballistic missiles: the *Ohio* now bears Tomahawk cruise missiles, which can carry either conventional or nuclear warheads; it isn't due for decommissioning until 2023. The remaining fourteen Trident submarines and their Trident II D-5 missiles will remain operational until 2040.

Research and design of a replacement nuclear-armed submarine has already begun.

LOW: "Missouri"
(*Secret Name* LP, Kranky, 1999)

The café seemed the first local place Sarah and I might claim, a small but not inconsiderable reminder of the college town we'd left only days before—Ithaca, New York—and of our former lives in New England and Toronto. Here in rural central Pennsylvania, where I would begin a teaching job in two months, we felt dislocated and freaked out. The front page of the local paper, the first morning we awoke in our new rental house, was given to photos showing our fellow townspeople, with coolers and lawnchairs, lining the shoulders of US Route 15 to cheer flatbed trailers carrying NASCAR cars south from one racetrack to another. A sidewalk preacher blessed us every time we visited the post office or CVS. In a small park downtown, the reverent congregated for a marathon day of prayer. The local hospital: Evangelical Community Hospital. Amish men drove lopsided single-horse carriages on the roads west of town, and Mennonite families piled out of drab minivans to shop at Wal-Mart. The local religion was religion, along with high school football, pickup trucks, chicken and waffles, and hunting. Sarah and I drove forty minutes, the first weekend, to a nearby town with a small state university so we could see a movie.

On the way back, we noticed the café and decided to stop. Students lounged around a table on the sidewalk. Inside the door, I glanced past a pile of pamphlets ("Support the Zapatistas!" I imagined) to a few shelves of worn books, stereotypically mismatched furniture, and, framed by velvet curtains and covering the entire back wall, an ironic, faux-naïve mural of a haloed Jesus kneeling beside a lamb. Sarah stepped to the counter to order our coffees, and, by habit, I turned to the bookshelf. A few mass-market paperbacks, I now saw, were outnumbered by copies of the New Testament and the Gideons Bible. The pamphlets advertised Bible summer camp and a motorcycle ministry. I looked back to the mural: Jesus held his palms open in a gesture of embrace, and his large brown eyes bored into mine. Sarah handed the cashier some bills, and I took a few wobbly steps toward the counter. "This may be a really stupid question," I said to the cashier. "Is—is this a Christian café?"

"Sure is!" she said, smiling. "That's the theme!" She pointed to a ceiling-mounted speaker above us. "We even have Christian rock on the stereo."

We sat at a corner table in stunned silence, unable even to laugh. I stared at my café au lait as if it might poison me. "We just gave five dollars to the religious right," I moaned.

▶

I'd dismissed and then scrupulously avoided the band Low—a trio from Duluth, Minnesota, known for playing fragile, repetitive, slow songs that sometimes seemed more concerned with testing their microphones' ability to pick up the entire decay of a plucked guitar string than with melody—when I learned that two of the band's three members were practicing Mormons. Religious fervor of any sort has always made me uneasy, and, despite the praise critics and fans lavished on Low's records, I didn't want to support a band I imagined as fringe fundamentalist Christians. I based my poorly thought disavowal not on any specific knowledge or principle (my consumer boycotts were half-hearted at best) or, you know, actually listening to the band and determining whether I liked the music—exactly the sort of ignorant snap judgment I derided fundamentalists for making.

But by 1999, stuck in Pennsylvania, I finally included Low's new album, *Secret Name,* in a mail-order purchase: everyone raved about this double LP, it was issued on a label I respected, and I figured I should probably hear it. Even before I learned that "Missouri" probably alludes to Mormon settlers in that state and the persecution they faced until their eventual eviction in 1838, I found the song's brief opening lines evocative: "Oh, speak to me, Adam and Eve / Oh, Missouri." (Of course, these lines also confirmed my apprehensions about being proselytized to.) Guitarist and vocalist Alan Sparhawk sings in a shaky falsetto, conspicuously pronouncing "Missouri" as "Misery," and the words suggest the tensions between pre- and post-lapsarian language, the wish to communicate with one's ancestors, but especially the miseries of separation, the miseries of geography, and the miseries of religion: three sorrows I felt keenly at the cusp of the millennium, when an end-of-days vibe often seemed palpable, and even the dentist's waiting room was stocked with religious pamphlets.

Still, "Missouri" was—and remains—undeniably beautiful. And if, like much of Low's music, it captures a sense of dread in its melancholic minimalism, then it may be less spiritual than I think: the second coming is supposed to fill true believers with indescribable joy, but I've yet to hear a song by Low I'd regard as joyous. I have no idea what the three members of Low might or might not believe (given a number of the band's public statements, I suspect their theology is far more liberal than I once assumed), but their music both exhibits and responds to the dread many of us felt from certain events of the 1990s and beyond—L.A. riots and D.C. snipers; Branch Davidians, Aum Shinrikyo, Heaven's Gate; the Oklahoma City bombing and anti-abortion terrorism; armed militias and white supremacists; a man beaten and dragged behind a truck because he was black; a man beaten and tied to a fence because he was gay. It didn't require the country's divisions of belief becoming outlined forever in red and blue, nor religious fanatics flying planes into the World Trade Center, to convince me of the dangers of fundamentalism.

All of which is to say, as Sparhawk once concluded an interview: "This moment is as doomed as the rest."

CEX: "Enter Carter"

(*Get Your Badass On 7"* EP, 555 Recordings of Leeds, 2000)

It almost certainly required the Internet—and the early Internet, at that: a bunch of isolated mid-'90s obscurists seeking anonymous congress and debate with other freaks via 2400-baud dial-up line—to invent a musical genre name as self-obliviously stupid as "Intelligent Dance Music," or IDM. And yet, deep in the Bill Clinton years, before the Hale-Bopp comet flickered past and businesses bought ad space to reassure us they were "Y2K compliant," IDM was an accepted, if ridiculed, descriptor for synthesizer- or MIDI-based music never intended for clubs, but that—if you were a sensitive, slightly misunderstood fancier of vintage drum machines, C++, weed, and soldering irons—might well have provided insistent clicking background rhythms on your minidisc player as you sat in your school's computer lab, toggling between some listserv digest on the ASCII-formatted screen of your Pine e-mail client and a search of rec.music.marketplace.vinyl for old Aphex Twin 12″s.

Rockism was so suspect by the latter half of the 1990s that everyone I knew had traded in their guitar records for techno, ambient, and trance; trip-hop, illbient, drum 'n' bass, and jungle; techstep, dubstep, and grime; digital hardcore, chiptune, laptronica, electroclash, and all manner of other absurdly narrow, precisely taxonomized subgenres of electronic music. I own records produced by sampling the stutters of intentionally scratched CDs, records "programmed in Music 2000 on a Sony PlayStation," records made by modifying the circuits of handheld electronics, records comprised of "analogue tone poems" made by trading tapes through the mail—not one of which has been on my turntable for years. When everyone except the futurist diehards tired of records that didn't sound appreciably better or worse, just slightly different, whether played at 33⅓ or 45 RPM, some listeners found even terrible rock bands like the Strokes and the White Stripes refreshing.

The earliest records by Rjyan Kidwell—then a Maryland high school student making music under the name Cex (does it need saying that most electronic bands are one or two people at the most?)—were electronic pastorals, tentative keyboard melodies twinkling atop distorted beats and granular dissolves, with the occasional vocal sample. From the start, Kidwell mocked the electronic music scene, with sleeve notes such as his list of "alternate song titles for the 'IDM' crowd who demand meaningless gobbledeegook: Fff, Zadda Zoo, F?, Cpckes, Dol-Ell.i.zit, Zoo!d" and actual song titles—"Your Handwriting when You Were a Child in the Winter"—that punctured the fake nostalgia so many synthesized instrumentals seem designed to inspire.

"Enter Carter," a seventy-second goof, samples a dude who sounds almost shocked by how stoned he is: "So when something is *weird,* you've *got* to get a picture of it!" "I see what you're saying," another dude responds. "Weird things deserve pictures of them. As *proof* that they're *weird.* The pictures will then in turn make people think differently about the world and society." An android voice chimes in, deadpan: "Woooord up. I hear that." This conversation occurs over mournful synthesizer chords crossfaded into gentle feedback that wheezes briefly and is suddenly cut off. It's the sound of artificial intelligence getting high and spending all day surfing—a verb that, in its sense of adventure, still pertained—websites where Flash animation had only begun to overtake flying toasters and purple text on black backgrounds. The track's brevity, the dialogue's simultaneous pretensions and inanities, and the swift, unexpected ending all seem fitting tributes to IDM's historical moment: within months, Kidwell had moved on to spaz rap he improvised on stage, sometimes while stripping to his underwear. The only nostalgia the melancholic digital textures of IDM seem likely to inspire today is a yearning for what now seems the ease and prosperity of the pre-millennial years, when our traumas were small and isolated, and we coded our machines to sing them for us in the haunted voices of 1s and 0s.

PIXIES: "Break My Body," "Something Against You," "Broken Face" (*Surfer Rosa* LP, 4AD/Rough Trade, 1988)

Halloween afternoon, my senior year of high school. At the end of the school day, shadows already stretch from the huge white pines near Newton Square. The Pixies' record *Surfer Rosa* came out in the US at the end of summer, and, as we climb into my friend B.'s old blue Toyota in the upper parking lot, we slide a cassette of that album into the tapedeck and crank down the windows. The unseasonably warm air makes us frisky, as do the Pixies: last month we would've played *Rocket to Russia* or *This Is Boston Not L.A.*, but now the speakers in B.'s car vibrate and shudder with Joey Santiago's rough, whiny guitar. Unlike those other records, this one, still new and undiscovered, feels like it belongs to us alone. "Now let's not get too preachy-preach about kissy-kiss," Black Francis advises. I sit shotgun; Tim, floppy bangs covering half his face, sits in back.

On the floor at my feet, half a dozen cans of Silly String roll: B. has stolen them from his part-time job at Cumberland Farms.

Cars from two parking lots slowly creep downhill toward Highland Street and wait to turn. A year ago, two years ago, I would've been headed to cross-country practice, my running sneakers and shorts and T-shirt in a duffle bag at my shoulder; Coach Donahue would've handed us training schedules still damp from the mimeograph machine. A year earlier than that, I would've been walking home in Converse All-Stars, pegged jeans, and my dad's US Navy wool shirt, trying to look cool though I felt anything but. Now, I grab one of the cans of Silly String and shake it. Younger, backpack-burdened kids stream around the cars in twos and threes: I have no idea who any of them are. From the speakers, Black Francis shrieks and sputters. By the time he and Kim Deal harmonize, "Break my body, hold my bones," we've turned left onto Highland Street, still barely rolling in an almost entirely adolescent traffic jam. I hang out the window, then spray ribbons of pink foam on a troop of younger kids walking by: they lift three-ring binders as shields, shout at me, give me the finger, turn and run. Inside the car, Tim cackles, doubled over, and B. pounds the steering wheel. I haven't yet buckled my seatbelt—we're going five miles an hour, then maybe ten as I grab another can. We leave behind the foam-wreathed kids as, ahead of us, cars slip through the Newton Square rotary in four different directions.

"Somebody got hurt, somebody get hurt, somebody got hur-r-r-rt!" Kim Deal and Black Francis harmonize again, and then immediately the next song starts with a twangy guitar lick and a ferocious drumbeat. Black Francis's voice, run through some filter, sounds monstrous, chromed: "I've got something against you!"

"Get them, get them," Tim says, pointing at another cluster of kids.

We're heading up Pleasant Street toward Coffee Kingdom, starting to pick up speed. My arms and shoulders out the window, I aim the nozzle at the kids. Silly String shoots over the sidewalk as the kids try to dodge it, but I get their jeans, their sleeves, their shoes. I ease back into the car, laughing, and look at B. He's facing me, eyes nearly closed as he chokes out laughter, one hand on the wheel, the other pointing at the kids I just sprayed. Then I look through the windshield—where, a few car lengths in front of us, a pickup truck has stopped to make a left turn.

"Stop!" I shout, and then B. looks too and stomps the brake pedal. Screeching tires drown out the Pixies. I don't know how fast we're going when the hood of his Toyota crumples against the pickup truck's bumper: when I open my eyes, I see B. hitting his chin with his hand to force his face out from where it's wedged between steering wheel and dimpled safety glass. I too have left the impression of my skull in his windshield. In the backseat, Tim has torn his pants and cut his leg. We totter out of the car and sprawl on the strip of grass between sidewalk and curb, clutching our heads and groaning. The middle-aged guy driving the pickup truck comes over and shrugs, his hands palms up to the sky. "I'm really sorry," B. says. The kids marked with gobs of mostly wiped-off Silly String walk past us, laughing and pointing at the crushed Toyota. The speaker mounted in the open passenger door still plays music:

Black Francis yelps that he has a "broken face, uh-huh, uh-huh, uh-huh, uh-huh, oooh!"

FAUST: "Untitled: All on Saxes"
(*The Faust Tapes* LP, Virgin, 1973)

In 1901, Mrs. Elise Boyer Hall, president of the Orchestral Society of Boston, paid Claude Debussy five thousand francs to compose a rhapsody for saxophone—an instrument then some fifty years old, though it had yet to acquire much role in classical or popular music. Mrs. Hall informed the composer that she would perform the rhapsody herself. She had begun playing the saxophone after typhoid fever damaged her hearing: her late husband, a cocaine-addicted surgeon who had himself died of typhoid following an erroneously diagnosed appendectomy, suggested that learning the instrument might help prevent further impairment because of the pressure it would exert on her Eustachian tubes.

Debussy had "described the composition as 'ordered, paid for, and eaten'" for some time, but had done no work on the rhapsody when Mrs. Hall arrived unexpectedly at the composer's Paris home in the spring of 1903: "[This] lady, who is not satisfied being American but also allows herself the bizarre luxury of playing saxophone…ask[ed] me for an update about her piece! …I had to get down to it," he complained in a letter to conductor André Messager. To his wife, Debussy wrote that he was "trying to finish this goddamn piece as quickly as possible," and that "la Femme-Saxophone" "will never suspect how much she bored me. Does it not appear indecent to you, a woman in love with a saxophone, whose lips suck at the wooden mouthpiece of this ridiculous instrument?"

Still, the composer began work on the rhapsody. Debussy biographer Edward Lockspeiser notes that in the "following year, 1904, Mrs. Hall gave a public performance in Paris of another work she had commissioned, the *Choral varié* by [Vincent] d'Indy. Debussy 'thought it ridiculous to see a lady in a pink frock playing on such an ungainly instrument; and he was not at all anxious that his work should provide a similar spectacle.'" But the events of Debussy's own life in the weeks following Mrs. Hall's performance offered Parisian society sufficient spectacle: he left his wife and fled to Jersey with a married woman (who would shortly become his second wife, and with whom he'd soon have a child); his first wife shot herself in the chest in the Place de la Concorde, but survived; Debussy, gossipers claimed, left his first wife for the wealth his second wife possessed. The scandal and subsequent lawsuits consumed the composer's time; he wrote to a friend that he would "try to find again the Claude Debussy of old," but admitted that he was not working as much as he would have liked.

By 1905, Mrs. Hall's rhapsody existed only as a sketch; in 1911, the composer, suffering from cancer and, according to biographer Oscar Thompson, "apparently abandoning the task in despair, ...sent the rough draft, obviously incomplete, to Mrs. Hall." Mrs. Hall, now almost completely deaf, received the orchestrated score in 1919, a year after Debussy died.

"It is a stillborn work and hardly ever performed," Lockspeiser writes.

▶

Among the more gruesome situations of the early-to-mid-1980s—at least, among those I witnessed—was the sudden vogue for saxophone in pop music. This trend inspired at least a few of my classmates to pick up the saxophone as part of that same elemental urge prompting most kids to plug a scuffed-up, detuned Stratocaster clone into a borrowed amp and spend an afternoon plucking out "Smoke on the Water" or, more ambitiously, learning the barre chords to "Stairway to Heaven." The kids selecting the saxophone attempted some other strange template of cool, or felt a need for devotion to one's instrument that a casual guitarist never requires.

I can't use modifiers such as "blistering" or "furious" to describe a saxophone's music the way I might apply them to a guitar solo, can't equate a spit-soaked reed with a bloodied finger callus, can't explain how or why the instrument's unusual sound infected kids' minds: and none of these kids, I'll hazard, were listening to Charlie Parker, John Coltrane, or Sonny Rollins, nor their parents' old Stax and Motown records. I can easily envision a bored kid somewhere in America right now strumming a guitar—or learning how to cross-fade and beat-match, or to program Cubase—but find it difficult to imagine a kid working his or her fingers up and down a saxophone's curved form, or saying, as one saxophone-playing sixth-grade classmate once told me, "It's saxy!"

Every time I sat in Dr. Melanson's padded chair having my braces tightened, I endured the memorable sax riff in Wham's "Careless Whisper." A year or two earlier, radios everywhere had honked with the sax solos in Men at Work's "Who Can It Be Now?" Foreigner's "Urgent," Quarterflash's "Harden My Heart," Huey Lewis and the News's "I Want a New Drug." The first LP I ever bought—I admit with as little shame as possible: I was eleven years old—was Duran Duran's *Rio,* featuring a sax solo in the title song. Clarence Clemons, the saxophonist from Bruce Springsteen's E. Street Band, seemed to be everywhere in the 1980s, his face inflated like Dizzy Gillespie's as he blew so mightily that at times he overshadowed even the Boss. And the instrument glittered in so many MTV videos: Sade's cinematic "Smooth Operator," in which the camera zooms into the horn as if to penetrate its mysteries; Glenn Frey's AOR soundtrack songs, including saxophonist Beverly Dahlke-Smith dancing—in oversized suit jacket and skinny tie: the 1980s equivalent of the pink frock—as she played.

I found all these saxophones hooting over cheesy pop songs, in the alleged aim of cool, simply embarrassing: the instrument's pleading, lurid, look-at-me whine, its selfish-yet-smooth bleat, too often matched pop stars' needy sensibilities, and its very tone delineated the tenor of the decade.

▶

"It is at most a mongrel instrument," Léon Kochnitzky, adopting the viewpoint of a saxophone antagonist, wrote in the 1949 pamphlet *Adolphe Sax and His Saxophone,* "a somewhat unnatural blending of the clarinet and the English horn...severely criticized and vilified by many an important critic or a famous conductor. A stillborn invention, doomed to oblivion.... I wish it had never been born."

▶

When Adolphe Sax—son of an instrument maker, conservatory-trained clarinettist, and inventor of the saxophone—exhibited some of his musical instruments at the National Exhibition of Brussels in 1841, he included among them a new bass clarinet he had devised, as well as an early saxophone prototype. The latter instrument had never before been seen in public, and, when Sax briefly stepped away from his exhibit, an unknown assailant kicked the saxophone to the floor. Not long thereafter Sax left his native Belgium for Paris. For the remainder of his life, his strange instrument—patented in 1846—would lead him into a tangle of business rivalries, lawsuits, and bankruptcies; privilege and disfavor as French government changed in the wake of the revolutions of 1848 and the Franco-Prussian War; and accolades, including Grand Prize at the 1867 Paris International Exhibition and the cross of the Legion of Honor.

Nor did his entrepreneurial spirit stop at the invention of

the saxophone. Sax also proposed the *Saxotonnerre* (a musical "instrument with the diameter of the Colonne de Juillet"), the *Goudronnière Sax* (a device "to impregnate the air of a room with the scent of tar, creosote, or other antiseptic"—of which Louis Pasteur requested several samples), and the *Saxocannon,* which would fire a "mortar-bullet, 11 yards wide and weighing 550 tons," in order to "demolish a whole city..., smash entire walls, ruin fortifications, explode mines, blow up powerhouses—in a word, exert an irresistible devastation." In the next century, his saxophone alone would impose such mayhem.

▶

After a Christmastime drug raid in his home, during which his wife flushed heroin down the toilet and he brandished a handgun at police, Stan Getz tried to kick his addiction cold-turkey during a brief tour just before he was due to be sentenced. An hour after arriving in Seattle for an evening concert, he wandered, strung-out and shaking, into a pharmacy across the street from his hotel, pretended he had a gun in his pocket, and told the pharmacist to give him some morphine. (According to the *Los Angeles Times,* "Mrs. Mary Brewster, 44, the drugstore clerk, reported the holdup man threatened to 'blow my brains out.'") Brewster didn't believe he had a gun and didn't give him the morphine, and Getz ran back to his hotel, telephoned an apology to the pharmacy, and attempted suicide by downing some barbiturates. Police found him rambling the hotel hallways and brought him to prison, where he fell unconscious; he was taken to King County Hospital, given an emergency tracheotomy, and lay in a coma for three days. "God didn't want to kill me," he wrote from jail in a letter to the editor of *DownBeat* magazine. "Next time I'm sure he won't let me live."

Getz, twenty-seven years old, had been a heroin addict for a decade. After his release from jail, he began snorting the drug so that his probation officer wouldn't notice track marks on his arms.

While Getz toured the country, an escaped mental patient strangled his wife nearly to death outside the family's home in Laurel Canyon. Weeks later, his wife and two of his three children almost died when the driver of a car they were riding in fell asleep and crashed into a bridge; a steel truss split the car in half. On tour, Getz had become infatuated with Monica Silfverskiöld, a Swedish student and the daughter of aristocrats—and, as his wife lay in her hospital bed, immobilized in a body cast due to the fractured spine she suffered in the wreck, Getz told her he wanted a divorce. Then he fled to Sweden to be with Silfverskiöld, arriving "deep in the throes of withdrawal and with no idea where his next fix might come from," according to biographer Dave Gelly. He ended up detoxing while straitjacketed in a Swedish hospital.

A decade later, in 1964, Getz's gentle saxophone helped "The Girl from Ipanema" introduce bossa nova to the United States, though his affair with singer Astrud Gilberto meant he would not work again with her husband, João Gilberto, until 1976.

"I never played a note I didn't mean," Getz often said, before his 1991 death from liver cancer.

▶

James Siegfried, a scrawny dropout from the Wisconsin Conservatory of Music, left Milwaukee for mid-'70s New York, taking his saxophone, a sculpted pompadour, and the new name James Chance. After a brief period playing with Lydia Lunch in Teenage Jesus and the Jerks, he formed the Contortions—who dressed in suits like a '60s soul act, though they played a broken, atonal, frenzied free-jazz take on punk. On stage, Chance danced and spun like a stiff, white James Brown, but became better known for punching audience members:

> Those SoHo people...really bugged me. They would just stand there with a kind of blank attitude like they really thought they were so cool. I just didn't feel any real enthusiasm coming, so I thought, You motherfuckers, I'll get you to pay attention. A lot of it was just coming from my own emotions—my own total rage and hate.... It just came out one night at this gig at the Millennium. This overwhelming thing came over me and I just started running out into the audience and like pushing and shoving people. I just started grabbing people and slapping them around.

The Contortions' "I Can't Stand Myself" (itself a loose cover of James Brown and the Famous Flames' cut) and "Dish It Out," both from Brian Eno's *No New York* double-LP distillation of the No Wave scene, groove and swing despite—or because of—carnival keyboards, repetitive basslines, scratchy guitar, and Chance's freaked-out vocals: "When you touch me, I can't stand myself," he barks in the first song, then, in the latter, yowls, "I wanna see some emotion, not the usual fluff." But the songs sound most disturbing when Chance funnels his aggression through his saxophone. The horror of that screech surpasses all his theatrics, all his microphone-bellowing, and matches the self-hatred of the lyrics far better than the buzzsaw guitars in similarly themed songs by contemporaries like the Ramones or the Sex Pistols—both of whom sound tame and poppy in comparison.

▶

Raphael Ravenscroft may be simultaneously the most famous and least known saxophonist: his solo in Gerry Rafferty's 1978 hit "Baker Street" is unforgettable to anyone who experienced that era, and has long been credited with reviving the instrument for pop music, but he released only one LP under his own name. "The sax solo as we know it today would not exist without Gerry Rafferty," Rob Sheffield wrote upon Rafferty's death in 2011. "His 1978 soft-rock classic 'Baker Street' has to be the *Ulysses* of rock & roll saxophone, giving the entire chorus over to Raphael Ravenscroft's sax solo, creating one of the Seventies' most enduringly creepy sounds." *The Cambridge Companion to the Saxophone* refers to "what can only be described as the Baker Street phenomenon," claiming that,

> following the success (and consequent air-play) of this number, ...every self-respecting band had to include a saxophone. Soon after that an enormous percentage of

> TV advertisements had a sultry tenor or wailing alto taking prominence, and in the mid-1980s the saxophone became the most popular instrument for youngsters starting out.

An early episode of *The Simpsons* resurrected the song for a new generation when Lisa Simpson played it in a duet with her saxophone mentor, Bleedin' Gums Murphy.

Ravenscroft, a session player, was in the studio when Rafferty recorded "Baker Street." "And where," asked Ken Emerson in a 1978 *Rolling Stone* article about Rafferty, "does the magnificent saxophone line that everyone is humming come from? At first it was part of the melody, and Rafferty reckoned he'd sing it. Then he tried it on guitar, and that didn't sound quite right."

"'Most of what I played was an old blues riff,'" Ravenscroft told the *Scotsman* in 2008:

> "If you're asking me: 'Did Gerry hand me a piece of music to play?' then no, he didn't." Ravenscroft's fee was a cheque for £27, which he says bounced anyway and is now framed and hangs on his solicitor's wall. Rafferty has not attempted to make further payment, and Ravenscroft has chosen not to pursue the matter of a song that guarantees Rafferty a yearly income of £80,000.

Ravenscroft still seems to respect the pursuit of concerns other than financial ones, as he suggested to his 147 Twitter followers not long after that interview: "As the Alchemist advised I am following my dream."

▶

J.D., the sexy-but-murderous hipster played by Christian Slater in the 1988 cult film *Heathers,* is asked the famous "lunchtime poll" question: "Check this out. You win five million dollars from the Publisher's Sweepstakes, and the same day that that big Ed guy gives you the check, aliens land on the earth and say they're going to blow up the world in two days. What do you do?"

"Probably row out to the middle of a lake somewhere, bring along a bottle of tequila, my sax, and, uh, some Bach," he tells the clearly intrigued Veronica, Winona Ryder's character.

It's only later in the film that Veronica, perhaps reflecting on this response, says to J.D. "And to think there was a time when I actually thought you were cool!"

▶

Fifteen-year-old "nice Jewish girl" Susan Whitby played saxophone, like Elise Hall, in a pink frock—the "pink uniform she'd worn to her good private school," as Greil Marcus reports. Six months later, she responded to an ad in *Melody Maker,* joined London punk band X-Ray Spex, and began calling herself Lora Logic. Just after the band released its first single—1977's "Oh Bondage Up Yours!"—she was forced out, her saxophone parts entrusted to a new player. Still, it must be either Steve Mackay's saxophone on the Stooges' *Fun House* or Lora Logic's saxophone on this single that gave the instrument a place in punk: "Lora Logic kicked off her saxophone solo as if she were kicking down a door, which was exactly what she was doing," according to Marcus. Singer Poly Styrene, a fashion industry refugee and hippie runaway turned punk—and, like Lora Logic, a suburban teenager—shouts tunelessly until her voice cracks, but Lora Logic's keening saxophone, for all its potency, does have a few moments of fluttering delicacy as her notes decay into the rest of the band's chug. Poly Styrene's screams and Lora Logic's saxophone form an aggressive call and response, the two young women claiming the most audible aspects of the track. ("Some people think that little girls should be seen and not heard," Poly Styrene says, to introduce the song.) Early photos of X-Ray Spex show the teens front and center on stage, forming the band's visible presence as well—in one, they wear raincoats against the crowd's spitting—so it's unsurprising that, as Lora Logic told an interviewer, "Poly saw that I was getting a little too much of the spotlight and I was just replaced without any notice after a year."

After her ouster, Lora Logic formed Essential Logic (a band that began with *two* saxophonists), released a few singles and an LP, and then—"[I] was dallying with drugs a little too much, living the rock lifestyle," she admitted later—joined the Hare Krishnas. "I know we're not just a body and there's more to life than putting safety pins through noses," she told an interviewer in 1982. Poly Styrene was soon visiting the same temple. "She had been going through a lot," Lora Logic said, "and I understood. We formed a reggae-ish band with other Krishnas…"

▸

On the first day of June, Democratic presidential candidate Bill Clinton's motorcade, on its way to his speech at the West Angeles Church of God in Christ, rolled under clouded skies through burnt-out and boarded-up buildings in South Central Los Angeles where, a few weeks earlier, days of rioting following the Rodney King verdicts had destroyed neighborhoods. On the second day of June, while California primary voters cast the ballots giving him the state's delegates and, with them, the party's nomination, Clinton addressed rallies in the Central Valley, Oakland, and UCLA; offered brief victory remarks at the Los Angeles Biltmore; talked to CBS's Dan Rather on a call-in show; then, on his beachfront hotel balcony, practiced his saxophone. He played an old song based on a news story about a suicide—a man who jumped from his own hotel window, leaving only a one-sentence note: "I walk a lonely street."

Even for the famously extroverted Clinton, the line may have matched the moment: Clinton edged California governor Jerry Brown in the primary, but still trailed in national polls: Gallup showed Ross Perot at 39 percent, George H. W. Bush at 31 percent, and Clinton at 25 percent that month. A year earlier, following Operation Desert Storm, Bush had seemed unbeatable; now, "Perot mania" seized voters around the country, and, in the wake of Clinton's various missteps and scandals—his affair with Gennifer Flowers, his alleged draft-dodging to pursue his Rhodes Scholarship, his admission that he smoked weed but "didn't inhale"—few gave Clinton a chance.

On the third day of June, Clinton waited on Stage 29 of the Paramount Lot in Hollywood, cradling the saxophone slung around his neck and joking with the Posse, Arsenio Hall's house band: "If I mess up, play louder," he told them.

"Hey, if this music thing doesn't work out," drummer Chuck Morris replied, "you can always run for president."

Standing nearby, Clinton's staff criticized his boring outfit: dark suit, white shirt. They made him remove his neutral tie in favor of a yellow-and-blue patterned one from the host's own collection. Just before the show went live, campaign spokeswoman Dee Dee Myers handed speechwriter Paul Begala's Ray-Bans to Clinton: "Governor, you have to put on the sunglasses."

The Posse played the show's intro music, and Arsenio Hall walked onstage, blew a two-finger kiss to his crowd (a Secret Service detail occupied the front row), then pointed and smiled at Clinton, who stood at one edge of a riser, cheeks puffed and eyebrows waggling as he blew. But Clinton kept playing "Heartbreak Hotel" as the Posse laid down the eight-bar blues and the audience freaked. After a last flourish of sax notes, the song ended in a storm of cymbals, bass notes, and keyboard glissandi. Clinton high-fived bandleader Michael Wolff and adjusted his shades. "The big man!" Hall shouted, gesturing toward Clinton, "and the Posse. Boy, oh boy. You can't beat that!" A bit later, after Clinton, sunglasses removed, played Billie Holiday's "God Bless the Child" with the Posse, Hall added, "It's nice to see a Democrat blow something besides the election."

Following this appearance, Clinton began a steady climb in the polls—helped by the dismal economy and Perot dropping out of the race for several months after the Democratic convention. Commentators viewed Clinton's sax performance as vulgar and undignified, as another announcement (welcome or not) of the increasingly multicultural influences on American politics and culture, as part of Clinton's strategy to court the youth vote through new media. "A sad John Belushi wannabe," sniffed Bush's press secretary. "Saxophone playing for a president...? Forget it. It's a very bad idea," advised Richard Nixon's former White House counsel. "He plays like a politician because everything was confusing. You couldn't tell one note from another," joked jazz saxophonist Stanley Turrentine. But a young assistant to the curator of American music at the Smithsonian told the *Washington Post* that "the sax...has sex appeal," and she preferred "candidates with sex appeal." The few minutes Clinton played saxophone on live TV became a crucial part of the narrative that began with his declaration of himself as the Comeback Kid in New Hampshire and ended with his election to the presidency.

But other narratives also demanded attention. "Could Governor Bill Clinton make a living playing tenor sax when his political days are over?" asked the *Los Angeles Times'* Dennis Hunt. Hunt found Clinton's rendition of "Heartbreak Hotel" "tentative," but noted that, in his take on Billie Holiday's "God Save the Child," "Clinton demonstrated a surprisingly warm tone.... Rather than clinging to the traditional melody, Clinton put it through some twists and turns." Another reporter noted that "ever since Bill Clinton appeared on Arsenio Hall's TV show, saxophone sales have shot up 20 percent.... Whether it's a resurgence of traditional musical values or just a fad, the saxophone is gleaming again."

▶

Music, Roland Barthes claimed, "is only ever translated into the poorest of linguistic categories: the adjective.... The adjective is inevitable: this music is *this,* this execution is *that.*" The saxophone's distinctive sound renders such translations even less escapable, the descriptors even less variable. Whenever I imagined I'd come up with a decent way to characterize the saxophone's sound, I soon realized how worn-out were my words. The saxophone, as the clichés claim, is smooth, sultry, sexy, silky, seductive; it is mellow; it is intense. But adjectives administer effects; to narrate the instrument's expressions is to rely on similarly impoverished verbs: the saxophone squawks. It wails, or moans. Screeches, squeals, squalls, sings, sobs, snorts. Howls, honks, hoots, toots, whines, wheezes, bleats, blasts, blows, blares.

Perhaps, most of all, the saxophone skronks. "Skronk" may have been coined by Robert Christgau, as Lester Bangs would have us believe—"Christgau calls it 'skronk.' I have always opted for the more obvious 'horrible noise'"—but Bangs provided the service of linking the word to Ornette Coleman's saxophone ("*he* played 'skronk'"), a pairing that, ever since, has become mandatory.

Still, the skronking saxophone—the saxophone played by the amateur, or played by the expert uninterested in wedding-background, Dave Brubeck niceties—is nearly the only saxophone I can bear. My favorite saxophone songs are those in which the instrument invents an unwelcome injury, or maybe mimics whalesong—anything that sounds as awkward and strange as the instrument itself has always appeared to me.

▶

"I played in the first punk band in Zürich but I played saxophone.... You weren't allowed to have a saxophone in a punk band at the time," Marlene Marder told an interviewer in 1998, recalling the humble beginnings of the Swiss punk scene twenty-one years earlier, in the wake of the Sex Pistols: apparently X-Ray Spex had not yet reached Switzerland. Marder quit, and—ditching her saxophone for the few simple chords she knew on guitar—joined her friends Klaudia Schiff, Lislot Ha, and Regula Sing in the band Kleenex.

Recorded just before Kleenex received a cease-and-desist from Kimberly-Clark's lawyers and changed its name to LiLiPUT, "DC-10" is straightforward compared to the primitively yelped, sing-song gems that made Kleenex a sensation in England after John Peel played their first Swiss single on his radio show and Rough Trade issued two more singles. "DC-10" didn't appear on those joyous, raucous records, perhaps because the song attempted a more serious mood in response to the notable McDonnell-Douglas DC-10 crashes and safety incidents of the 1970s, though it shares the singles' intensity and drive. Ha's ferocious drumming, Marder's simple chords, and Schiff's eighth-note bassline capture the feel of powerful machinery on the verge of disaster, but a baleful saxophone blat punctuates Sing's warnings: "If you wanna fly / with DC-10 / keep open your eyes / keep open your eyes / 'cause there's a lot of risk / in the DC flights..." Amid the chaos of the song—which ends with Sing shouting "Emergency!" and the rest of the band shrieking in the background as another DC-10 goes down—the restrained saxophone notes seem mere texture, about as unnoticeable as the instrument ever gets. Angie Barrack, who joined LiLiPUT for the reconstituted band's first single—itself featuring squawky saxophone—appears to have played the sax in "DC-10," but Marder had found a way, like Lora Logic before her, to make saxophone punk.

▶

The Psychedelic Furs' debut record may have been the first time I heard a saxophone in a rock context and didn't hate it. Duncan Kilburn embroiders the entire album with curlicued melodies and the occasional solo—the typical ways sax is integrated into a guitar-bass-drums lineup—but occasionally, as in "Fall," he wails more wildly, and his runs trade off with the guitar's to fill in the song around Richard Butler's raggedy sneer and hoarse cynicism. In the droning, spooked "Imitation of Christ," Kilburn's horn sounds almost the only melodic notes in an insistent dirge of flanged guitars, snare snaps, and tom-tom fills like miles-away thunder. The record sounded bracing, but also stiff and British. I could possibly have admitted that its saxophone approached cool. Sax riffs like the one in "Dumb Waiters," from the band's next record, haunted me in the '80s, suggesting the potential implicit in all the decade's lame saxophone noodling.

▶

In Wümme, West Germany, at an isolated old schoolhouse—transformed, with music journalist Uwe Nettelbeck's praise and

Polydor's money, into a high-tech recording studio—six long-haired weirdos known as Faust and their assorted producers, guests, and hangers-on spent the early 1970s living communally, tripping on Swiss LSD-25, playing darts naked outdoors, racing (and wrecking) Porsches and Volvos on the local roads, and, occasionally, creating their own now-legendary music—the band members often recording their takes while lying in bed, microphone cables and patch cords stretched from pillows to control room.

In the late '60s, in search of rock cred, Polydor executives had asked Nettelbeck to find an underground band the label could sign: Nettelbeck helped assemble the members of Faust, designed their record covers, produced their records, and managed Faust's daily business, an experience he compared to "looking after a sack of fleas day and night." The first record—a clear vinyl LP, packaged with a transparent lyric sheet, inside a transparent sleeve printed with an X-ray of a fist—consisted of three lengthy avant-rock congeries and sold very poorly, after which Polydor demanded a tour, a more marketable sound, and some return on their continuing investment. The second record—a black vinyl LP, packaged in a black sleeve and accompanied by a set of illustrations for each song—featured shorter tracks and better production, but little that might be construed as pop. The tour involved jackhammering bits of concrete on a darkened stage. Polydor cut its losses.

Richard Branson had recently founded Virgin Records, and, after a successful run importing and distributing early-'70s "Krautrock" records (the name would be applied to the genre retrospectively, after the lead song on Faust's fourth LP), had come to Hamburg to scout and sign some German bands. Nettelback sold Branson a Faust album collaged from various home recordings made at Wümme between 1970 and 1973. These experiments, exercises, cut-ups, and other sonic fragments were spliced with a Frankenstein elegance and packaged as *The Faust Tapes,* which Virgin sold for 48p as a loss leader. The strategy worked too well: the label sold 50,000 copies of *The Faust Tapes* in 1973, meaning that perhaps some 48,972 bewildered Brits wondered what they'd just heard, never mind the LP's disclaimer ("The music on this album, drawn from Faust's own library of private tapes, was recorded informally and not originally intended for release.... These tapes have been left exactly as they were recorded—frequently live—and no post-production work has been imposed on them").

Among those whom the record affected deeply, Julian Cope called *The Faust Tapes* LP "the social phenomenon of 1973, and it finally brought the true avant garde into everyone's living room, for a short while at least." The LP's two side-long movements weren't labeled or subdivided, so as needle tracked vinyl, a pretty pastoral folksong might displace treated drums crashing against a battery of overloaded guitar amps, or human voices made to sound like accelerating motorcycles, or a free jazz-inspired workout, or a rhythm & blues groove gone askew, or what might be TV audio overlaid with the sounds of footsteps and flushing toilets. Later reissues divided the material into twenty-six discrete tracks, most of them only brief sketches. "Untitled: All on Saxes" showcases the instrument's "aquatic" timbres Debussy noted: for ninety-three seconds, several members of Faust make saxophones squeak an uneven alien dialogue. The track's energy is hushed, but a looping two-note bass heartbeat running beneath the saxes and the rising, atonal harmonies summon a wilderness melancholy. I've heard the saxophone sound stranger; I've heard it sound farther-out; I've never heard it sound this creepy.

▶

The kids who took music lessons after school carried their instruments to our sixth-grade classroom in scuffed black cases that banged their knees as they walked, then left them beside their desks or by the cubbies at the back of the room: a few half-size rented violins and violas, two girls' clarinets, one kid's trumpet, and a saxophone. The saxophonist had arrived at our school a few years after the rest of us, who'd all started together in kindergarten, and still seemed like a new kid—a little strange, a little unknowable. During afternoon recess kiss-and-catch the year before, he was often the head kisser, and now he spoke of his instrument's "sax appeal" as if he knew something the rest of us would learn later.

The monotony of our school days was relieved by occasional outliers I never knew when or how to expect: we picked teams and spent an afternoon playing spelling baseball in class; we wrote stories at our desks in the morning, and read them aloud in the afternoon; we trooped down to the dim gymnasium for a school talent assembly, the folding wooden bleachers pressed against the walls so we all sat crosslegged on the court. One girl sang an a capella version of "Rhiannon"; another strummed something on an acoustic guitar; two sisters danced the Irish jig.

I want to tell you that the sexy saxophonist honked out "Yakety Sax" and "Tequila" while we stood and cheered, but I don't remember ever hearing him play. I don't remember him ever opening the snap-locks on its case and lifting the smudged brass horn from the velour interior. What I remember is that a year or so later, the saxophonist seemed to have given up his instrument. He'd renounced saxiness in all its forms and now wore a white-elbowed jean jacket collar-up, an Iron Maiden patch with grinning, long-haired skulls across the shoulder blades. His own hair hung untrimmed and lank, and moustache wisps curled at the corners of his mouth. He exhibited a paunch. Was his saxophone the crude and tawdry agent that had mutated him into this new self, or had it been the only thing keeping him, until now, from metalhead delinquency? I didn't know: his was the first case of saxophone derangement I observed, and mostly I wanted to avoid whatever infection he'd caught.

Only later did I realize that he, like rebellious teens worldwide, had simply learned an eternal truth from Frank Zappa: "If ever there's an obscene noise to be made on an instrument, it's going to come out of a guitar. On a saxophone you can play sleaze [but]... the guitar can be the single most blasphemous device on the face of the earth.... The disgusting stink of a too-loud electric guitar: now that's my idea of a good time."

SHUGGIE OTIS: "Aht Uh Mi Hed"
(*Inspiration Information* LP, Epic, 1974)

"Nothing special—'You could dance to it,' as we said," my mother told me when I asked her to recall Little Anthony and the Imperials' version[1] of the Teddy Randazzo- and Bobby Weinstein-penned "Goin' Out of My Head."[2]

1 "'Goin' Out of My Head' was never a No. 1 song for Little Anthony, but when the Lettermen combined it...in a recorded medley, the tunes became pop classics, recorded by a gamut of industry giants, from Frank Sinatra to Dionne Warwick. 'I've lost count on how many versions there are,' [Randazzo] said." (Wayne Harada, "Teddy Randazzo, '50s Rock Legend, Dead at 68," *Honolulu Advertiser,* Nov. 24, 2003.)

2 See also the aforementioned medley version by the Lettermen, or the bossa-nova-lite version by Sergio Mendes & Brasil '66, or perhaps the slightly funked-up version by the Delfonics, or the wah-wah-'n'-horns disco version by Gloria Gaynor, or any number of countless others. But, e.g., the Lettermen's version is too unsoiled by any emotion—how can any listener believe that these four clean-cut young men, all with perfect enunciation and matching sweaters, are even close to out of their heads? They've calculated every move of this medley; even the sound engineer cranks up the artificial enthusiastic applause from the imaginary audience (themselves all well within

"For a slow dance?" I asked.
"Oh, yeah," she said. "A slow dance."[3]

▶

"I want you / I need you / I want you to want me / I can't think of anything but you."[4, 5] Little Anthony, in a girlish, prepubescent voice,[6] intones these lyrics as part of a teenage passion play; from

---

their crania) at each segue between "Goin' Out of My Head" and "Can't Take My Eyes Off You." And though disco was, at root, all about reaching a state of being out of one's head—from cocaine and alcohol, marathon dancing, post-pill and pre-AIDS sex; about a state purely physical, not at all cerebral—and though a disco version of "Goin' Out of My Head" seems appropriate, still Gloria Gaynor's version is again too crisp, too studied. The uptempo rhythm suggests that this pain is not real, no deeper than a snub from someone at a singles bar. Is this song the place for a bouncy bassline, for disco's swollen string arrangements, for an extended instrumental break with laser noises and tabla?

3 "The word 'desperate' is apt for his early work, because no one spoke more for the agonies of very young love than did Little Anthony—and his high-pitched falsetto was a most appropriate instrument." (Unattributed liner notes, *The Very Best of Little Anthony & the Imperials,* United Artists, 1974.)

4 "Yearning hurts, / and what release / may come of it / feels much like death." (Heraclitus, *Fragments: The Collected Wisdom of Heraclitus,* trans. by Brooks Haxton, Viking, 2001.)

5 "Melody / especially when it grieves / (arioso dolente) / takes your hand. / Leads you / willing or unwilling / to the pine-lit / wedding chamber, / you are married / to the fact of it, / the light goes out / on all you've felt / or failed to feel. / Grief / is the distance / between loves…" (Robert Kelly, "Section 9, Sonata in A-flat: The Essay on Form," *The Loom,* Black Sparrow Press, 1975.)

6 "Effeminacy of character arises from a prevalence of the sensibility over the will; or it consists in a want of fortitude to bear pain or to undergo fatigue, however urgent the occasion.… [These persons] have been so used to a studied succession of agreeable sensations that the shortest pause is a privation which they can by no means endure—it is like tearing them from their very existence…They are completely wrapped up in themselves; but then all their self-love is concentrated in the present

Ella Fitzgerald's lips, these words hum with the worldly electricities of physical desire.[7] Never mind her characteristic improvisations and asides, her utterly distinctive phrasing, the force of her breath; consider instead how she caresses the words "into your heart" before, a moment later, summoning that breath's full measure for the refrain "outta my head"—localizing these parts of the body as she turns the song from the melodramatic tale of a weepy and passive crush to one of adult longing and obsession.[8] The production of her version—a fairly sloppy live recording—in no way rivals the sophisticated production of the versions by Little Anthony and the Imperials or the Lettermen, and yet she imparts the lyrics with a depth of expression no amount of studio wizardry can recreate.

---

minute." (William Hazlitt, "On Effeminacy of Character," *Table-Talk,* Oxford UP, 1933 [reprint].)

7 "Her presentation is casual and matter-of-fact. In one hand she holds a small hand mike. In the other she clutches a colored kerchief with which she dabs at perspiration on her brow or dries the corners of her eyes, which water very easily in the presence of smoke. So she keeps her eyes closed when she sings and, keeping time with her shoulders, her arms and her body, floats airily through familiar ballads, gently expanding or rephrasing the melodic line, or she rolls out chorus after chorus of darting, silver-quick scat singing.... 'Music today has a different beat,' she was saying one afternoon in her suite at the Americana as she reflected on the songs she has sung and still continues to sing. 'The style of music has changed.... If you don't learn new songs, you're lost.... Everybody says there are no good songs now. But there are two from this generation that I like—"Goin' Out of My Head" and "Sunny."'" (John S. Wilson, "Ella Changes Her Tunes for a Swinging Generation," *New York Times,* Nov. 12, 1967.)

8 "When I desire you a part of me is gone: your lack is my lack. I would not be in want of you unless you had partaken of me, the lover reasons. 'A hole is being gnawed in [my] vitals' says Sappho.... 'You have snatched the lungs out of my chest'...and 'pierced me right through the bones'...says Archilochos." (Anne Carson, *Eros the Bittersweet,* Dalkey Archive Press, 1998 [reprint].)

▶

The *Oxford English Dictionary* posits the head "as the seat of mind, thought, intellect, memory, or imagination; cf. BRAIN" and "often contrasted with *heart*, as the seat of the emotions: see HEART." To be *off one's head*—"out of one's mind or wits, crazy. *colloq.*"—did not, apparently, enter the lexicon until the nineteenth century; to be *out of one's head* is the same phrase contemporaneously Americanized. But if mind is in some ways synonymous with head—the former perhaps the inhabitant of the latter's vessel,[9] though the two are inseparable—such definitions bring us no closer to understanding this odd turn of phrase.[10] In what ways does grief over love—or

9 "The perceptions we refer only to the soul are those whose effects we feel as being in the soul itself, and for which we do not normally know any proximate cause to which we can refer them. Such are the feelings of joy, anger and the like.... We need to recognize also that although the soul is joined to the whole body, nevertheless there is a certain part of the body where it exercises its functions more particularly than in all the others. It is commonly held that this part is the brain, or perhaps the heart—the brain because the sense organs are related to it, and the heart because we feel the passions as if they were in it. But on carefully examining the matter I think I have clearly established that the part of the body in which the soul directly exercises its functions is not the heart at all, or the whole of the brain. It is rather the innermost part of the brain, which is a certain very small gland situated in the middle of the brain's substance...." (Rene Descartes, "Passions of the Soul," *Selected Philosophical Writings,* trans. by John Cottingham, Robert Stoothoff, and Dugald Murdoch, Cambridge University Press, 1988.)

10 Off the top of my head: the Rolling Stones: *Out of Our Heads.* Lupe Fiasco: "Out of My Head." John Newman: "Out of My Head." Ashlee Simpson: "Outta My Head." Madchild: "Out of My Head." Deetron feat. Ovasoul7: "Out of My Head." Swearing at Motorists: "Going Out of My Head." Kylie Minogue: "Can't Get You Out of My Head." Electric Light Orchestra: "Can't Get It Out of My Head." The Blake Babies: "Outta My Head." M. Ward: "Outta My Head." The Go-Betweens: "I Need Two Heads." The Go Team: "My Head Hurts." Etc., etc. Yes, I know I missed most of them.

the desire for love—affect the seat of intellect? In what ways does the head here trespass on the realm of the heart?[11] How does grief, at least metaphorically, resemble decapitation, or perhaps more accurately trepanation, some severance of one's faculties from the skull that contains them?[12]

"I *think* I'm going out of my head"[13] is, at any rate, a difficult line for me to believe. If one were going out of one's head, wouldn't one *know* it was happening? And if one *is* out of one's head, or about to approach such a state, how can one retain the self-consciousness to narrate such an advent?[14] Perhaps Randazzo and Weinstein hoped to convey such confusion as an elemental part of the young lover's grief, just as a teenager smoking pot for

11 "The mind does not understand the heart? Neither does the heart." (James Richardson, *Vectors,* Ausable Press, 2001.)

12 "For a hundred years, (literary) madness has been thought to consist in Rimbaud's '*Je est un autre*'; madness is an experience of depersonalization. For me as an amorous subject, it is quite the contrary: it is becoming a *subject,* being unable to keep myself from doing so, which drives me mad. *I am not someone else:* that is what I realize with horror." (Roland Barthes, *A Lover's Discourse: Fragments,* trans. by Richard Howard, Hill and Wang, 1978.)

13 Italics mine, though who can narrow the emphases the multitude of singers who've covered this song have suggested?

14 The original connotations of the word "ecstasy"—"to drive a person out of his wits," per the *Oxford English Dictionary*—suggest the uncontrolled experience, a "withdrawal of the soul from the body." As Milan Kundera has noted, "Ecstasy means being 'outside oneself,' as indicated by the etymology of the Greek word: the act of leaving one's position (*stasis*). To be 'outside oneself' does not mean outside the present moment, like a dreamer escaping into the past or the future. Just the opposite: ecstasy is the absolute identity with the present instant, total forgetting of past and future. If we obliterate the future and the past, the present moment stands in empty space, outside life and its chronology, outside time and independent of it (this is why it can be likened to eternity, which too is the negation of time)." (*Testaments Betrayed: An Essay in Nine Parts,* HarperCollins: 1995.)

the first time believes she is stoned long before she is—the force of the desire to experience the altered state increases, at least in her head, the amount of alteration. "Goin' Out of My Head" seems not so much to recount the actual grief of a lost love, the grief over a relationship ended, as to approach the idea of such grief in a sanitized and self-consciously pubescent way—i.e., in a way appropriate for the sort of slow dance my mother recalled, held Friday night in a sweaty gymnasium, wherein shadows and makeup have transformed the pull-up-induced facial contortions of one's daytime classmates into the sleek, romantic visages of one's new, mysteriously familiar evening companions.[15, 16]

▶

"Goin' Out of My Head" should, ideally, be performed not by a group but by a lonesome teen, constructed not in the impersonal space of a rented studio but on the edge of the same bed in which the lonesome teen cries him- or herself to sleep over the crush the song addresses. Accompaniment should consist of soft hums and finger-tapped thighs or windowpanes at least, out-of-tune guitar

---

15 "Even though the staple of rock and roll in the fifties was teen schmaltz of wondrous innocence and vapidity, and even though the popularization of black music meant romanticizing the hard-assed realism of rhythm-and-blues, the sheer physicality of rock and roll, its sexual underpinnings, always implied a negation of such escapist rhapsodies." (Robert Christgau, *Any Old Way You Choose It: Rock and Other Pop Music, 1967–1973,* Cooper Square Press, 2000 [reprint; expanded edition].)

16 "…soon life began to unfold, beautiful and passionate and sad, while still the young men and girls entered, scented and sibilant in the half dark, their paired backs in silhouette delicate and sleek, their slim, quick bodies awkward, divinely young…" (William Faulkner, "Dry September," *Collected Stories,* Vintage, 1977 [reprint].)

at most. The volume of this solo performance should not exceed a dB level capable of escaping the bedroom walls. All of this begins to approach Shuggie's "Aht Uh Mi Hed."[17, 18]

▸

"Who's Shaggy[19] Otis?" my stepfather asked me on a recent visit. I'd laid the LP atop one speaker after listening to it sometime prior to his arrival, and now he squinted through his spectacles—if not closely enough—at the photo on its odd, nearly monotone cover: Shuggie sits, skinny legs elegantly crossed, in an Adirondack chair amid a strangely shaggy garden; the cover's only color is a sort of rainbowing to the album title.[20] My copy of the LP, a promo originally loaned to a radio station—has a scuffed and ringworn

---

17 "Though blessed with a sweet, buoyant voice and a knack for subtle inflections, Otis was too shy to record with anyone in the studio." (Tom Moon, "Shuggie Otis' Classic Returns," *Philadelphia Inquirer,* March 25, 2001.)

18 "Three years in the making, *Inspiration Information* is flamboyantly arty, the work of a young musician determined to get it all in. It is also remarkably accomplished. In the tradition of R&B auteurship that stretches from Stevie Wonder to Prince to D'Angelo, Mr. Otis wrote every note and played nearly every instrument on the album." (Jody Rosen, "Luxuriating in the Sprawl of That Early '70s Sound," *New York Times,* July 29, 2001.)

19 "Shuggie—it's impossible to call him by any other name..." (Jeffrey Lee Puckett, "Soul Inspiring," *Louisville Courier-Journal,* March 31, 2001.)

20 The reissue features entirely different jacket art: the portrait of Shuggie from his second LP has been warmed with a self-consciously retro palette of red and orange; his Afro has become mere abstraction. The new cover seems designed around a current college student's idea of what an LP from the '70s should look like: garish, bold, iconic. The image is as easy and unearned as the plastic repro tiki drink glasses one can now buy for ten dollars a dozen at certain shops, along with butterfly chairs, paper lamps, and T-shirts with artfully—artlessly?—faded logos of imaginary high school sports teams; it loses completely the sense of the original artwork's weirdness.

sleeve, a clipped corner, taped edges, and a radio station sticker with tracklist on the front. Despite such evidence of wear, I doubt this copy was much played at whatever radio station it was sent to; none of the "recommended cuts" have been checked off, and the vinyl is pristine.[21, 22]

Luaka Bop, the record label that reissued *Inspiration Information* more than ten years back, offers on its website a sampling of the reviews that greeted the reissue: "An expansive creativity that appeared unlimited," says *Rolling Stone;* "more than justifies the cult following garnered in the years since its (largely ignored) 1974 release…[u]nbelievably wonderful," promises *Billboard;* "nothing short of a '70s psychedelic pop Rosetta Stone," claims Barnes & Noble's online review.[23] I bought my copy of *Inspiration Information* at a used record store before the reissue, at a time before I really

---

21 "The album proved too futuristic, too stubbornly unique for the rock marketplace of 1974." (James Sullivan, liner notes to *Inspiration Information,* Luaka Bop, 2001 [reissue].)

22 In his review for *Pitchfork,* Jonny Pietin argues that *Inspiration Information* was ignored upon release not because "the world wasn't ready" or because "some evil executive quashed it," but because it was "designed to be" overlooked: "*Inspiration Information* is a stubbornly small album, free of the grandiosity and posturing of similar records of the time, like *What's Going On* and *Superfly.* There are no social issues at stake here, and no 60-piece orchestras swelling our hearts. There's just the sound of one extremely talented young musician exploring his craft's limitations, and his own." (Jonny Pietin, undated review on Pitchfork.com.)

23 "But, no matter how much the partisans claim[,]…this isn't revolutionary, even if it's delightfully idiosyncratic. So, don't fall for the hyperbole. This isn't an album that knocks your head off—it's subtle, intricate music that's equal parts head music and elegant funk, a record that slowly works its way under your skin…. But it isn't a record without precedent, nor is it startling. It's a record for people that have heard a lot of music, maybe too much, and are looking for a new musical romance." (Stephen Thomas Erlewine, Allmusic.com.)

knew who Shuggie Otis was—and since this was the sort of record store where almost all the used LPs cost $3.99, regardless of rarity, the shopkeeper—a long-haired Merseybeat fan rather than a condescending young hipster—seemed not to know who Shuggie Otis was either. Shuggie, of course, was always busy defining and reinventing himself anyway, or being defined by others,[24] beginning as a teenaged blues guitar prodigy who wore fake moustaches to play nightclubs, moved from blues to the "psychedelic soul" of "Aht Uh Mi Hed" and other tracks, turned down an invitation to join the Rolling Stones after Mick Taylor quit the band, and ended, sometime after *Inspiration Information*'s commercial failure—when Shuggie was twenty-one years old—as a musical recluse: someone, we might say, *lost in his head.*[25, 26]

▶

24 "Most present, however, is the sense and beginning of a totally new struggle for Shuggie. The thirteen-year-old who made his recording debut with the Johnny Otis Show, and later came to national attention through the Al Kooper sessions, is a man and an artist now. He is creating in the Seventies, a time whose conflicts are being shaped by information—and the lack of it. One gets the feeling that even as the information changes, so will the inspiration." (Winston Cenac [Scoops], liner notes, *Inspiration Information,* Epic / CBS LP, KE 33059, 1974.)

25 "It is possible that this solitude is dangerous only for those idle and vagrant souls who people it with their own passions and chimeras." (Charles Baudelaire, "Solitude," *Paris Spleen,* trans. by Louise Varèse, New Directions, 1947 [reprint].)

26 "Otis was not exactly sunny—he had a fragility that bordered on melancholy—but he was insular and hermetic and emphatically apolitical; his music has timeless appeal because it never belonged to its time to begin with." (Ben Greenman, "Lost Soul," *The New Yorker,* June 11, 2001.)

"Aht Uh Mi Hed" burrows its way into the listener's head[27]—a miniature headphone symphony,[28] an ornate lite-funk pop pastiche of echoing drum machine, swirls of organ, skeletal ska-style rhythm guitar, some subtle strings, and Shuggie's sweet vocals. Call it delicately persistent.

While simple headphones—such as those worn by telephone operators—existed for most of the twentieth century, John Koss is generally credited with inventing the first modern stereo headphones for consumers in 1958, the Koss SP/3. By the 1970s, headphones weren't much less bulky or comfortable than the SP/3, but studio production values had improved enough that a pair of padded headphones often accompanied many home stereo systems. The six-foot tether of copper wire kept the listener near the stereo, but the headphones effaced much of the rest of the world by thwarting its sounds. Stereo pans, crossfades, multitrack recording, and other studio effects made music appear to originate from some point at the center of one's brain.[29] This location became

---

27 "One is hardly ever *completely listening* (which requires a devotion to time of the wild leap), therefore what follows such reduced attention generates little but quick opinion, and you can feel the mass of all you missed draining away. Music must *be* the room you are in, for the duration." (Clark Coolidge, "Rova Notes," *Sulfur* 17 [1986].)

28 "The headphone music experience is qualitatively different from a typical concert situation. Undesirable sounds, such as the coughing, rustling of programs and emergency-vehicle sirens that are often heard at concerts, are almost completely masked. And while at a concert one shares in the community space of an audience, one enjoys a direct personal relationship with sound when listening with headphones; the sociological and cultural accessories of music are eliminated." (Durand R. Begault, "The Composition of Auditory Space: Recent Developments in Headphone Music," *Leonardo,* Vol. 23, No. 1 [1990].)

29 These same studio technologies are what allowed Otis to write and record the entire record himself: the one-man band, like the writer, arranges, assembles,

critical once the Sony Walkman helped shrink the headphone: now a cranial music was portable.

Inspiration Information—both the original release and the reissue—coincides with two important moments in the history of the headphone: first, the moment in the early '70s when it became a fairly common household consumer product—a way of shutting out the sounds of the family home and concentrating on a private experience of music rather than a communal one; next, the more recent moment when its ubiquity, indicated in part by its free inclusion with many portable electronic devices, signifies both our near-inability to exist in silence (both because we bring music with us everywhere, and because music, as unwanted noise, is imposed upon us[30]—the former condition perhaps a response to the latter), as well as the way our listening now often takes place somewhere other than the home. Headphones permit us to transform any public space with the addition of our own soundtrack,

---

overlays, produces; the performance is not live but constructed, a series of revisions that occur over time. Stephen Thomas Erlewine: "Otis crafted all of this essentially alone...and it's quite clearly a reflection of his inner psyche..." (Allmusic.com).

30 "Mass music is...a powerful factor in consumer integration, interclass leveling, cultural homogenization.... Beyond that, it is a means of silencing, a concrete example of commodities speaking in place of people, of the monologue of institutions.... But silencing requires the general infiltration of this music, in addition to its purchase. Therefore, it has replaced natural background noise, invaded and even annulled the noise of machinery. It slips into the growing spaces of activity void of meaning and relations, into the organization of our everyday life: in all of the world's hotels, all of the elevators, all of the factories and offices, all of the airplanes, all of the cars, everywhere, it signifies the presence of a power that needs no flag or symbol: musical repetition confirms the presence of repetitive consumption, of the flow of noises as ersatz sociality. (Jacques Attali, *Noise: The Political Economy of Music,* trans. by Brian Massumi, University of Minnesota Press, 1983.)

or indicate the noise with which the world surrounds us and the desperation of our need to reclaim what we hear, or suggest the circumscriptions of our private lives and our private spaces, which now often extend no further than the limits of our own bodies: so we colonize our headspace before some other does. If the head is a space that can be trespassed against our will, it seems unsurprising that Shuggie's record invites the intimacy of headphone listening.

▶

"Nothing special—he has two or three good songs: 'Inspiration Information,' 'Aht Uh Mi Hed,' and that ten-minute-long one on *Freedom Flight,*" my friend Hua told me when I asked him what he thought about Shuggie Otis.

"'Strawberry Letter 23'?" I prodded.

"Yeah, that one too," he agreed.[31]

▶

31 When I e-mailed him this brief paragraph to confirm its accuracy, Hua responded: "I do think Shuggie Otis was someone special. I guess what I meant to say was this: he's the type of artist that invites hyperbole. There's a 'Shuggie discourse' that's formed around all the strange aspects of his life—prodigy turned recluse, famous pops, almost a Rolling Stone, black and psychedelic. And, in his more sublime moments, he is unrivaled: 'Strawberry Letter,' 'Aht Uh Mi Hed,' 'Freedom Flight,' and the all-time facemelter 'Inspiration Information.' But generally I think his albums rarely rise to those heights—I haven't really sat with the third one (my favorite) in a while but the first two have a lot of run-of-the-mill stuff on them. I've always associated him with Fugi, Rotary Connection, Black Merda and all those other post-Sly psych dudes, and in retrospect, they were all probably as 'big' as they should have been."

"At that time," Shuggie Otis told *Philadelphia Inquirer* music critic Tom Moon in a 2001 interview, referring to 1974, "there was the understanding that you could write lyrics and they didn't have to have any meaning.[32] Well, I wanted the songs to mean something, at least along the lines of a fantasy or something outside of your normal experience....[33] That's what I was striving for, to free the mind of the listener and free my own mind."

A freed mind, at least since the 1960s, has variously connoted a mind altered by drugs, uncolonized by political or social propaganda, unburdened by systems of labor, untroubled by preconception or prejudice, or enlightened through Zen Buddhism (as

---

32 "Outta my head / it's growing / outta my head / it's glowing / outta my head / 'cause I heard / something said / in a word / from your voice / did I hear / only choice / dear / outta my head / she tells / from shots that shot above / outta my head / things are different / outta my head / of a time / in the bed / for a rhyme / flashin' back / to your air / and the good / there," etc. The first and second person here are the usual subject and object of most pop music, but apart from the refrain, the heavy parataxis and obscure referents of the lyrics give them enough ambiguity that we might read them as the random words singers sometimes sing when writing lyrics to first get the melody right. But the depth of Shuggie's passion is so evident as he sings—his voice ranges from whispers to cries, breathy ooohs to strained cracks—that we have to assume they do "mean something" liberating to him: "it's about time / something new," he croons near the end of the song.

33 "We penetrate the mystery only to the degree that we recognize it in the everyday world, by virtue of a dialectical optic that perceives the everyday as impenetrable, the impenetrable as everyday.... the most passionate investigation of the hashish trance will not teach us half as much about thinking (which is eminently narcotic), as the profane illumination of thinking about the hashish trance. The reader, the thinker, the loiterer, the *flâneur,* are types of illuminati just as much as the opium eater, the dreamer, the ecstatic. And more profane. Not to mention that most terrible drug—ourselves—which we take in solitude." (Walter Benjamin, "Surrealism: The Last Snapshot of the European Intelligentsia," *Reflections,* trans. by Edmund Jephcott, Schocken, 1986.)

interpreted by US counterculture); it signifies a utopia in which the physical world can be transformed as one's consciousness is transformed. We can also read the idea back further, to André Breton's 1924 *Le Manifeste du Surréalisme,* in which Breton described the socially constructed mind that surrealism would liberate: "Under the pretense of civilization and progress, we have managed to banish from the mind everything that may rightly or wrongly be termed superstition, or fancy; forbidden is any kind of search for truth which is not in conformance with accepted practices." Surrealism, as Breton defined it, involved "psychic automatism in its pure state, by which one proposes to express—verbally, by means of the written word, or in any other manner—the actual functioning of thought. Dictated by the thought, in the absence of any control exercised by reason, exempt from any aesthetic or moral concern."

Shuggie's apparently associative, possibly automatic lyrics don't relate a narrative so much as they conjure a mood. Part of that invocation may be due simply to Shuggie's reliance, like most pop songwriters, on cliché: we all speak in clichés so readily that pop music is popular in part because it borrows our most familiar language to give voice to feelings we think we already feel, feelings we cannot articulate except through debased expression. These inarticulate articulations generally reflect some relatively temperate emotion: the sunny-and-harmless, the socially-acceptable-passionate, the bittersweet-and-safely-depressive, the mildly-political; when we hear a pop song that speaks to a starker desperation through cliché—such as Joy Division's "She's Lost Control" or Beyoncé's "Crazy in Love"—the effect is, as in "Aht Uh Mi Hed," memorable. Whether or not the mood Shuggie's lyrics summon represents the experience of being out of one's head, whether or not it frees the listener's mind,[34] it does, unlike Randazzo's and Weinstein's version of a similar sentiment, feel ecstatic in all senses of the word.

▸

A common trope for pop music criticism invokes Emily Dickinson's famous comment[35] to propose the site at which music affects one both physically and as close to cerebrally as a pop song might achieve: the head (a song "took my head off" or "knocked my head off," etc.). Perhaps in an even more familiar idiom—often, but not

34 Like all distinctive, memorable songs, "Aht Uh Mi Hed" does, at least, free the listener's mind in that, after hearing it, our notion of the possible in the four-minute pop song has been expanded.

35 "If I read a book and it makes my whole body so cold no fire can warm me, I know that it is poetry. If I feel physically as if the top of my head were taken off, I know that it is poetry. These are the only ways I know it. Is there any other way?" (Thomas Wentworth Higginson, "Emily Dickinson's Letters." *The Atlantic Monthly,* Vol. 68, No. 4 [1891].)

always, a complaint—the song has become "stuck in one's head."[36], [37] But the brain can, apparently,[38] inscribe music into itself as a way of remembering it—our heads offering us storage space for our music that's not too different from the external hard drives onto which we cram excessive iTunes libraries, so that our preferred music is always in our heads, even when it may be driving us out of our heads. "Aht Uh Mi Hed" is too subtle a listening experience,

---

36 "German music fans have adopted the term 'ohrwurm' (earworm) to describe" those "annoying snippets of pop songs that get lodged in your head and won't go away." (Barry Willis, *Stereophile* "News Desk," February 2, 2003.)

37 "This was the first study to examine the earworm phenomenon. It documented the pervasiveness of the phenomenon and sought to lay the groundwork for a theory of 'cognitive itch.' The primary focus was on identifying 'sticky' properties of music that make becoming an earworm more likely. It appears that music characterized by simplicity, repetitiveness, and incongruity with listeners' expectations is most likely to become 'stuck.'" (James J. Kellaris, "Identifying Properties of Tunes That Get 'Stuck in Your Head': Toward a Theory of Cognitive Itch." In Susan E. Heckler and Stewart Shapiro, eds., *Proceedings of the Society for Consumer Psychology Winter 2001 Conference,* American Psychological Society.)

38 "All of us (with very few exceptions), can perceive music, can perceive tones, timbre, pitch intervals, melodic contours, harmony, and (perhaps most elementally) rhythm. We integrate all of these and 'construct' music in our minds using many different parts of the brain. And to this largely unconscious structural appreciation of music is added an often intense and profound emotional reaction to music. 'The inexpressible depth of music,' Schopenhauer wrote, 'so easy to understand and yet so inexplicable, is due to the fact that it reproduces all the emotions of our innermost being, but entirely without reality and remote from its pain.' ...Much that occurs during the perception of music can also occur when music is 'played in the mind.' The imagining of music, even in relatively nonmusical people, tends to be remarkably faithful not only to the tune and feeling of the original but to its pitch and tempo. Underlying this is the extraordinary tenacity of musical memory, so that much of what is heard during one's early years may be 'engraved' on the brain for the rest of one's life. Our auditory systems, our nervous systems, are indeed exquisitely tuned for music." (Oliver Sacks, *Musicophilia,* Knopf, 2007.)

too mellow in its particulars to knock anyone's head off, but it's long been stuck in my head.

FLYING SAUCER ATTACK: "Beach Red Lullaby" (b/w "Second Hour" 7", Planet, 1995)

Driving westbound on the Massachusetts Turnpike's thirty-mile Berkshire run between Exits 3 and 2, on a late October morning after a rainy fall when the foliage never achieved much grandeur, only muted oranges and burnt-out reds and dusty greens amid curled-up browned leaves, much of the foliage now stripped from the branches anyway so that the bare white birches rising roadside are more visible than the top of the illuminated McDonald's / Gulf rest-stop sign lost in low fog, the morning's drizzle just enough for slow interval wipers, I climb in light traffic past Blandford into Otis, the wind-ravaged trees here stunted and crook-limbed, the fog lower and lower until even the mile markers and the tops of the eighteen-wheeler's trailers fade into it ahead of me, cruising at seventy-some miles per hour, running lights catching the guardrail's white reflective strips, the massive three-bladed 600 kW wind turbine absent amid clouds, a few hilltop leaves' reds vibrant against the utter grayness of asphalt and sky and dynamite-exposed granite and day itself, and the iPod spins up Flying Saucer Attack's "Beach Red Lullaby," a lossy file I digitized and ripped at 320 kbps, a fidelity almost as fuzzy as this weather, though even listening to the vinyl record (via nude, line-contact diamond stylus; 0.8 mV moving-coil cartridge; 1:5 amorphous-core step-up transformer; vacuum-tube phono preamplifier, etc.) I've wondered what Rachel Brook's singing: "Red, red glow"?—"Red, wet glow"?—"the earth less whole"?—who knows: the track's mix favors the guitars over her voice, and anyway she's nearly whispering, but the four-minute song's wistful melody and finger-picked guitar whelmed by wind-tunnel distortion accompany the drive and the weather and my mood, so I keep thumbing the steering wheel's rewind button and letting it replay itself, again and again and again, before the iPod can shuffle away, even though the roadside sign warns "emergency stopping only," and then the low-pressure system cycles in another wave of rain, the defogger warms the windshield and my face, and the car's so comfortable I wish the landscape could recycle itself like that in a Hanna-Barbera cartoon and I keep driving endlessly through it, because everything's both fleeting and worth preserving, especially these minor moments of self-awareness that rupture my tiresome routines, or because I don't yet know that within twenty-four hours a freak early snowstorm will blow through these hills and split leaf-heavy trees and literally alter the landscape for good—"pics or it didn't happen," we demand of any unbelievable claim, a belief that the only real experience can be proven, and revisited, and ever since my phone's included a camera I too have often wanted to stop and photograph something I've witnessed, whether sun-backed clouds over the Catskills or a coyote watching a cow herd in a pasture: the wish to stop time, to undo a moment's happening, simply acknowledges that the camera lens, by making something seem worth capture, helps our eyes notice whatever imperfect beauties they might otherwise miss, but however potent my desire to make visible to someone else—even only my future self—the minor significances I've seen, I almost always refuse to stop for the snapshot, whether because I think I don't have time to make the document, or because I want the moment to exist only as memory and so sustain its unverifiability, or because I know that no one else can value my own abstracted reveries in a way that will affirm what they mean to me—but already I'm descending the hills' far side, passing the pond in Becket, ducking the Appalachian Trail's overpass, and the yellows of phragmites and greens of tiny pines emerge from the gray now resolving itself into layered clouds stretching ahead toward the Taconics, and plumes of mist rise from the Housatonic valley as a string of eastbound headlights approaches the past I've just exceeded.

MY BLOODY VALENTINE: "To Here Knows When" (*Tremolo* 12″ EP, Creation, 1991)

Green River Road, Halifax, Vermont: a corduroyed gravel stretch tracing the curves of hills and river. The dry weeks of August and September, passing cars and pickups kicked stones into wheel wells, lifted dust that settled on ditch grass. I lived here one year in college, in a basement apartment at a trout farm, with my girlfriend—who, during the fall semester, seemed gradually to inhabit a reality unobservable to anyone else. She interpreted her odd dreams (children with glowing eyes, etc.) as prophesies, stopped talking much to me or anyone else, and then dropped out, but not before her mother, in some sort of cleansing ritual, placed small seashells from a Cape Cod beach in the apartment's four corners and smudged the rooms with sage. Another friend's mother died, and that friend, too, dropped out. A third friend confessed one afternoon that she found little to admire beyond

Tess of the d'Urbervilles, and that she was contemplating dropping out. Mornings, I watched through the window as my landlord, Mr. Dalrymple—now retired, in matching green workshirt and workpants, his combover undone in the wind—flung handfuls of what seemed to be dog kibble into the old aboveground swimming pool that served as his trout hatchery. The water churned, brown and hysterical. Afternoons I didn't have classes or work-study in the college bookstore, I'd lie on the couch wearing a pair of red Snoopy sunglasses I'd bought at a yard sale, drinking gin and tonics, and writing so many short stories that my professor nicknamed me Josh Carol Oates.

My car rarely ran reliably, so I lugged my Fender Precision bass uphill two miles to campus for band practice: it was 1992, and Rebecca, Sean, and I called ourselves Uma Thurman's Death Posse. On clouded or moonless nights, walking home, I followed the mostly invisible road by looking for the strip of slightly lighter darkness between the trees on either side of it. Still, I drove when I could—to get to town, to get away from my girlfriend, to listen to music in solitude. Though I knew how to make a low-tech tape loop—loosen the tiny screws clamping the halves of a cassette; slice the two pieces of leader tape and discard; cut a length of tape to suit your desired loop; splice the ends; reassemble the cassette; record—I opted instead to fill one half of a ninety-minute cassette with a fake loop I created by playing the coda of the first song on My Bloody Valentine's 1991 EP, pressing pause, replaying it, pressing pause again, and so on, until I had forty-five minutes of seesawing drift. (With iTunes, it's easy: set "To Here Knows When" to start playing at 4:42.778—the slight bit of staticky fadeout from the actual song is necessary, in my version; select repeat; press play. The track's blurry, minute-long tail—a bunch of processed guitar tones and chords that might be the best thing Kevin Shields ever recorded, a perfect soundtrack for anything lost—will go on forever, if you let it.)

My tape—agitated and peaceful, confused and confusing—sounded like something that might be the noise clouds make when their movements are sped up in a student film. It matched the rhythm of winds disturbing the unmown pastures along Green River Road, Ames Hill Road, Lucier Road. The rhythm of blood in my ears when, on hands and knees to retrieve a dropped pen, I discovered the tiny whelk my girlfriend's mother had hidden under my desk. Of a twenty-one-year-old girlfriend sobbing in a dingy stall shower in a dingy basement apartment, and my own worthless, unuttered guilt. Of the freight train the woman I soon found way more interesting than my girlfriend told me she'd jumped one afternoon while we sipped hot tea with cheap whisky from plastic dining-hall mugs and yellow maple leaves spiraled down around us—and of those leaves themselves. Of so many short afternoons I wasted watching the sky outside my windows darken, and contemplating how to describe it. Of my skittery heart, the night during finals when two friends and I crushed ephedrine tablets and stayed up in the music library, playing records and grinding our teeth until dawn.

That afternoon, still humming, I wrote the last eight pages of a final paper on Faulkner's *Absalom, Absalom!,* pinned it to my thesis advisor's door, then drove back to the trout farm and packed up the last of my junk. I'd heard that my former girlfriend had driven to the west coast with some trust-funded guy, and married him, or had a kid with him, or both—no one knew, exactly. Mid-May, and exams had almost ended, but it still felt cool in the hills. Did I miss her, or was I glad she'd vanished from my life? That winter, at one of Uma Thurman's Death Posse's three public performances, I'd torn in half a picture of myself and shouted, "Fight the real enemy!" Most of my friends had already dispersed for summer, and I drove home having said few goodbyes. A month or two later, I sold my Subaru to a junk dealer for $125, then bought a used Telecaster for the exact same amount. Sean had graduated; Rebecca had transferred. Sometime that summer, I lost the cassette I'd made. But it didn't matter: my mother had recently sold the house I'd grown up in, and most of my childhood leftovers had been dumpstered. Anyway, every time I heard "To Here Knows When," my mind let its ending wander on and on down back roads.

Twenty years after I left the trout farm, My Bloody Valentine's repeated excerpt could have scored the fury of Hurricane Irene's rains and the floods that followed, temporarily erasing Green River Road from the map. The rebuilt road is, the *Brattleboro Reformer* reports, now paved.

LOOK BLUE GO PURPLE: "Circumspect Penelope"
(*Bewitched* 12″ EP, Flying Nun, 1985)

My youthful travels—bounded by the meager means I possessed for escape: junker cars, slender bank accounts, impoverished imagination—never took me as far as I desired or dreamed. In our junior year of high school, a friend and I concluded one night that instead of doing homework we needed to see the ocean, so we lit out for Rhode Island in his parents' Ford Country Squire. Forty-five minutes later, we bypassed the faint lights of Providence—another world entire, it seemed—and continued south, but lost our nerve someplace well before Point Judith or whichever beach we fantasized we'd stand upon while wild waves soaked us, and turned back. A year later, a different friend—a manic-depressive who wore her hair in a red-dyed quiff and broke the hearts of boys and girls at Coffee Kingdom—moved out from her parents' place but kept a house key and, though she didn't drive, a car key. Occasionally, on school nights, we'd wait until after her parents' windows went dark and then sneak into their garage, and I'd drive—hands at two and ten o'clock until we'd slipped through the Mass Pike tollbooth, when I'd test the accelerator, since, unlike my 1980 Mercury Bobcat station wagon, this car didn't rattle my teeth if I pushed it over seventy. We'd zip into Boston, shoot out of the Copley Square exit, and park. Neon-lit city before us, we might've done almost anything, but usually we went to get a deep-dish pizza at a chain restaurant, and ate it while complaining about whatever bistro-punk injustices and misfortunes we felt we'd suffered that week. On the way home, we'd refill the tank to its previous level, readjust the rearview mirror, and ease the car into her parents' garage as if returning a rental.

Distance always seduced me—distance from whatever was most familiar, especially myself—but the difficulties in achieving such remove vexed me. Records by British bands and place names like Macclesfield and Ladbroke Grove offered me one form of cultural tourism, but the New Zealand music scene I discovered in college afforded an even further flight, maybe because the music sounded so near to what I loved already. Everyone knows the Clean and the Chills, the Verlaines and the Bats, Toy Love and the Tall Dwarfs—and should know the Pin Group and the Renderers and Dadamah and the Terminals and the Dead C—but Look Blue Go Purple, who put out only three EPs over the course of four years, is, song for song, among my favorite bands of any country. "Circumspect Penelope" sketches departure and return, and sounds urgent enough to make you jump out of your chair and run as soon as Kath Webster and Denise Roughan start speed-strumming their guitars, Norma O'Malley chips in a wheezing sixties-style organ, and Kathy Bull's bass joins Lesley Paris's terse snare-ride-cymbal-and-kick-drum beat. The song's lyrics may seem cribbed from an English-class lecture on *The Odyssey* in their thumbnail version of that epic's events, but the five women in Look Blue Go Purple clearly sympathize less with Odysseus's exploits than with Penelope's endurance: "She's been waiting twenty years / and you just walk in / telling stories of the sea / She should hate you, your Penelope."

Before my girlfriend moved out of our trout farm apartment, but when our split seemed inevitable, I vanished from that basement as often as I could. One cloudy night my car's alternator fizzled out in front of the dirt-road workshop of an artisan who, on hand-carved signs hung from tree limbs, advertised "Wooden Toys," "Dawn 'til Dusk." My dashboard lights dimmed and then winked off, and October-bare branches reeled in the winds. I cranked the ignition: the starter only clicked. I abandoned my car there until daylight and scurried home in the dark, glancing over my shoulder every few paces for axe-wielding toy-makers. Later that week, the car still in the shop and my girlfriend sitting in our windowless kitchen squinting at *The Mill on the Floss* for class the next day, I roamed uphill to campus on foot.

Our minuscule college had no ivy, no brick, no columns, no quad, only some drafty old farmhouses where we held classes and a barn-turned-dining hall, all built upon the steep slopes atop a hill, with newer dorms and cottages half-hidden amid the trees behind. The white clapboards and twelve-over-twelve windows looked glorious against green grass, yellow leaves, or two feet of snow, but at night we could see only the moon, the stars, and a bright security light above the maintenance garage. I drifted into the campus center—nearly deserted until the rush downhill from the library at ten minutes before close, when the work-study kids shouted "FREE COFFEE!" to all comers instead of dumping whatever unsold brew remained in the pots—and down through the mailroom, where a few kids played pool and smoked, then out into the brisk Vermont air and back down past the dining hall, thinking I'd head to a friend's cabin. Instead, two figures approached. We were always squinting into the dark and asking each other "Who's that?"—or else tucking our heads and hoping to pass unnoticed. But I recognized the laugh of a woman who'd transferred here that fall. We shared none of the same classes, but I'd noticed her short dark hair, big dark eyes, and Charlie Brown striped sweaters. She and her roommate were carrying a bottle of cheap mezcal to their cottage. "Come with us," she said, hooking her arm around mine, and I did.

At their place, we shook salt on our hands, chugged shots, bit down on lime slices. Charlie Brown sweater girl told me that Codeine and Galaxie 500 and the Pale Saints and the Swirlies—or whoever else I mentioned listening to—were pretentious. "It's all so whiny," she said, and slid a Jesus Lizard tape into her boombox. There was no clock on the wall, no watch on my wrist, nothing but dark night beyond the floor-to-ceiling windows and the bottle on the table we sat around. Her roommate slurped one more mezcal and slouched down the hallway to her bed. I understood the evening's probable endpoint, and however eager I might have been for such an outcome, I thought about my still-sort-of-girlfriend at home, halfway through the tiny type of a five-hundred-page novel I would never read. Was she awake, reading about Maggie Tulliver—and, like her, withdrawn from the outside world—or had she gone to sleep early? I can't remember if we'd even said anything to each other when I left that night. A month and a half into our nine-month lease, we'd already realized the profundity of our mistake in living together, and I spent long days away from the trout farm, planning my exit, though those plans didn't involve Charlie Brown sweater girl or anyone else. "I'm a fool to believe in love and its channels, / I'm a fool to believe in it at all," Norma O'Malley of Look Blue Go Purple sings on the band's last record, two years after "Circumspect Penelope." I was such a fool, then, wanting both the comforts of home and the excitement of travel, and believing them not incompatible. No siren songs seduced me save those I invented for myself to hear.

Dribbling mezcal across the tabletop, Charlie Brown sweater girl filled both of our shot glasses and pointed to the agave larva curled in the half-inch of alcohol still in the bottle. "Do you want to eat it?" she asked.

"You'd better," I said, standing up and knocking my chair backwards.

She laughed, she swallowed the worm, we drained the bottle, we briefly made out with lime-sticky lips on her couch, and then somehow I was stumbling uphill toward campus, then back downhill along Moss Hollow Road toward the trout farm. Every winter a few students drove their cars into the ditch along this steep gravel curve. The boozy blood rushing in my head rolled and swirled like the guitar chords of the whiny and pretentious bands I liked.

The woods along Moss Hollow sheltered only a few houses, and even the ramshackle one called J.K.'s—which half a dozen or so students rented in ever-changing combinations—was unlit. A mile farther, the trees opened to a pasture where three Clydesdales freaked me out every time I walked past: first all three would turn and stare, then they'd slowly trot toward me, soundless but for their hoofbeats. Were they standing in the dark, watching me now? I wanted to stop and sit on a leaf-banked stone wall, but kept blundering through the night, catching my toes in potholes I couldn't see.

At last I crossed Green River Road, then a small bridge over the Green River itself, and trudged up the rutted driveway to the trout farm. From the one side of the apartment with windows, lights glowed. I opened the door, lurched into the jamb, and stepped inside. That dank and dismal space, now warm and bright, bore some magical-but-familiar scent I couldn't quite name. A chair scraped linoleum and my soon-to-be-ex-girlfriend stood in the doorway to the kitchen, wearing pajamas and glasses instead of contacts, holding her half-open novel.

"Where the hell have you been?" she said, almost whispering. "I've been baking cookies since 2:00 A.M.!"

I stepped closer: she'd heaped chocolate chip cookies on a plate on the kitchen table. I stared at them, at her, at my feet, but could think of nothing to say, so I staggered into bed.

The poet we know as Homer wrote, in Richmond Lattimore's translation of *The Odyssey,*

> Circumspect Penelope said to him in answer:
> 'If, my friend, you were willing to sit by me in my palace
> and entertain me, no sleep would be drifted over my eyelids.
> But it is in no way possible for people forever
> to go without sleep; and the immortals have given to mortals
> each his own due share all over the grain-giving corn land.
> So I shall now go back again to my upper chamber,
> and lie on my bed, which is made a sorrowful thing now, always
> disordered with the tears I have wept, ever since Odysseus
> went away...'

"She should hate you," Kath Webster sings to the Odysseus figure in "Circumspect Penelope," perhaps thinking of such passages, but Penelope doesn't hate him. Maybe my almost-not-girlfriend hated me, or should have, but I didn't hate her, not even after she'd cheated on me that summer. We'd reconciled just long enough to move in together, and then I'd turned aloof and withdrawn: by that October night, I was no longer willing to sit by her in the trout farm and entertain her. My girlfriend's eyes may or may not have been tear-reddened behind her glasses. Was she waiting for me to return home, or, finally, to leave? Did she truly believe—as she told a mutual friend that year, who then told me—that she and I had been destined to be together, but evil forces were driving us apart, just as Poseidon kept Odysseus from returning to Penelope?

In the Lattimore translation, following the consistencies of *The Odyssey*'s oral origins, Penelope is always circumspect; Odysseus is always resourceful; the young Dawn always shows again with her rosy fingers. At twenty-one, I found everything about my life worth dramatizing in similarly simple and repetitive terms: a friend would tell me a story, or something mildly interesting might happen to me, and a week later I'd have written a faintly altered version of it for my fiction workshop. Life seemed to exist for me mostly so it could appear in my own retellings of it, versions in which I controlled when scenes began and ended, which details received description, which points of view were privileged and which silenced. But there was nothing worth mythologizing, nothing remotely epic about the sorry, slow-motion undergrad break-up between my girlfriend and me, and in any case I used none of my scanty resources as I wandered the gravel roads and woods-trails of my campus, delayed only by obstacles of my own making. She saw and understood far less of me than she thought she did, though when I returned home it required neither Penelope's circumspection nor Athene's gray eyes to discern that I'd been drinking all night and kissing another woman.

Dawn may have shown again with her rosy fingers through the windows of the trout farm, but, hungover in my bed, I didn't notice. When I awakened, my girlfriend had gone to class. I ate one of her cookies, then another, and looked out the window at low gray clouds, bare trees, aboveground swimming pool teeming with trout. Amid the steep hillsides and narrow valleys of southern Vermont, where dawn arrived late and sunset came early, it was always hard—even for those of us not blinded by selfishness—to see very far.

U2: *Boy*
(LP, Island Records, 1980)

> Finding out, I'm finding out the things that I've been talking about,
> Finding out the things that I've been missing out,
> Finding out the things that are on my mind
> —"Boy/Girl"

I once dated U2. We went steady throughout my junior high school years. Ours was a serious, committed, exclusive, long-term relationship. I felt smitten, heartstruck, crushed, lovesick, moony. Sure, I looked at other bands—who doesn't?—but those other bands only confirmed for me how special U2 was. If I flirted, I never strayed. Not at first.

What exactly did I see in these four young men with artfully scruffy haircuts, flannel shirts and peacoats, the grit and roughness of Dublin nearly visible on their smooth faces? In those days their own peculiar take on anthemic stadium rock had only begun to fill stadiums; they'd yet to revise themselves into a slick, MTV-ready package, as heavily processed as one of the Edge's guitar riffs. I may have been attracted to their sensitive posture coupled with their propensity to rock: unlike much of the post-punk and new wave of their era, they had no aversion to the sort of guitar heroics most thirteen-year-old boys, myself included, require in their music. Or it may have been the fact that while many of my contemporaries mauled air guitars to Van Halen's *Diver Down,* Led Zeppelin's *II,* or AC/DC's *Back in Black,* and watched idealized versions of themselves on screen in such movies as *Sixteen Candles* and *The Breakfast Club,* I—who never owned those records, who never saw those films until my late twenties, and then mostly to participate in Sarah's semi-ironic nostalgia—looked across the Atlantic for my role models. Because I played soccer—in 1983 and 1984, a profoundly unpopular sport in my hometown—the Scottish film *Gregory's Girl* (about an awkward, soccer-playing teenage boy confused about girls) was my John Hughes movie; the Irish band U2 was my Van Halen. Even at twelve and thirteen, I imagined I possessed a discriminating sensibility, one that spurned mass-market pop culture in favor of something that I naïvely believed was more genuine, less commodified—if only because it was foreign, unknown amongst my peers.

Afternoons, I'd sequester myself in my bedroom, where I'd switch on my silver Sony receiver and cue U2's *Boy* LP on the old Harman-Kardon turntable I'd inherited from my parents. I played that LP so often, light would have shone through its grooves if I'd held it up to the window. I studied the album cover—the four deliberately distorted portraits of the US pressing—for so long I might have been looking into a mirror. I read the lyrics printed on the inner sleeve, sang along when I knew no one was listening, fumbled out Adam Clayton's bass lines on my cheap birthday-present bass guitar.

The songs on *Boy*—which, in such titles as "Twilight," "Stories for Boys," and "Out of Control," or such lyrics as "A boy tries hard to be a man / His mother takes him by the hand" and "In the shadow, boy meets man" delineated the confusing, liminal state in which I found myself—seemed to explain something essential to me during those repeated listens, or perhaps served as an affirmation that my feelings were not as unique as, at my most self-pitying moments, I sometimes believed. When Bono sang, "Look from the outside to the world I left behind," I could sigh with some combination of recognition and gratitude. The pulsing bass, the galloping drums, the reverberant guitar arpeggios—all these instruments played with a kind of nervous turbulence—the very sound of this album suggested my own restlessness, my own inability to inhabit myself.

If not *Boy*, I listened to *War*. Or *October*. I believed that these one-word titles evoked the same sort of complex, inchoate feelings blitzing my hormone-sullied self. Like *Boy*, these other two LPs offered their own metaphors, ones I could conveniently personalize: the lyrics on *October* repeated images of burning and falling that indicated less the autumn leaves than my own adolescent fluster; *War* depicted conflicts political and personal, so I could reckon the troubled state of the world—which I barely understood anyway—a mere outgrowth of my own inner cosmos. These three documents seemed profound—nothing about my love could be anything less—and I became their scholar, their apologist. But among them I returned most often to *Boy*—slurred and reckless, raw, recorded seemingly in a single take, its initial mistakes preserved out of a youthful indifference. Forget *Pet Sounds* and Brian

Wilson's multi-tracked "teenage symphonies to God": *Boy* was for me the genuine article.

I preferred side two to side one, which opened with "I Will Follow," U2's earliest hit, a song whose seductive qualities always seemed too simple to me; I felt most captivated by *Boy*'s subtler depths, and, on side two, U2's songs seemed more nuanced if no less bombastic. "Stories for Boys" announced itself with a reverbed guitar riff and a thunderous drum roll; "The Ocean"—with its tape-effect water gurgles and rope creaks, bass chords, and near-whispered vocals—struck me as profound; "A Day Without Me" offered the album's poppiest moment—though this was lurching and off-kilter pop, driven by rattling drum fills, piercing guitar riffs, buoyant chords, and the Edge's tape-sped, chipmunked vocals in its long fadeout. "Another Time, Another Place" seemed, despite a simple bass pulse and crisp rhythm, the most musically ambitious song on the album, with the Edge's melancholy harmonics, a key change midway through, an extended guitar solo, and Bono's throatiest vocal lines, including one verse declaimed in—Gaelic? Latin?—certainly not English. "Electric Co." sounded as furious as the shock treatment it portrayed, and from its closing rumble rose the indeterminate acoustic narrative of "Shadows and Tall Trees." Those many hours in my bedroom wedged these six songs into my memory so incontrovertibly that twenty years later I can still hear them there, note for note.

▶

> Spirit of the rising sun, lift me up
> Hold me there and never let me fall
> Love me till I die, my heart won't wait
> Soon I will be gone…
> —"The Three Sunrises"

To get to know my better half better, I sought everything I could: import singles with rare B-sides or remixes; the hagiographies already appearing in the record stores; oversized, tape-cornered posters that slowly sagged under their own weight. In my bedroom I assembled, except for two or three impossible-to-find items, U2's complete discography, as if doing so were proof of both my feelings and the depth of my commitment, as if love were a case of consuming one's partner.

A local radio station would, every afternoon at five o'clock, play the "Top Five at Five." During the weeks when U2's "Pride (In the Name of Love)" was a staple of this countdown, I would tune in daily—perhaps believing that such sanction vouched for my own brilliance and good taste, perhaps checking that my band's reputation had not slipped in the estimation of others.

Another radio station would, from time to time, late at night, play a band's entire oeuvre in alphabetical order—"U2, A to Z," for example. Even though such an undertaking would require hours—how quaint it seems even mentioning this now, after the Clear Channel era, after radio in general—I would ready a blank tape and sit, one finger hovering above my tapedeck's record button, through the whole program for those few super-rare songs or alternate takes I might not have owned.

Our first meeting is somewhat hazy to me now—there was no momentous, across-the-room meeting of our eyes, no introduction through a mutual friend; I was too young to have picked U2 up in a bar. Instead, we became aware of each other over time. I watched the videos for "Gloria" and "A Celebration" on the USA network's *Night Flight* as Friday night became Saturday morning; I'd twist the tuning knob on my receiver to the left end of the dial and grip my antenna for better reception to listen to a static-stuttered "New Year's Day" on the college stations from Boston and Providence, before that song was broadcast on my hometown's airwaves; finally, at my seventh-grade birthday party, a friend handed me a flat package wrapped in the Sunday comics page—my first U2 LP.

U2 and I saw each other, as often as possible, at the Centrum, a venue they sold out a surprising number of times in those years—once, I believe, three nights in one week. Why did they come so often to a city to which the Boston and New York newspapers referred, if they referred to it at all, as a "fading milltown"? Simply to see me, I was convinced: the center of my own tiny world, I believed it only natural that U2 would entertain me there. I sat by the rotary telephone those mornings the tickets went on sale, breathlessly dialing and redialing the box office until I broke through the busy signal and secured myself a seat, borrowing my father's credit card instead of my father's car to arrange my date. A $16.50 ticket was a small price to pay to celebrate our relationship by wearing a crisp, yet-unwashed U2 concert T-shirt to homeroom the next morning.

Through the smoke of smuggled-in pot, I gazed at the faraway object of my affection, on a stage surrounded by thousands of other people who didn't understand U2—people who stuck fingers into their mouths to whistle, who lifted the meager flames of Bic lighters as if they were at a Rolling Stones show. Perhaps I should have known—by the way Bono pranced and strutted and waved flags, by the hysterical shrieking of the girls who imagined that Larry Mullen, Jr., had winked at them as he pounded the beat to "40," by the sheer number of people who had shown up to watch four Irish guys with bad hair belt out their dramatic take on rock music—that things between us couldn't last, that what now seemed so endearing, cool, and endlessly fascinating would so quickly come to disgust me.

▸

> Like a song I have to sing,
> I sing it for you.
> —"Like a Song"

It is a curious thing, dating a band. I had no interest in U2 sexually, but my interest transcended the platonic. I wanted to be them, to have them explain myself to me, or at the very least have my affiliation with them somehow verify my own worth to others. They might elevate me. I admired their moody rock star poses in fields and snowscapes, and practiced their pouty-yet-piercing gazes.

When you date a band, you want everyone else to know how special your relationship is, so you ink the band's name across your arm, your hand, your jeans, your notebook. If there is a mention of your band appearing on the radio, or on TV—even a song you have heard several hundred times, perhaps even several times that same day—you hush everyone around, in order to better hear the song, and to draw attention to it. Dating a band means laying claim, marking an off-limits sort of ownership: when I wrote "U2" on my notebook, I may as well have written "JH + U2 TLF." Although your relationship with your band begins under the most private of circumstances—you, a stereo, a closed bedroom door, perhaps even a set of headphones—it becomes a declaration to anyone who'll listen, especially in seventh grade when your allegiances in everything from sneakers to polo shirts to sports teams to hairstyles define your very soul; it is as clear a system of signs and signals as public handholding or a wedding ring. You must somehow perform the equivalent of kissing your band at your locker between classes. My best friend at this time dated ZZ Top—too young to grow a beard, he etched the word "Texas" into the finish of his guitar, and, during games of twenty-one at my driveway basketball hoop, explained to me the mythology of that red car and its mysterious keys on the double-Z keychain.

Of course, dating a band also involves a certain level of paradox; often—at least in the case of bands such as U2—the entire point of being in a band is to become popular and sell millions of records, and yet someone dating a band both desires and fears this outcome. Once the band attains that popularity, you'll spend a lot of nights waiting up with the lights on, but they won't come home.

▸

She is a pretty face
But at the wrong time,
And in the wrong place
—"The Refugee"

One of my fiercest rivals during eighth grade was a girl in my class who also dated U2. Because she transferred to our junior high from out of state that year, her claim surprised me: it might have been valid at whatever school she'd attended before mine, but, caught unawares, I saw it as a threat. She made her relationship with U2 an even greater and more obvious part of her life than I did. In January 1985, on our first day back at school after the winter holidays, she bragged to me, "I played 'New Year's Day' eighty-five times in a row the other day." Conversations with her quickly turned into U2 trivia contests—could I, she wanted to know, name the Edge's wife (Aisling), the school at which Larry posted a flyer seeking classmates to form a band (Mount Temple), the band's first incarnation (the Hype)? I sulked and raged inside whenever it seemed that someone viewed her as a bigger fan than I: for her, dating U2 seemed to be more about Bono's blue-eyed gaze and the Edge's high cheekbones than the music. Worse, in my opinion, she expressed a desire to date me. Her friend told me that she liked me—*liked me* liked me—and for a few months I received prank phone calls every night—I'd answer to hear a moment of silence, the muffled sounds of two girls giggling, and then the line going dead. Perhaps she saw our shared appreciation for U2 as a potential bond. I preferred to view it as a barrier as firm and impenetrable as the Berlin Wall seemed in those years.

I like to think that some part of me realized that, early in our relationship, U2 served as a surrogate for the girls I was too shy to ask out. But by ninth grade, I had somehow acquired a steady girlfriend, and after school most days would walk two miles to her house, where we sat on her couch kissing through the short autumn afternoons. Half-heard, the local, non-cable video channel V-66 played in the background: teenage mood music. I sometimes felt as awkward with my girlfriend as, a year earlier, I had felt muddling my way through "Sunday Bloody Sunday" on my bass guitar, but was determined to muddle through this new territory as well. It still seemed possible to date both U2 and a girl without either party feeling resentful, and without my loyalties feeling too divided—U2 didn't make many demands, didn't expect much, came over whenever I touched needle to vinyl and left whenever I lifted the tonearm. Still, as if secretly jealous, the boys from Dublin would sometimes appear in a video on my girlfriend's television screen, and, during such potentially awkward moments, I'd pause my explorations to watch, the cathode-ray light flickering over us in her darkened living room.

▶

I like good times
But I can feel it's going wrong
You sing the same old song
Now I think it's time we get it right
—"Treasure (Whatever Happened to Pete the Chop)"

As in any long-term relationship, my partner occasionally embarrassed me: the chanted beginning to "Red Light" kept me from appreciating that song for years, and Bono's histrionic grunts throughout U2's records seemed, in my dispassionate moments, absurd—nearly blushing, I'd turn down the volume so no one else would hear them. In his Journals, John Cheever wrote that his daughter "makes the error of daring not to have been invented by me, of laughing at the wrong times and of speaking lines I have not written," and I came to feel similarly selfish about U2; I could not imagine them existing beyond the fantasy versions I had conjured in the space of my bedroom. No one else could understand them as I did, I thought, until that point in time when I realized I no longer did understand them—and even then I saw that lack of understanding not as a flaw of my own, but rather an error on their part: their once-perfect sense of aesthetics and propriety began to diverge from mine. Bono's increasingly self-aware antics onstage—wrapping himself in white flags, putting a foot on a monitor to reach an upraised fist over the crowd—made me cringe. Didn't he see that such theater was unnecessary, that the music had power enough? Soon these quibbles became difficult to ignore, and the music's power over me faltered within these gestures; the idea of living together began to seem impossible.

We never fought that I can recall: my disappointments went unspoken, as if I thought that keeping them to myself would mean U2 would cease disappointing me. But instead, the disappointments became more apparent. When U2 released *The Unforgettable Fire* in 1984, I felt conflicted. There had been hints that the album would be something of a departure: Bono noted, in a 1983 interview with the Irish rock magazine *Hot Press,* that he saw U2's first "three albums as the end of an era." For me, this declaration also marked the moment a personal era began to end. Perhaps, for the first time, I saw how much their album titles strained for portentousness, this one more so than any other. Perhaps I finally noticed the band's unabashed fascination with my familiar and mundane America—their songs were now titled "4th of July," "Elvis Presley and America," and "MLK"—which to my mind stripped them of their essential Irishness, and much of their appeal. Perhaps *The Unforgettable Fire* was a more mature and subtle record, less anthem and more texture, for which I was then unready; perhaps, despite my own atheism, I liked Bono much better when he'd sung about the messiah than when he began to believe that he was the second coming. It was a confusing time in our relationship: as U2 finally achieved top forty status in the US, more and more of my friends and classmates asked me about them, and yet I could already feel us drifting apart.

▸

> Find yourself in someone else,
> Don't find yourself in me
> —"Love Comes Tumbling"

As do most relationships at that age—perhaps through an intermediary, or to a chorus of that crucial question, "Who dumped who?"—ours ended in a drawn-out and messy way. By the summer of 1985, when U2 appeared at the Live Aid concert and released the EP *Wide Awake in America,* it became pretty clear to me that they'd long been cheating behind my back, seeking out new fans indiscriminately (and hadn't discrimination, the ability to see in each other what no one else could, been the very foundation of our relationship?). But I'd cheated, too: the vast possibility in the bins at Al Bum's had entranced me. Things between us turned cool and strained—I'd already rolled up most of my tattered U2 posters, wrapped them in rubber bands, and put them in my closet; for a while there had been other bands' posters on my walls, and the flat gazes of Bono, the Edge, Larry, and Adam seemed to express a growing unhappiness at their displacement in my bedroom.

In 1987, dismayed at what I saw—ponytails, leather vests, so much dabbling in a cowboy affect—I bought *The Joshua Tree* mostly to confirm how irreconcilable the differences between us had become: by now, it was an anomaly in my record collection. Within weeks, half my high school attempted to lay claim to my former beloved: kids who a year ago might have worn Mötley Crüe T-shirts now showed up at school with the same U2 T-shirts I once wore, or ventured tiny ponytails in imitation of those worn by Bono and the Edge.

More distressingly, U2 had changed in ways I didn't understand: videos shot in Las Vegas, or filmed on a Los Angeles rooftop, seemed obviously populist efforts to assimilate themselves into the world of Van Halen. (If I may pursue this comparison further: Bono's theatrics were mere variation on David Lee Roth's—and let us note the affinity for tight leather pants that both men shared. Where Roth played to the libido, Bono played to the conscience. Each turned into a narcissistic, caricaturish preacher. the Edge's guitar heroics, too, came to seem not unlike Eddie Van Halen's—

instead of blazing fretwork and finger-tapped strings, the Edge used banks of delay and reverb and echo, but the effect was nearly as wanky, just in a more nerdy way.)

I could try to pretend that U2's music still mattered to me, could try to pretend that my heart was still in it, despite the absence of some key ingredient. The one thing I did understand was that—despite what I'd once felt—I needed to cut my ties. I gathered up all of my U2 records—the debut single, all the imports, the albums, everything—and sold them to a girl in school, someone who could appreciate the new version of U2 without seeing it forever overlaid with the old one. Perhaps, in such a betrayal, I hoped to hurt U2 as they had hurt me. I tried not to look over my shoulder as I walked away. I was certain I would never need those records again. Yes, I dumped U2. Only later did I realize that what I had in fact dumped was the soundtrack to my early adolescence.

▶

> We thought that we had the answers
> It was the questions we had wrong
> —"11 O'Clock Tick Tock"

U2's popularity grew to the point where they no longer needed fans to date them; they could, and did, date supermodels. For a while, they were the most popular act in rock and roll—"rock's hottest ticket," as one of their live bootleg titles had it—something which always surprised me given the way I remembered them: endearingly scruffy, dewy, still in the process of figuring themselves out. If nothing else, they've long since figured out what the rock-listening public wanted, and in so doing cemented their place in rock and roll history. Of course, it occurred to me years ago that I was the one who never understood U2; those people whistling and shrieking and lifting lighter flames in their fists had grasped U2 completely.

For a brief while I felt like someone who watches an ex achieve everything that had been impossible during the relationship. I can vaguely recall U2 collaborating with B.B. King and Johnny Cash—forever seeking that elusive, mythic America, it seemed to me—but at that time my ex and I moved in such different circles that this information reached me only indirectly, the sort of thing a friend of a friend might report offhand, having forgotten our earlier connection.

I take some solace in discovering that I am not the only one who feels that U2 squandered something special. In the 1985 second edition of *The New Trouser Press Record Guide,* editor Ira A. Robbins judges U2 in rhetoric typical of the contemporary critical opinion:

> With a unique, passionate sound, individualist lyrical outlook and youthful guilelessness, Ireland's U2 made a big splash quickly, both in the UK and US... The four Dublin lads have become well-deserved stars, both popularly and critically.... An unquestionable masterpiece, *Boy* has a strength, beauty and character that is hard to believe on a debut album made by teenagers.

But by the time of the book's fifth edition, published a decade later as *The Trouser Press Guide to '90s Rock,* Robbins distanced himself from the band and his earlier acclaim:

> The boys tried hard to be men, and within a few years had lost every bit of their childlike grace, with mounting self-obsession and concomitant inability to see themselves develop into world-class prats.... Last laughs can be mighty bitter, and Bono is hardly in a position to be pointing fingers at little rock gods who've lost their way.

Or, as Robert Christgau succinctly put it in his *Village Voice* review (accompanied by a grade of "B-") of U2's *October:* "What a stupid band to expect purity from."

As I finished high school and for years to come, I had no concern with the goings-on in the world of U2. In the expanding universe of my musical tastes, they had become a dim and distant point in my past. If I thought of them, it was with the understanding that I had been an unformed person then, and that my feelings had been blurred with the hasty and senseless passions of youth. ("Look from the outside to the world I left behind"—or, to paraphrase Hemingway, ours had been only a boy and band affair.) Some part of my consciousness registered that the Edge was balding and goateed, Bono flaunted getups not unlike those worn by Madonna's concert dancers, Adam was rumored to have a drug problem, and Larry still had not changed his haircut since 1984. I heard, at parties or on the radio, their reinvented sound in the string of hits they had in the early 1990s, and went into another room or changed the station—not out of sorrow, or anger, or bitterness, but simply indifference.

▶

> Oh oh on borderland we run
> and still we run, we run and don't look back
> —"A Sort of Homecoming"

I emerged blinking from the intensity of my relationship with U2, uncertain of how to proceed. All the bands I'd ignored during those years I was dating U2 had gone elsewhere, found other partners, given up on me. I tried to date other bands, but could never fully muster the passion. I'd missed my chance with Joy Division and Wire, Buzzcocks and the Clash, A Certain Ratio, the Slits, and Section 25—they'd all broken up. R.E.M. wore a beret and too many Greenpeace and Amnesty International badges on an army-surplus backpack. The Smiths, whiny and dramatic, spent too much time in front of the mirror, in drama club, and reading arch British poetry looking for quotations to print beneath their yearbook photos. I wasn't sure I could really be seen in public with the Fall, much genuinely stranger than the greasy-haired, philosopher-quoting kids smoking clove cigarettes on the quad during lunch. Sonic Youth, intelligent as they were, seemed to have dropped out of school and were spending all day getting stoned in someone's borrowed apartment—would I ever be able to bring them home to meet Mom? Throwing Muses, the Pixies, and My Bloody Valentine each tempted me in the last few years of the 1980s, but by then I'd decided I was too old to date bands. All these relationships were mere dalliances, a string of one-night stands, cheap and empty thrills compared to the onetime depth of my feelings for U2. I sometimes wondered if I'd ever rediscover true love, or if I'd turn into that bore at the party still talking about the person I went out with years ago. My burgeoning LP collection seemed a testament to the hold U2 had once had over me: I could keep hoping to replace them, but would never rekindle a similar spark.

I grew up. Matured. At some point—until I started writing this book, at least—I no longer needed the self-assurance that came from positioning myself in relation to pop music. And there were, after all, girls to date.

But now, after years of running from U2, I have risked a look back. They remain, in the landscape of rock music, inescapable, and, as Bono insisted in "New Year's Day,"

> Though torn in two we can be one.
> I will begin again, I will begin again.
> Oh and maybe the time is right,
> Oh maybe tonight.
> I will be with you again.
> I will be with you again.

In the course of my usual visits to used record stores, I've tried—discreetly, when clerks who don't know me are working the till: buying U2 records more than twenty years after the fact is decidedly uncool—to reassemble some of my old collection. I've told myself I'm only doing research to write this essay.

The albums were easy to find; any used record store has some of them. The import singles I'd once prized were slightly more difficult, but not dauntingly so, and I now have about ten of U2's early records. Late at night, after Sarah has gone to bed, I slip them from their sleeves, ease on my headphones, and, in the living room's darkness, allow myself to get reacquainted. "Two Hearts Beat as One," indeed: "I try to spit it out / I try to explain / the way I feel." The last few nights, I've stayed up past two o'clock in the morning, then hidden the U2 records in the bins and sneaked into bed beside my sleeping wife.

It feels good, familiar, almost too easy. Still, I swear I'm not committing to anything this time.

ALTERED IMAGES: "Sentimental"
(c/w "Dead Pop Stars" 7″, Epic, 1981)

A little more about *Gregory's Girl:* "It's a tricky time for me," Gregory tells his football coach, who's demanding goals. The movie has only just begun, and already we've watched Gregory and his friends admire, through a window, a nurse removing her "brassiere." The next day, Gregory's team loses its eighth game in a row. The coach demotes Gregory from striker to goalie, and replaces him with the only viable option an open tryout produces: Dorothy—a "lass," a "dear"—who's far more skilled a footballer than all the boys she competes against.

A fourth-year student—a bit older than I was the first time I watched the movie, the same year my Under-14 soccer team, the Barons, won the championship—Gregory offered me some uncomfortable parallels. He, like me, was tall and gangly; he played soccer; he felt too shy to ask out girls; he played drums (I was learning the bass); he'd thumbtacked posters (Rush, the Specials, the Jam, Patti Smith) across his bedroom wall. Music, soccer, girls: a holy trinity for us both, the negotiations among them inevitably tricky.

Later in the film, talking to his friend Steve, Gregory grumbles, "Look, pal, I don't know whether you've noticed, but I'm going through a crisis." Gregory's crisis is that of every teen desperate to belong—he cheerfully betrays his friend Andy to retain his own endangered place on the team; he has a crush on Dorothy, a girl Steve's called "unattainable," but no idea how to attain her. And though his complaint's rhetorical, Gregory does believe his friend hasn't noticed. He's clumsy, vulnerable, confident and insecure in the manner of most teenage boys. Late for school one morning, he trots in evasive patterns across the empty football field, and, in a modified version of the film's first scene, two teachers watch him from the faculty lounge window: "He must think he's invisible," one says, laughing. Of course he did. Few boys that age are wise enough to know that everyone else generally feels as out-of-place and overlooked as they do; few can observe the world's machinations. I wasn't; I couldn't.

Dorothy *was* unattainable—so devoted to her training that while the other characters are busy being teenagers and dreaming about each other, she's running laps around town in the darkness. Though everyone's infatuated with her—both her own team and the opposing team mob and kiss her when she scores a goal; in the boys' bathroom, there's a thriving trade in photos of her—she never seemed as intriguing to me as her lab partner, Susan, who wore an in-her-eyes Louise Brooks haircut, a beret, and lots of eyeshadow.

▸

My own desperation to belong sometimes endowed even the simplest, most banal events with import I felt but didn't understand. My mother, late to pick up a friend and me from afternoon soccer practice at the nearby community college's athletic field, gifted us that many more minutes to kick a ball between us, then gossip about classmates as we took off our shin guards and lounged on the clipped grass. He was our team's goalie, I the center fullback, and we hung out at practice, in school, and on weekends. We slipped into a not-uncomfortable silence. The things at which I'd excelled in grade school—drawing, kickball, running fast, making up stories—had lost all currency in junior high, and so these idle moments helped me reinvent myself with my friends and the people I hoped would be my friends.

Squinting into the low sun, I watched a boy and a girl about my own age stroll across the field and through a gap in the chain-link fence on its far side. I couldn't see their faces, but felt convinced that they were girlfriend and boyfriend by the close-but-casual postures of their bodies. The moment meant nothing—two kids walking across a soccer field late some October afternoon—but I managed to idealize it: this brief vision haunted me, suggesting, though I couldn't have explained it then, their obliviousness to everything but each other, their ease with another person that I'd yet to feel—and, I realized later, that my own hyper self-awareness prevented me from feeling. When would I be so at ease, unwitting part of someone else's imagined narrative, participant instead of observer?

▶

Madeleine, Gregory's younger and far wiser sister, accompanies him to the mall to help him pick out new clothes. She gives him sensible advice: buy Italian trousers, take an interest in himself if he expects anyone else to do so, don't script conversations for his dates. After shopping, they sit down at a café, where Madeleine orders "ginger beer and lime juice, with ice cream, please, but don't stir it"—unlike her brother, she asks for exactly what she wants. "The nicest part," Madeleine tells him when the drink arrives, "is just before you taste it. Your mouth goes all tingly, but that can't go on forever. . . ."

If we experience adolescence through its perpetual delay, its apparently endless liminality, Madeleine's line offers perhaps the most crucial of the film's many reassuring lessons: the anxiety of anticipation happens interminably and confusingly, and life's nicest moments are fleeting. So are its worst, we can infer, even if it never seems that way. When Gregory finally does end up on a date—if not the one he expected—he has to be instructed several times to loosen up: "You can't enjoy yourself if you don't relax!" But who can relax when the world seems to postpone what we want most? One of the movie's most painful (and painfully funny) scenes occurs when Gregory, in a borrowed white jacket that doesn't fit him, stands beneath a massive ticking clock awaiting his date's arrival, rehearsing his greeting, sniffing his armpits, and checking his wristwatch.

Like many comedies (but especially *A Midsummer Night's Dream*, which the characters read for school, and which the film's events sometimes mirror), *Gregory's Girl* involves delay, misdirection, and crossed purposes. Even if Gregory feels brief hope—as when Dorothy sends a friend to ask Gregory to meet her—it turns out that she only wants a goalie to help her practice shots. "I just wanted to know what you're up to at lunchtime," she says, when he arrives at the break room the cool kids occupy. His answer nails teenage resignation: "Oh, nothing that can't wait a million years."

Gregory's even dorkier, more hapless friends, Andy and Charlie, resolve early on in the film to stop waiting: "Look, Charlie, we've got to get some girls. We've got to make a move. Even Gregory's at it now. We're falling behind. I don't think there's any advantage in putting it off any longer. Besides, it's making me depressed." When it's unclear why what seems deferred for you has been fast-tracked for everyone else, falling behind becomes your primary concern, and the couple making out in the hallway behind Andy and Charlie only reinforces that anxiety—for them, and for the falling-behind eighth-grade viewer watching at home alone some Friday night when the movie ran on the USA Network.

▸

Our far-flung soccer games took place Saturday mornings in the fall, and our parents drove us through early fog along hilly back roads until we located a field surrounded by old maples at the edge of some small town, or fresh chalk stripes drawn across a sandy baseball diamond where someone had assembled two opposing goals and narrow wooden benches along the sidelines. Often we'd meet at some obvious location and caravan to the game so no one got lost. One morning, as we waited for stragglers in a Dunkin' Donuts parking lot so we could head forty-five minutes north, my friend the goalie asked if I wanted to ride with his mother. I assumed he meant with him and his mother, but when I accepted the offer, he hopped into another teammate's car, and as we all pulled out of the Dunkin' Donuts lot, I sat buckled in the front seat of his mother's Chevette, alone with her, wiping my palms on my shorts and wondering what I should say. A single-mom graduate student who grew hot peppers on her windowsill, who insisted I call her by her first name (as her son did—and as Gregory called his father), and whose boyfriend looked like a cross between John Lennon and Joey Ramone, she always unnerved me. She wore her spiked hair short, seemed younger than everyone else's mom, rented out space in her sprawling, ramshackle house to other students, and had filled her living room with books and LPs I loved to look through whenever I had the chance. I found her both cool and very intimidating—in part because she never spoke to me as if I were a dumb fourteen-year-old.

But when I was fourteen, the world was only just losing its power to intimidate me. At the end of practice after a rousing victory halfway through our season, Coach Barton called us together while he gathered balls into mesh bags. We'd begun the season not unlike the hapless losers on Gregory's team. In the mid-'80s, soccer was not televised, so we probably knew the intricacies of Australian Rules Football—which ESPN used to broadcast early weekend mornings—better than those of the beautiful game. Our hometown of 165,000 people afforded us barely enough thirteen- and fourteen-year-olds to field a team of eleven with a few reserves. We understood the terms slide tackle and bicycle kick, but had few skills to execute either. Coach Barton had to explain how our defense could run the offsides trap, or the difference between direct and indirect free kicks. Now that we'd embarked on a winning streak, he ran his hand through his short gray hair, spun the whistle he kept on a lanyard, and singled out some of us for praise. "Josh," he told me, "you used to be Timmy Timid, but lately you've turned into Thunderfoot."

Thunderfoot? Thankfully the nickname didn't last as long as the boost in my self-esteem. After the speech, Coach Barton had me take all of our team's goal kicks, and some of our corner kicks—though, given my height, he also began putting me in front of goal on our corners, so I could try to score on a header. After the drive with my friend's mother, during which I realized that I felt happier being asked serious questions about myself than sitting crammed in a backseat punching and joking with my teammates, I received my first yellow card of the season, for an aggressive challenge.

▶

Susan, the character in the film who does notice Gregory—"He's got a nice laugh," she says to Dorothy—is played by Clare Grogan, whose band Altered Images put out their debut single, "Dead Pop Stars," a month before the release of *Gregory's Girl* in 1981. "Dead Pop Stars" skidded through the bottom of the UK singles chart for two weeks, but had vanished by the film's opening night. Altered Images, circa 1981, played a poppy post-punk they'd adapted from elder contemporaries such as Siouxsie and the Banshees: echoing, minor-key guitars create a tenebrous mood, but Grogan's breathy, girly voice brightens the gloom.

My fondness for *Gregory's Girl* inspired me to seek out Altered Images. The lyrics to the vaguely gothic "Dead Pop Stars"—"And now I've had my fifteen minutes / I'm just another memory, / An embarrassing part of your youth"—suggest that Grogan was already realistic about her own career's potential longevity, but I didn't care about the vagaries of the pop star life when I was fourteen. Selfish like Gregory, I wanted music to cover my own youthful embarrassments, to validate my own invented crises: what use was a pop song if it didn't sound cool, didn't lend some of that coolness to its listener, didn't also function as a mirror? "Sentimental," the B-side, reminded me of the early U2 records I liked so much then: insistent drums, repetitive bass, delayed and flanged guitar, and lyrics that expressed teenage confusion. "Enter the vast arena," Grogan sings. "Where do you, where do you, where do you go from here? / Can't you see, don't you know, don't you know the way? / Forget the past and it'll go away." "Sentimental" had just enough post-punk energy and just enough winsome new wave chirpiness to appeal to me, and its naïve introspection made my naïve self want to replay it.

I could have construed Clare Grogan's call to "enter the vast arena" as denoting the band's ambition—naming the place they wanted, like U2, to end up playing—or as a reference to the soccer fields where I was handicapped by rules and boundaries I'd yet to master, but I heard it as an allusion to the unknown, perilous site into which I was stepping, where, my mistakes and successes visible before some audience that could vote on my fate, I might or might not survive. The time for choosing was ending. "Enter" was an invitation, but also a command.

At my vulnerable age, I felt welcomed by even the most minor affirmations. A song whose enthusiastic bluster and jumbled lyrics I could make bear my immature, inarticulable feelings, and a film whose characters endured my own worries—both helped usher me into the vast arena of adolescence. Both encouraged me to stop waiting and to accept the world's messiness as it was, and as it remains. Still, plenty of other bands and movies had represented teenage bewilderment in ways that spoke to me. In *Gregory's Girl,* the welcome I found wasn't the fact that Gregory turns out to have an admirer, and that, through Susan's elaborate ruse, he finally realizes it: no, that story only reinforced the basic boy-meets-girl tropes; even though the boy who gets the girl is a dork, he does get the girl, and, at the end of the film, we last see him lying in bed in his borrowed white jacket, flower between his teeth, at peace with himself and his world.

Halfway through the film, in class one day, Andy reads aloud a passage from *A Midsummer Night's Dream,* and quotes Puck: "My mistress with a monster is in love." Although, in the play, Bottom has an admirer, he's still a monster with an ass's head dressed in "hempen home-spuns," which describes pretty well how I felt as a hormone-fueled fourteen-year-old boy without the right clothes, right knowledge, right tastes. Didn't we all secretly fear that some aspect of our appearance—or our souls—was monstrous, and that that fact explained why our crushes failed to recognize us? "Why do they run away?" Bottom wonders, when his friends first see him transformed—a question I might have asked my teenaged self.

Andy and his sidekick Charlie—who, throughout the entire film, never opens his mouth to speak, only to stuff food into it—fill the role of foolish monsters: their idea of picking up girls in the cafeteria is to join them uninvited, and then explain such "well-known facts" as the velocity with which a sneeze exits one's nose, or the method of veal production. And as their desperation not to fall behind increases—particularly when they see Gregory with three different girls on a single night—they try to hitchhike to Venezuela, where Andy has researched the ratio of women to men (eight to one, he believes). In darkness dissolved only by passing headlights, Andy holds a handlettered sign reading "CARACUS," until Charlie finally breaks his silence to tell Andy that he's misspelled the name and they should go home. "There's some nice girls in third year," Charlie says, as they depart. "They always go for the older guys. At least, the nice ones do. There's even a couple of beauties in second year.... Andy. I think everything's going to be all right."

Everything's going to be all right: here was my affirmation, because clearly everything *wasn't* all right with Andy and Charlie as they slouched into the darkness. If such a sad case could admit this delusional hope to another equally sad case, then possibly I might be okay. And as I pondered such questions, the camera caught one last sight of Dorothy, in her tracksuit, running through the night: *Exeunt*.

Charlie's optimism seemed a fantasy, if a compelling one I wanted to believe. As in the midsummer Athenian woods, dreams and darkness obscure and transform the passions in Cumbernauld, the drab Scottish New Town where *Gregory's Girl* takes place, and a dream admits the presence of another in "Sentimental." "What a dream," Gregory sighs to Andy, the first time he notices Dorothy. Later, Madeleine asks Gregory whether he's dreamed about Dorothy, because "that means you really love her. It's the one you have the dreams about that counts." Twice during the film, Andy tells Charlie that he's "had that dream again last night"—and though we never learn the precise nature of this dream, we can imagine it. And, near the end of "Sentimental," the drums and bass drop out for a few measures, and Grogan sings, "In my head, I have a dream / A dream for you, for me / It's a nice dream, you'd like it."

John Peel, the famous Radio One DJ, claimed that, even into late middle age, he wept whenever he heard his favorite song, the Undertones' "Teenage Kicks." "A teenage dream's so hard to beat," Feargal Sharkey sings in that song's first line, and from the perspective of adulthood, it's easy to hear what Peel recognized in those words, and in the song. (Per his wishes, the lyric was chiseled onto Peel's gravestone.) Teenage dreams are so impassioned, and so meager: our most fervent adolescent yearnings so often involve little more than being noticed and appreciated.

As a teenager, I didn't yet realize how banal and absurd so many of my dreams were, nor how achievable, but I still treasured them, and many mornings when I awoke in the muddle of my narrow twin bed, those already departing visions seemed more real—and far more interesting—than the life I abided. In the film, it's crucial that we see Gregory alone in his bedroom, pensive for a moment after bashing his drum kit—and that we see Susan alone in hers, curled up in bed reading Shakespeare, but still attentive to the night-noises through her window. Given the performative nature of adolescence, the constant need to define oneself for others to avoid the risk of being defined by them, my bedroom offered me a retreat where I could consider both the person I hoped to become as well as the person I feared I was. Of course, the bedroom is also where we dream about that becoming. Maybe I needed only to see characters to whom I could relate have their dreams both met and frustrated in order to believe in my own. Madeleine had told Gregory how to realize what we love, and so within a year I'd quit soccer for the greater challenges of music and girls, the things I then dreamed about. *Gregory's Girl* and "Sentimental" both imply more than they state, and those occasional ambiguities felt true to my desires—confused and shifting, impossible to pin down.

ECHO AND THE BUNNYMEN: "Over the Wall"
(*Heaven Up Here* LP, Korova, 1981)
NEW ORDER: "Temptation"
(b/w "Hurt" 12″, Factory, 1982)

> "*Je suis comme le roi d'un pays pluvieux*..."
> —Charles Baudelaire, "Spleen (III)"

After I acquired a Walkman to carry while I walked—and, since I was too young to drive, too old to want to ride my ten-speed, I walked everywhere—I could take with me whichever songs felt crucial to my existence that week. If it rained on me, as it frequently seemed to do, so much the better: these often-mopey songs seemed best suited to the accompaniments of dripping hair, sodden sneakers, jeans dragged through puddles too large to leap. I shunned raincoats and umbrellas; I imagined my very presence, hunch-shouldered and glowering, to rebuke the sensible people in rubber slickers or dry inside their cars.

What is the teenage pleasure in appearing so abject? My developing aesthetic of estrangement required me to enlist weather into its ancient role as I paraded my desolation about town. Rain can be gloomy; rain can be rejuvenating: I was reborn, in those

Massachusetts rainstorms, a serious young depressive, and that I willingly fancied myself a sufferer says all one needs to know about the level of my suffering. Like most teens, I sought simultaneous visibility and invisibility, a public audience for my private woes, and the Walkman—with its obvious evidence of one's secret music—enabled such tensions. Though I was then mostly ignorant of previous generations' complaints, I would, as the Everly Brothers sang in 1962, "do my cryin' in the rain"—even though "raindrops fallin' from heaven / could never wash away my misery"—or, as the Dramatics suggested in 1971, I'd "go outside in the rain," because "I [didn't]"—i.e., did—"want you to see me cry." I hoped to find a girl who would recognize in me what Ronnie Spector, in 1964, imagined about her fantasy boy: "He'll be kind of shy, / and real good-looking, too / And I'll be certain he's my guy / by the things he'll like to do / Like walking in the rain..."

▶

I was hardly alone in my misery: everyone, it seemed, was miserable in the 1980s. Everyone still seems miserable—and though now we worry less about nuclear war than terrorism, less about AIDS than mutant strains of influenza, our anxieties about unemployment and the economy and all the uncertainties of an elusive, provisional world persist. But back then, our miseries evidenced themselves even more noticeably than do foreclosure signs staked outside houses, or the daily social-media appeals for attention we send to hundreds of people we barely know. Instead, I'm thinking of jagged, eye-obscuring haircuts; a mournful punk's deliberately rent black clothes; tears drawn on in eyeliner pencil—or, for terminal cases of misery, tattooed on in ink—weeping from the corners of the eyes of black-lipsticked kids who sat by the reflecting pool downtown. Still, the primary form our misery took in the '80s, its most obvious signifier, was that of the solitary and misunderstood figure walking alone in the rain. The decade's music reworked this trope endlessly: Echo and the Bunnymen, New Order, the Cure, the Wedding Present, Felt, Sad Lovers & Giants, the Wake, and countless other bands all walked alone in the rain *and* made sure to write a song about it so that the rest of us knew. Even Grace Jones—has there ever been a more confident, badass woman in music?—achieved some chart success with her 1981 cover version of Flash and the Pan's "Walking in the Rain," in which her *flâneur*-narrator delivers this crisp, monotone report: "summing up the people / checking out the race / doing what I'm doing / feeling out of place / walking, walking in the rain." (Walking in the rain *always* means feeling out of place.)

Still, it's unclear whether—at least for the adult musicians aestheticizing teen angst—this activity felt inherently sad because of rain's melancholic connotations, or because one lacked companionship and preferred rainy streets to empty house, or because of the time, effort, and hairspray (or egg whites, toothpaste, Jell-O, cornstarch) that went into maintaining the hair sculptures of Ian McCulloch, Robert Smith, and all their suburban disciples, and which rain would surely ruin (as Morrissey lamented, "The rain that flattens my hair / oh, these are the things that kill me"). Or was it because these bands were all British and simply writing about the local climate?

▶

A distance runner in high school, I loved running in the rain—the chill on my skin, the trees dark and shining, the city softened by clouds and fog, the hissing of cars' tires on wet asphalt, the way I thought my hair looked when drenched. One soggy afternoon I headed out to run seven miles, but forgot my house keys, and, when I returned amid a downpour, no one was home and the doors were locked. I went out behind our house, sat on a deck chair, and waited: it was warm enough, and pleasant enough, to sit there and get soaked. I leaned back, crooked my arm over my face, and listened to the slap and patter of rain.

Our street climbed a steep hill, and the house next door was a good story taller than ours—that is, my second-floor bedroom was about level with the Krausses' first-floor living room. (I will take this opportunity to apologize for all the music I blasted while Bill Krauss tried to watch the Red Sox.) Fran Krauss could, from her kitchen window, see me quite clearly on our back deck. And apparently I looked so pathetic and miserable, sitting in the rain, that she told my mother I seemed depressed. *Really* depressed. Fran taught English at a local private school, so she knew the look of privileged despair; Fran was also the first adult with whom I ever drank tea, in that same kitchen—during which (speaking of privileged despair) we discussed *The Catcher in the Rye.*

A night or two later, I'd once again scrapped the exterior world in favor of the Public Image Limited or Joy Division LP on my turntable when my mother knocked on my bedroom door and asked me if I felt suicidal. It was a laughably earnest question, and I did laugh when she asked it, then probably yelled at her to leave me alone while secretly feeling gratified by her concern. Still: did she ask because of the doomy music? My teenage sense of melodrama? Or the fact that I'd willingly waited in the rain?

▶

If the singer-songwriters and AOR artists of the '70s also seemed laughably earnest in their sensitivity (e.g., among endless possibilities, "There are times when a woman has to say what's on her mind, / even though she knows how much it's gonna hurt / Before I say another word let me tell you, 'I love you' / Let me hold you close and say these words as gently as I can"), and if the hard rock of the same era offered an aggressively masculine corrective to all those expressions of feeling ("Hey hey Mama, said the way you mooove…"), then the morose new wave of the '80s twisted and stunted the previous decade's straightforward, psychotherapy-inflected emotional declarations. Exhibiting one's feelings became acceptable again, sort of, as long as those feelings were couched in a bitter sarcasm, or expressed via an insolent wit, or muttered inwardly instead of spoken, or the result of a sensibility finer and rarer than those ordinary people possess. Rain-disguised tears were no longer required to indicate misery: elaborately disheveled hair, corpse makeup, and funereal clothing all indicated the death of one's inner self. Darkness never felt as appealing as it did when political ads insisted that it was morning again in America.

▶

While my friend's proposed method of junior-high seduction involved Def Leppard lyrics played over the phone, my more pathetic, less imaginative tactic involved researching in the telephone book the last names of girls I liked, and, since I almost never knew their fathers' first names, cross-referencing the resulting list of addresses with my knowledge of which neighborhood elementary school these girls had attended to attempt to triangulate the locations of their houses, and then incorporating these often far-flung sidestreets into my training runs. In the event one of these girls was contemplating life from her bedroom window, she'd see me—hair looking good in the rain—run past. I'd take the same route for weeks, until it was evident the girl had better things to do than watch the street all afternoon in case some boy from her World Civ class sprinted by at an unrealistic pace for a distance run, and then, for another few weeks, I'd run past some other girl's house.

This process exhausted me, and I never did manage to accidentally bump into any of these girls outside their homes. Still, after I'd quit the track and cross-country teams to spend more time hanging out at Coffee Kingdom with the other dropouts and wastrels—clove-cigarette-smoking would-be artists, retired skateboarders, medicated suburban poets, bedroom guitar stars, Nietzsche-quoting idlers, low-level weed dealers, 'zine publishers doodling on their hands—I retained my taste for restless Walkman-accompanied strolls on rainy afternoons and evenings, filled with what Charles Baudelaire describes, in *Paris Spleen,* as "the love of masks and masquerading, the hate of home, and the passion for roaming."

"The man who is unable to people his solitude is equally unable to be alone in a bustling crowd," Baudelaire's speaker continues. "The poet enjoys the incomparable privilege of being able to be himself or some one else, as he chooses." By removing the teenage listening experience from the bedroom to a slender pair of Walkman headphones and the city streets, we all became poets in Baudelaire's definition; we could not only soundtrack our journeys but add an entire metanarrative element to them in which we were no longer ourselves wandering our own neighborhoods, but the protagonists of the songs we played. "The Walkman," Iain Chambers notes in his essay "The Aural Walk," is "both a mask and a masque: a quiet putting into act of localised theatrics." Listening to vague, insipid lyrics like those in New Order's "Temptation"—"Up, down, turn around / please don't let me hit the ground / tonight I think I'll walk alone / I'll find my soul as I go home"—allowed me to fill that dumb lyrical template with all the dumb drama of being fifteen.

▶

Perhaps the earliest song I remember: "Raindrops Keep Fallin' on My Head," a *Billboard* #1 hit the year before I was born. On an end table, next to a dish of caramels I raided every visit, my grandmother kept a porcelain figurine of a boy holding an umbrella. I could wind up the figurine's base to make it slowly revolve as, inside it, a music box's metal teeth tinkled that song's familiar melody.

▶

September 1985: in the darkened gymnasium, humid in the aftermath of so many moving bodies, I hunted beneath wooden bleachers and in the locker room for the new Nike jacket I'd worn to the dance and left in the huge pile of other coats. A thin nylon windbreaker somehow supposed to be able to fold up into its own pocket, it seemed hardly worth stealing—not to mention hardly the sort of thing a would-be punk would wear, but though my musical identity had been fixed a few years earlier, my sartorial identity remained in flux. I knew my jacket would never turn up, but I told Juliette and Adam and the other kids walking home down June Street to leave without me so I could keep looking. A few moments later, after they'd gone, I walked alone into the Saturday night, where clusters of kids still stood smoking and talking in the darkness of the upper parking lot. The sky spit rain, and I strode past them, past kids in cars waiting to make the turn onto Highland Street, then cut across the school lawn until I was in no danger of anyone noticing me and calling my name. Arms bare, hands pocketed, I ducked down a sidestreet and walked home the long way.

November 1985: My girlfriend lived two miles away, and most afternoons that fall I'd walk to her house and back by dark. We sat on her living room couch, alternately making out and watching music videos on V-66, a local music video station her TV received but mine didn't, and which thus seemed far cooler than MTV. Her parents, both of whom worked, didn't know I was there—no one was allowed to be there except her, doing her homework—and as those brief afternoons grew dark and the videos flickered over us, she'd light lamps, and then I had to knot my black Converse All-Stars, put on my father's old US Navy wool work shirt that I wore as a jacket, and head home. Like a lot of ninth-graders, she liked public displays of affection that discomposed me far more than public displays of misery—I blushed when our Biology teacher commented as my girlfriend clutched my shirt and kissed me before class. I liked those swift afternoons on her couch, but I also liked the walks home in the rain, through Tatnuck Square and the gas station's oil-rainbowed cement, past cars waiting at the red light where Chandler Street met Pleasant Street, rain spangling streetlit powerlines and smearing parking meters, the smell of wet wool filling my nose as my Walkman played some tape I'd made and I thought about what I'd say when, after dinner, I called my girlfriend.

October 1986: Before two kids from Colorado forever changed the garment's meaning, I owned a dark brown sharkskin trenchcoat, purchased at the vintage clothing store I'd later manage. Its deep pockets comfortably held my Walkman and a few cassettes, and until one of my dissolute friends bumped a lit cigarette against it and the fabric melted away in an almost perfectly round O, I wore it around town: it was as far from the Nike windbreaker as I could get for twenty bucks. Brian Edge, in his book *Joy Division + New Order* (a creased copy of which I consulted regularly that year), summed up pretty clearly the meaning the garment then held for me: "Joy Division had attracted...serious young men wearing severe haircuts and moody, downcast expressions, and the badge of this particular tribe, the '*angst*-ridden' raincoat."

My hometown annually receives an average of 49.05 inches of rain. But for most of the 1980s I'm pretty sure it rained daily.

▶

What desired outcome did I seek, parading my self-involved feelings and invented problems through the streets and hoping strangers would notice? What can result from such attention, beyond the attention itself? Did I want someone in a passing car to stop, roll down his window, offer condolences, tell me he felt that way, too? How embarrassing! Did I have no other outlet for my repressed emotions, no real confidant except the stretch of Pleasant Street from Newton Square to Chamberlain Parkway?

"I'm walking in the rain / to end this misery // I'm walking in the rain / to celebrate this misery," an apparently distraught Ian McCulloch moans in "Over the Wall." At fifteen, I felt far more interested in celebrating misery than trying to escape it: I imagined misery less minor ailment than eternal condition. And yet my city's streets were not promenades where everyone turned out to stroll. There were, then, no surveillance cameras transforming every intersection into a panopticon. Rather, like Hawthorne's character Wakefield, my "quiet selfishness" and "peculiar sort of vanity" persuaded me that someone would observe me haunting the neighborhood and gazing at lighted windows. No one did. I crept unseen along darkened streets, one shadow among others, accompanied by nothing and no one but the despondent songs whispering in my ears, unremarked no matter how much I wanted to be the subject of someone's story—anyone's story but my own.

MOVIETONE: "Late July"
(*Movietone* LP, Planet Records, 1995)

Despite plastic's longevity, vinyl is a degradable medium. LPs scratch, chip, fracture; warp from long-term leaning or horizontal stacking. Sliding a record from its sleeve can scuff it. The static charges in spinning LPs attract dust, hair, pet fur. Mold spores bloom in vinyl's tiny grooves. From these simple facts, a complex industry: anti-static guns, preservative and cleaning fluids, ultrapure distilled water rinses, "ricepaper" replacement sleeves, carbon-fiber-bristled brushes, ultrasonic stylus blasters, vacuum-cleaning machines, LP demagnetizers, LP flatteners. Attempting to commute volatile vibrations in air into inert physical material is a formidable business, in several senses of the word. And if record collectors desire to preserve the past (or versions of the past), and to possess regular access to it—out of an anxiety of forgetting or otherwise losing contact with it—how to deal with the deeper anxiety of losing the fragile physical objects offering such preservation? A solution: I own five copies of Movietone's debut LP.

THE PICTURES: "Renewal"
(*Interior Monologue 7″*, Tiny Shoes, 1997)

Because the vinyl renaissance of recent years has been LP-centric—and original pressings of vintage LPs accordingly expensive—singles bins still brim with overlooked salvage. I paid one dollar for the Pictures 7″, persuaded not by the record store sticker ambitiously name-checking the Sea Urchins, Orange Juice, Tricky, the Field Mice—a hard sell for a buck!—but by the sleeve's blurred monochrome photo of bare trees, field, stone wall: all signifiers, I suspected, of sensitive, post-adolescent yearnings the yearner hoped might've impressed Alan McGee. "Renewal" begins with a drum fill recorded so poorly it sounds more like a cheap drum machine, and immediately a rollicking, delicately-picked Stratocaster riff and nearly-buried bassline spring forth. Two-finger Casio SK-1 chords texture the choruses, and some guy—the one playing everything except drums—sings softly about how he doesn't "want to go home tonight," etc. It's all as tame and wary and plagiarized as I'd imagined it would be—six years passed between purchase and the bored Sunday afternoon I finally played the record. When I did, I maybe loved most the audible clicks of someone pressing the Tascam Portastudio's record button at the ends of overdubs; and the vigorous, almost-out-of-tune guitar strumming; and the distortions where the cassette tape wrinkled after too many takes, too many bounced tracks: all the presences of the shy-but-fervent disciple, the dude so moved by admiration for his records that he wants to make one like them, though he can't quite pull it off. My friend Rebecca and I once locked ourselves in a bedroom for several July weeks to record our own earnest attempts at melancholy pop songs, capturing them on tape as soon as we believed we'd mastered the notes and chords: thankfully we didn't have the money to press a 7″ ourselves. I can assume so much about the Pictures' equipment and instrumentation because it sounds so much like ours did.

"Renewal" is, if charmingly sincere, derivative and deservedly unknown—the record's bland titles render it virtually un-Googleable, and until recently even Discogs, a website that catalogs the obscurest vinyl, failed to include it. Indie kitsch, its pretensions to truth and beauty founder beneath vapid music and lyrics. I can't help recalling Susan Sontag's famous denotation that camp's "essential element is seriousness, a seriousness that fails." The song's clumsy rendition of the basic gestures and clichés of Byrds-jangled, early-'90s lonely-boy British indie-pop attempts to meet that scene's specific expectations: of course, the record also contains a photocopied booklet conspicuously similar to the

Sarah Records inserts, and venturing the same serious-but-breezy delivery that Sarah's Clare Wadd and Matt Haynes achieved. "Style without substance, youth culture has reached a complacent plateau," the booklet's writer warns, oblivious to how this statement condemns the accompanying record.

Still, the insert dedicates *Interior Monologue* to "the ones who believe that these things matter, because they do," and somehow I can't disagree with that sentiment: my favorite records, not unlike this one, are those that probably shouldn't have existed, often made by people with only the shakiest command of their music, and far more passion than the means to articulate it. It's hard to get excited by a record with such a low risk/reward ratio, but nevertheless I've played "Renewal" about twenty times this morning: the song's appeal resides not in how easily it can be overlooked, but in how familiar it already sounds, as though I've been listening to it for years.

THE CURE: "Just Like Heaven"
(*Kiss Me Kiss Me Kiss Me* LP, Elektra, 1987)
UNREST: "Teenage Suicide"
(*Kustom Karnal Blackxploitation* LP, Caroline, 1990)

After briefly contemplating the uninspired choices on our junior prom theme song ballot, my friend Ben and I proposed a write-in campaign for the Smiths' "Girlfriend in a Coma." No one heeded our endorsement. Instead, the Cure's moody pop song "Just Like Heaven" somehow defeated more obvious candidate, "(I've Had) The Time of My Life," Bill Medley and Jennifer Warnes's hit from that summer's *Dirty Dancing* soundtrack. Rumor was the field hockey team got out the vote for the Cure. But within days, the election had been vacated: someone's mom had objected to the winning theme song, the new rumor went, on the grounds that it was "about suicide."

Those of us who'd spent some solitary evenings with earlier Cure LPs *Faith* and *Pornography* found it a little tough to see much darkness in this varsity-approved, soft-goth iteration of the Cure.

By 1987, the band had mostly renounced doom and gloom, and only the bracing shimmer of the analog string synth in "Just Like Heaven" recalled those earlier records. The song's chiming, rose-water guitar riff, its tinkling piano solo, and its lyrics—"I promise that I'll run away with you," "why won't you ever know that I'm in love with you," and "you're just like a dream"—seemed aimed right at the hearts of fragile fourteen-year-olds. That said, we were mostly fragile sixteen- and seventeen-year-olds. Halfway through sophomore year, without explanation, one of my friends stopped showing up to school and quit talking to us, and after that we saw him only in his driveway, shooting baskets: when another friend visited him shortly after he'd begun his retreat, he didn't get out of bed, and my friend reported that "there were Legos on his floor."

Like every high school, mine had the kid who OD'ed, the girl who was molested on the school bus, the one who died in a drunk-driving crash, the date rapists, the bulimics, the institutionalized, the gay-bashers, the druggies, the depressives, the bullies, and the bullied, each person's story complicated and unknowable and unique even though outwardly it resembled some clichéd teen drama. One mom's crusade against a song she thought invoked suicide would not help us. Still, that mom's complaint trumped the collective will of Doherty Memorial High School's junior class, so we were left with the vapid promotion of teen sex ("With my body and soul / I want you more than you'll ever know // So we'll just let it go / Don't be afraid to lose control") and a song that might drive us to suicide, even if it didn't describe it.

▸

Ben and I had been born three years early for a perfect write-in candidate. Unrest elaborated the snippet of fictional song "Teenage Suicide (Don't Do It!)" from the movie *Heathers* ("They're playing our song," Christian Slater's character tells Winona Ryder's, before drawing a pistol and shooting the radio) into their own downer version with expanded lyrics: "Staring at a razor blade / from all of these things I was made..." In Unrest's ominous take, the overdriven guitar and punchy bass repeat a descending, dead-end riff. The thumping, compulsive beat isn't really danceable, just strangely stirring. The song's satire, like the film's, resists simple decoding, but the nihilistic, sing-along chorus feels empowering: "Teenage suicide / Don't do it // Teenage suicide / Yes, I can!"

The most terrible words of those years, spoken at us first by teachers and parents, but eventually, and most damningly, by our own peers and friends, were "Grow up." This imperative connoted not only the speaker's belief in the superiority of his or her status to ours, but also the socially approved necessity that we murder our most irresponsible selves if we too wanted to achieve this superior status. Worse, these words foretold our coming capitulations to routinized labor and lives we were already anesthetizing ourselves against at weekend keggers in the woods above Newton Square, at parties at someone's absent parents' house, and by shutting ourselves away in our rooms and turning up the music on our headphones. Rock music, until it starts earning a profit, is generally made by teenagers (or the recently teenaged) for teenagers, and its simple 4/4 rhythms almost always pound out a refusal of something, especially the refusal of maturity. My parents' generation, not mine, turned Jack Weinberg's warning "Don't trust anyone over thirty" into a catchphrase, but we agreed—especially when our over-thirty parents who'd once affirmed that slogan now expected our trust.

Whoever's busybody, censorious mom believed that changing our prom theme song—especially to one as vile and trite as "(I've Had) The Time of My Life"—would lead us to embrace life instead of death had herself grown up too much, had forgotten that to be a social being amid late capitalism is perpetually to annihilate one's inner self, the self that contemplates other, better options than those the market provides. I don't think many of my equally cynical peers saw prom night involving "dreams" or "souls"; mostly, it offered an excuse to dress up, get wasted, and have frantic sex in a hotel room, and to wake up feeling—and thus being—transformed.

After the prom I dropped off my date, changed out of my rented tux, and rode around with friends until dawn, eventually using the car to bash a mall parking lot's abandoned shopping carts over a guardrail and into a drainage ditch. My laughter as Seth nestled the front bumper square against the back of a cart, accelerated from zero to fifty miles an hour, and then stomped the brakes was, perhaps, the clearest indicator of my self-imposed exile from the grown-up, time-of-one's-life-having, suicide-denying world. Seth let me out in a light rain a few blocks from home—I wanted to walk—and on sidewalks I'd strolled most of my life, apple blossom petals, luminous in low light, were pressed to wet asphalt. No one else was out and not a single window glowed, but even with a pair of new suede creepers and the world to myself I could never imagine that a single spring night in my teenage years would be the best my life would offer me, would make my inevitable disappointments and travails all worth it in the end.

A CERTAIN RATIO: "All Night Party"
(b/w "Thin Boys" 7″, Factory Records, 1979)

A naked man nobody recognized danced on the beam stretching across the living room's cathedral ceiling. Despite the wall of windows thrown open, smoke choked the room. The Mad Hatter's Tea Party had been Jennifer's idea; we'd served gallons and gallons of Long Island iced tea. Homemade hats stitched from vintage gowns, draped with lace, veiled with tulle, and lofted with hidden wire now sagged, though my stereo still boomed Soul II Soul and Technotronic, and straight girls in black cocktail dresses, elbow-length gloves, and heavy makeup danced with bare-chested gay boys wearing eyeliner or swathed in feather boas. Beyond the parking lot, toward Highland Street, blue lights spun. Michael shimmied in from the hallway and said that the cops had set up a DUI checkpoint for departing partygoers at the end of our block. (That summer, he and Jennifer had wagered fifty dollars on whether or not I'd come out by the age of nineteen—sorry, Michael.) Tracey, who worked for a realtor and had found us this place, was hunting for Steven, and someone said he'd taken a gang of friends down to a vacant unit on the second floor to do lines. Weeks after the party, exploring other vacant units—only ours and one other on the fourth floor were rented, and the management company left all the rest unlocked—I found a sink brimming with moldy vomit in one of the first-floor apartments. It could have been disgorged by one of our friends from the suburbs; it could have been disgorged by a drunk who'd wandered in from Highland Street, since the building's back door didn't latch. I never returned to that unit.

In my bedroom, Richard—an older gentleman with an Afro and a thrift-store sport coat who was, except now, never not hanging out at Coffee Kingdom—had disassembled the metal shade of my floor lamp, then one of the few items of furniture I owned besides my futon and a butterfly chair, and in its stark incandescence was reading Amy's aura before a few stoned onlookers. Half-blinded, I saw only the tracers glowing cigarette tips etched in Jennifer's and Sarazar's darkened room. My ninth-grade sister, her hat tipped at a jaunty angle, leaned against the living room wall, absorbing these tableaux. Or was she talking to Phil, who'd famously traded his Chevette for two grams of coke the summer before I'd met him? After a while, Ben and I took her down to Theo's twenty-four hour diner and fed her French fries. When we got back, Michael, cigarette clamped in his lips, collected plastic cups and beer bottles while a few stragglers still whirled and bobbed on our filthied carpet.

Our apartment's spiral staircase, twenty-five foot skylit ceiling, neutral wall-to-wall, urban setting, and $1000-a-month rent must have been some developer's attempt to lure that era's famed young professionals, not four eighteen- and nineteen-year-olds who'd share bedrooms and co-sign the lease. Tracey had mentioned how fucking cool this place was during a New Year's Eve party at Tim's father's house, and a few of us, seized with the night's spirit (or with the night's spirits), had resolved to move in together and forsake our educations: Sarazar and I, seniors in high school, had no interest in going straight to college. Jennifer said she'd drop out of UMass. Tracey had already decided to skip school for the working life. A year earlier, we'd all partied in Seth's mom's condo, or Tia's parents' basement, or Jeff and Paige's apartment, where swollen, white-creased 1960s and '70s sci-fi and philosophy paperbacks lined the windowsills, and where we turned the electric oven to 450 degrees, opened its door, and sat in a circle on the scuffed linoleum after their heat got shut off. Now, a few months before I graduated high school, I moved into a brand-new, four-story brick building, six units per floor, surrounded by nineteenth-century three-deckers, halfway houses, and offices, and just off the slightly sorry commercial strip of Highland Street, where I worked managing a vintage clothing store.

For a few spring weeks I walked to school in the opposite direction from the house in which I'd grown up: except for our parties, I liked the idea of living in our apartment, and the fact that my classmates knew I lived there, better than the reality of living there, and anyway I still carried my laundry home, still ate dinner at my mom's house when I could. By graduation, I worked forty-hour weeks in a store that always smelled of mothballs, incense, and, when I'd steam some 1950s sequined sweater or Pendleton wool shirt to tag and put out on the floor, years-old sweat. One afternoon, a classmate browsing the racks told me that the Levi's 501 jeans we were selling to local college kids for $15 would fetch at least $50 on the street in Athens, and escape seemed suddenly possible.

Within a few months, all of us but Tracey had found subletters and left that apartment: Sarazar and I bought one-way tickets to Greece; Jennifer moved to her boyfriend's. I'd already abandoned my dying car in the parking lot, then returned months later with a former co-worker about to drive cross-country. I'd bumped into him one night at Coffee Kingdom, where he'd explained how his ex-girlfriend had turned out to be a witch trying to steal his soul; he was heading west to escape, too. He wanted a stereo for his car, so I told him to drive us to my old parking lot, where I let him pry the tapedeck out of my dead car's dashboard with a screwdriver. "Thanks, dude," he said. For some reason, I locked the car as we left, and looked up at the wall of lighted windows in my former apartment—my name was still on the lease. Some woman I'd never seen before gazed down at us.

Ben, Tim, and I had practiced a few times in that huge, acoustically lively living room, the year we were trying to sound like a graveyard funk band. Ben and I would cover A Certain Ratio's "Thin Boys" when Tim didn't show, since the song was just guitar, bass, and voice. Ben, a classically trained cellist, ran a beat-up Stratocaster through some inherited effects pedals. I, a mostly self-taught mediocre bassist, plucked my strings with a pick like

Peter Hook. Tim's dad bought him some drums that summer, but he struggled to keep time. We were listening to Public Image Limited's *Second Edition,* the Slits, A Certain Ratio, the Pop Group, Maximum Joy, Delta 5, and Rip Rig & Panic, but even these bands' sloppiest, most ramshackle records were beyond our capacities to emulate. Eventually we gave up trying. Ben and I wrote a fake folk song about a girl, a year behind us in school, who had a crush on both of us, and who used to come by the apartment to listen to us rehearse. Jennifer made us play it over and over, but only when the girl was sitting there.

I should have been composing different songs. A large number of the girls I found attractive in high school, I recently noted, inscribed my yearbook with some version of this sentence: "Yes, I'll come to the apartment tonight!" As best I can recall, none of them ever did. Had I been so obvious? Still, at least the girl busted for drunk driving before she was even old enough to get her license seemed impressed: "You and your parties! You guys are just crazy."

THE BEATLES: "While My Guitar Gently Weeps" (*The Beatles* LP, Apple, 1968)

One rainy Monday morning in the shiftless months after I'd graduated high school, I unlocked the steel-and-plate glass door to Shaky Jake's, the musty vintage clothing store where I worked. Before I hit the lights or reversed the OPEN/CLOSED sign in the window, I went up to the cramped office to switch on the stereo, and whatever station it'd last been tuned to began playing the familiar opening guitar strum and piano chords of the Beatles' "A Day in the Life." I'd heard the song numberless times, but now, alone in the store, surveying racks of polyester shirts and faded Levi's and tie-dyed Grateful Dead T-shirts and plaid sportcoats and floral-print broom skirts, and the wall of curling postcards friends and customers had sent the shop over the years, and the cars passing on Highland Street beyond rain-streaked windows—going somewhere, anywhere—I spent five minutes transfixed. Even though my days began with as much routine as the speaker in Paul McCartney's section of the song, I hadn't read the news that morning, or any recent morning. Daydreaming as remotely as John Lennon's echoing sighs suggest, I hadn't noticed that the lights had changed, that almost everyone from my high school class had left town while I still lived and worked half a mile away.

At the time, I didn't own a single Beatles LP, though my mother soon gave me a reissue of *Sgt. Pepper's Lonely Hearts Club Band* after I'd asked her some questions about the band when I couldn't get "A Day in the Life" out of my head. As is probably true for a lot of kids, especially white kids, born at the cusp of the 1970s, I've always had a burdensome relationship with the Fab Four. During childhood, I heard the Beatles' music everywhere: the radio, my mom's records, friends' parents' homes, friends' older siblings' bedrooms, even—"Here, There and Everywhere," or "In My Life"—on the easy-listening radio station that my grandmother played before Sunday dinner. Beatles songs suffuse my earliest memories so irrevocably that I never understood the band's musical or cultural significance, never grasped the strange mythologies and esoterica, never knew the music as much more than the background tracks to my own insipid days: the Beatles seemed just another part of the weather. I knew I'd missed a complicated history—if only from the way the Beatles' hairstyles changed on their LP covers and posters—but I also knew that that history belonged to other people. By the time I began establishing my own musical identity, I hated the whimsy, hated the sing-a-longs, hated the cartoonish psychedelia, hated that parents who only listened to classical music would make an exception for the Beatles. I resented the ongoing, ever-present Beatlemania—in part because the band's importance was undeniable, in part because the kids exalting the Beatles seemed so satisfied to celebrate a past they'd never experienced. The reverential Boomer nostalgia toward all things Beatles—the mock outrage when Nike used "Revolution" in an ad campaign, the hype when the White Album was released as a compact disc—haunted me. The Beatles also haunted many of the albums I bought, and this too aggravated me: why did so many bands feel a need to record a version of "Tomorrow Never Knows"? Why, if I had the good taste to like a band's music, did that band have the poor taste to admire the Beatles?

I wasn't one of the kids who choreographed dance routines to certain Beatles songs, who watched all the films, who memorized all the lyrics; I wasn't one of the teens who learned to pluck a passable version of "Blackbird" on an acoustic guitar with a chipped veneer to woo a sweetheart. I knew the most popular songs by ear but rarely by name. My mom had a few Beatles records—the only leftovers her younger brothers hadn't filched—filed in the living room cabinet with her old Motown and folk LPs: years earlier, she'd inked her maiden name onto the sleeves, another property line that excluded me. After her gift of *Sgt. Pepper's Lonely Hearts Club Band,* I listened to it a few times, then didn't bother picking up any more Beatles LPs for another decade. I did so finally out of a sense of obligation—didn't a decent record collection need at least a handful of Beatles records?—and also because I couldn't find much else worth buying at the one used record store near the small town in central Pennsylvania where I then lived.

One of my college girlfriends told me that her father, after he'd decided to leave her mother sometime in the mid-'70s, had driven an hour or two away from home when "Hey Jude"—a song that McCartney wrote for Julian Lennon as his parents were divorcing—came on the car radio. My girlfriend's father heard McCartney singing directly to him; he turned around and headed back to his family. I realized only recently that so many Beatles songs sound sad to me less because they accompany a depressing jumble of images from the first half of the 1970s—cold, sparsely furnished houses heated with woodstoves; macramé owls hanging on painted plaster walls; boxes of herbal teas; toothpicked avocado pits in glasses of water and enormous spider plants; mass-market paperbacks of *The Lord of the Rings, Future Shock,* and *Passages;* being sent outside to play with some kid and his broken Big Wheel while inside our parents possibly got stoned; small plastic garbage bags hanging from the knobs of AM-only car radios; straw-wrapped Chianti bottles plugged with half-melted candles; our young mothers drinking instant coffee from butterfly gold Corelle cups while we ran in and out of the kitchen seeking their attention—than because our parents, still listening to the Beatles in the aftermath of political assassinations and anti-war protests and race riots, in the depths of the Nixon era and the oil crisis and inflation, must have heard those songs through the prism of failure, and probably felt sad themselves, remembering when their relationships with each other were uncomplicated by kids, mortgages, careers. The Beatles' sudden and prolonged break-up—with its various walkouts and brief reconciliations and press releases and ultimate years-long legal battle—prefigured the divorces my parents and so many of my friends' parents would soon experience: even "Hey

Jude" only delayed the inevitable for my girlfriend's family. It's one thing to listen to songs of hope and love when change seems possible, and another thing entirely when change as social and personal utopia has been diminished to a barely winterized rental cottage on a lake, court-ordered monthly child support payments, and shared visitation rights.

So when a friend noted in her Facebook status that she was playing the Beatles' "Red" and "Blue" compilation double LPs for her young kids, "marveling" and "explaining," I felt a sudden desire to hear my own long-ignored Beatles records. I began digitizing the LPs as I went through them, late at night, listening on headphones.

▸

"Turn it up, dude," Sarah says, reaching for the volume knob before I can lift my hand from the steering wheel. We're headed north on the Taconic State Parkway, the iPod plugged into the Volkswagen's stereo, and she's asked me to play the Beatles' "While My Guitar Gently Weeps."

"You should write an essay about the Beatles," she continues.

"Really?"

"I heard this on my walk to work the other day."

She skips the track back to its beginning: the huge stereo separation makes the tinkly piano rise from somewhere to the left of the brake pedal, while the descending bass notes seem to float in from the window beside her.

"I mean, it's called 'While My Guitar Gently Weeps,' but this song is all about the bass," she says. "*Listen* to it." She turns the volume up a little more. "I think that bass inspired Led Zeppelin. Has anyone ever talked about that? When did the first Led Zeppelin record come out?"

"After this one," I say. "A year later, maybe."

"The bass is really crunchy and pounding and slow—not *weeping* exactly, but more like a dirge, like a weight being dragged along. And that wanky guitar—it's so Led Zeppelin," she says. "I can just picture Robert Plant and Jimmy Page listening to this and stealing the whole thing. And George Harrison even moans at the end of this, like Robert Plant."

"Well, not exactly like Robert Plant," I say. "Anyway, I think it's actually Eric Clapton playing the wanky guitar here."

"Did you ever read that Bugliosi book about the Tate-LaBianca murders?" Sarah asks. "I always associate this song with that for some reason. I read it when I was a girl, and it stayed with me way too long—especially the grainy picture of a dead Sharon Tate at the crime scene."

"This song's from the same album as 'Helter Skelter,'" I say.

"It just all seems so much about the end of the sixties, when love was supposed to be 'unfolded,' and abounding, but this love is still sleeping, and if so, what the hell have we been doing all these years? It's like he wakes up from some drugged-out haze and notices that the floor needs sweeping, everything's been bought and sold—"

"—and it was supposed to be free love," I say.

"Right! And he's bewildered at how the movement of love's all ended. He just realized the world's still turning. It seems so ironic when he says, 'Every mistake we must surely be learning,' since they're all stoned and barely noticing anything at all. Wasn't this song from the Summer of Love? When love was supposed to be changing the world, not sleeping? He sounds so disgusted when he says, 'Look at you all.' And all that energy's been diverted, perverted...."

"This record came out the year after the Summer of Love," I say. "But you should read Joan Didion's essay 'The White Album' if you never have."

"I don't think so," Sarah says.

"It's about the end of the sixties: Manson, the Black Panthers, campus protests, all that."

Clapton's solo, Harrison's falsetto, McCartney's grinding bass notes, Lennon's ringing acoustic chords, Ringo Starr's tambourine rattle lead us through the song's lengthy fadeout. I've always considered this song one of the Beatles' lesser moments, the lyrics contorted from the exigencies of finding rhyming words rather than anything as considered as Sarah's interpretation, and prefer *All Things Must Pass* as evidence of Harrison's songwriting skill to the few songs Lennon and McCartney allowed on Beatles records. "Now the two most interesting Beatles are gone," my mother lamented in 2001, when Harrison died. But the world always persists no matter the forms—weeping guitar, political protest, drugged stupor, rainy-morning epiphany, annotated pop song—in which we register our sadness or resistance to its outcomes. Didion's essay is less about the end of the sixties than about our desire for the imaginary security and orderliness of a narrative when our lives seem insecure and disordered—and the precariousness that

Didion noted as symptomatic of those years has not left us. "In what would probably be the middle of my life I wanted still to believe in the narrative and the narrative's intelligibility," Didion writes. When did I realize that I wanted to believe that those apparently endless childhood days scored by the soundtrack of the Beatles would not end? That a song I heard by chance on the radio might help me resolve some difficult decision—or explain myself to me? Maybe the Beatles endure because they've inspired untold conversations like this one. They grew up alongside their audience, and their music and fashions and public proclamations both responded to and affected the cultural tumult of the sixties—and for that reason seemed worth interpreting. Amid endless versions of who buried Paul and who was the walrus and who was counted in or out of the revolution, a listening audience learned to personalize the Beatles—about whom they spoke on a first-name basis—by composing narratives around the frameworks of their LPs, and learned to see all future pop music through similarly individual lenses.

In what will hopefully be the middles of our lives, Sarah and I keep driving, and the iPod plays the first notes of "Happiness Is a Warm Gun," a song I probably first heard when the Breeders covered it on their *Pod* LP in 1990. "She's not a girl who misses much," John Lennon sings.

"Don't you think it would make a good essay?" Sarah asks.

"Maybe you should write it," I say.

BOHANNON: "Gittin' Off"
(*Gittin' Off* LP, Dakar, 1975)
TALKING HEADS: "Stay Hungry"
(*More Songs about Buildings and Food* LP, Sire, 1978)

"I'm going to predict," Hua said, as we strolled down College Avenue, squinting against the warm April sunset, "that dinner will involve a stew. Or some kind of bean. Maybe lentils." He'd loosened the knot of his tie; I carried a bottle of wine in the crook of my arm. Across the street, our colleagues' pollen-dusted, Obama-stickered Saabs and Subarus filled driveways, an art historian weeded a bed of tulips, and a Victorianist's grubby kids colored sidewalk squares with pastel chalk. On this side, vintage ten-speeds were chained to rotting porches, and beer bottles cluttered the patchy lawns of dank rental houses. A bearded kid pedaled past us on a creaking bike—one hand gripping the handlebars, the other a paper cup of coffee.

Two graduating seniors—our former students—had invited us to dinner. They'd booked Dirty Projectors, Cause Co-Motion,

Mika Miko, High Places, and a bunch of other then-up-and-coming bands for packed shows in their off-campus living room as well as for the basement bar in the student center. Their snappy e-mail messages included reports such as this one: "I'm obligated to tell you that you missed an awesome outdoor show last night. Lau Nau and Teeth Mountain were transcendent...under a full moon atop Sunset Lake." Or this: "I'm going to New York this weekend...to see these excellent SF groovers named Tussle. Two drummers, keys, and bass—really on a shaggy Kraut tip." Their stances and pronouncements seemed simultaneously sarcastic and earnest, and often, ultimately, indecipherable—which was probably the intent.

They served us a chickpea curry, so Hua was right on both counts; they offered us some of their own homemade pickles from a jar they fetched from their basement. A moth fell from the ceiling onto Hua's plate; he plucked it out and kept eating. These two students reminded Hua and me of ourselves at their age—brimming with wacky ideas, way too invested in obscure music. When we imagined them outside of class, they read either architecture theory books or grimy copies of *Please Kill Me* while listening to Gang Gang Dance LPs. Still, despite their reputations as hipsters' hipsters on campus, they professed to hate indie bands and the indie scene, though they played in a two-drummers-with-tape-loops "project." As we ate our curry, one of them admitted his current musical affections: late-period Fleetwood Mac, and the Police. "I'm really into '80s production values right now," he told us.

When the floating signifier "indie"—an invented-as-it-happened DIY model that once indicated an oppositional stance to "corporate rock"—appears as a genre option in iTunes, and when most of Apple's millions of customers understand that term as it pertains to sound and style rather than economics, it's impossible to blame students for seeking cool elsewhere. Cool often involves obscurity, impenetrability—the initiate's secret dialect and knowledge, both safe from popular appeal because of the time and effort put into acquiring them; the records pressed only in minuscule quantities for those in the know. But once everything was born again online, few corners of pop culture remained obscure, and cool became merely a matter of knowing which search terms to input. Irony's always sufficed as a safe refuge when you feel your subculture's overrun, but when irony-as-subculture itself becomes overrun, I guess you head for "Gypsy" and "Little Lies" and "Synchronicity II." Since the mid-1990s, if not earlier, indie music has been mainstreamed and commodified in all the usual ways—to sell us itself as product as well as whatever junk it accompanies—but also in its transformation from music you once would've played to piss off your mom to innocuous background noise your mom hears at Starbucks or Gap and decides she likes, even though she thinks it's a little quirky. The music of indie bands like Scratch Acid cannot help sell lattés, but the music of indie bands like Vampire Weekend can.

Somehow our dinner conversation about the Police and '80s studio techniques turned into a pop quiz, and though I once enjoyed those first two Police records just fine and, like everyone in the '80s, was traumatized by "Every Breath You Take," I somehow failed to correctly answer my student's questions: I transposed the two LPs "Driven to Tears" and "Every Little Thing She Does Is

Magic" came from, or something crucial like that. The next part of the interrogation—Hua had rolled up his shirtsleeves and stolen a cigarette from the pack on the table, and grinned at me through a haze of smoke—concerned my favorite Talking Heads record.

"Probably *More Songs about Buildings and Food,*" I answered.

"Josh! That's so rockist. What about *Remain in Light?*"

"It's a really great record," I said.

"You're too into guitars. It's all about the groove," my student said, and now I had no idea how many layers his sarcasm had.

I'd once given this student a CD-R featuring bands such as Bubblegum Splash!, the Shop Assistants, Brilliant Corners, and the Pooh Sticks after he said, "I hate that *C86* shit," and, ever since, music had been our proving ground. Now he defended noise-gated drums and glossy synth overdubs as a protest against the indie trope of intentionally scuzzy recordings. The questions ended when Hua and I couldn't identify the producers of certain '80s LPs he deemed exceptional. We'd enjoyed the meal and the company, but, as we stepped into the suddenly chilly night, Hua turned to me and sighed, "Man. I didn't learn everything I needed to be cool from Wikipedia."

"It felt like they prepped for us with flash cards," I admitted.

Cool, of course, requires apparent effortlessness, the disguising of one's sources and influences, and as much as we like to pretend it's innate, no one's been cool in a vacuum: as a performed critique of social norms, cool demands an audience. I left Hua at his place, then kept walking home, thinking of David Byrne's murmured lyrics in "Houses in Motion," from *Remain in Light,* about the effort and study and ambition involved in becoming cool: "For a long time I felt / without style and grace / Wearing shoes with no socks / in cold weather / I knew my heart / was in the right place / I knew I'd be able / to do these things..." No, Hua and I didn't learn cool from YouTube and MP3 blogs—though, had those options existed back in the day, I'm sure we would have relied on them—but we still learned cool.

My student thought *More Songs about Buildings and Food* was a rock record, but the second half of "Stay Hungry" offers an epic disco shuffle that, had the band sustained it for another five minutes, would've choked dancefloors as easily as that year's other CBGBs-gone-disco hybrid, "Heart of Glass." Does anything on the busier, syncopated *Remain in Light* "groove" this much? Not to my ears. "I'm Not in Love" has its own stomper moments, though it's wound too tightly to say it grooves. "Warning Sign" borrows its rhythms and its tape effects from reggae and dub. And the album's best-known song, "Take Me to the River," is an Al Green cover. The bass-, keyboard-, and drum-driven funk so overwhelms the twitchy guitar on these tracks that I wondered whether my student even knew the record, or if he was making his argument based on something he'd gleaned online.

▶

Before Chris Frantz and Tina Weymouth messed around with congas in Nassau, before Brian Eno and David Byrne got lost *in the Bush of Ghosts,* before Talking Heads decided to cut a record inspired by Fela Kuti's *Afrodisiac,* before Jerry Harrison hired Bernie Worrell, Nona Hendryx, and Busta Jones to lend some plausibility to the band's new direction, before David Byrne tried his hand at rapping, someone in the band clearly fell hard for Hamilton Bohannon's records.

Bohannon played drums with a pre-superstar Jimi Hendrix, joined the young Stevie Wonder's band, arranged a number of Motown's hits, then started his own group in early-'70s Detroit and released six disco-struck funk LPs for Dakar between 1973 and 1976 before signing with Mercury and turning exclusively to disco. "No one has taken 'groove' as literally as Bohannon," according to Peter Shapiro's *Turn the Beat Around: The Secret History of Disco,* which names him "Motown's greatest rhythm mechanic." When my friends Jed and Claire first played Bohannon for me, I was gobsmacked by how precisely his records sounded like Talking Heads, despite appearing earlier—the intro to 1976's "Dance Your Ass Off" and the intro to 1975's "Feel Good at Midnight," with their repeating guitar riffs and jerky rhythms, might as well have come from *Fear of Music* or *More Songs about Buildings and Food.* Tina Weymouth and Chris Frantz later encoded this debt in their band Tom Tom Club's elaborately allusive "Genius of Love"—itself now an endlessly sampled cultural touchstone—but Bohannon remains an overlooked figure. The best songs on his mid-'70s LPs—such as the massive "Gittin' Off"—all have the same nervous urgency of the early Talking Heads, the same heavy pulse, the same popping basslines, the same scratchy, bent-string guitar licks: the main distinctions are the disco violins in some of Bohannon's songs, and the timbre of his voice compared to Byrne's—though Bohannon's voice anticipates Byrne's earnestness, if not his lyrical obscurity.

It's impossible to listen to these records and not hear the ways Talking Heads lifted bits of them.

Such pilfering forms the foundation of rock music: white musicians repurposing African-American blues for white audiences is foremost among the genre's complex origins. Talking Heads' appropriations of Bohannon during the late '70s didn't sanitize the music so much as defamiliarize it by displacing it into the context of deliberately uptight, ironic, "witty," white art school grads. And, with cool, context is key. Bohannon's music connotes something entirely different when he sings, "Make a lotta noise, make a whole lotta noise!" or "I'm tryin' to get to the floor / I gotta let myself go" than when, accompanying much the same sounds, David Byrne sputters, "Look over there! ...A dry ice factory / A good place to get some thinking done."

The postures of cool always involve some violence—at least, when those postures strip a cultural artifact of the cultural influences that produced it, when they modify that artifact to suit other aspirations (as, e.g., Bruce Springsteen learned when President Reagan tried to benefit from "Born in the USA" during his 1984 re-election campaign). Talking Heads made some great records by marrying a faux-naïve worldview to faux-naïve funk; still, I see their five-or-so-year trajectory from the studied eccentricities of their *Talking Heads: 77* LP to the studied new wave Afro-funk of 1980's *Remain in Light* as Borgesian. In Jorge Luis Borges's best-known piece, "Borges and I," the first-person narrator (in the James E. Irby translation) expresses the terrors of both fame's public persona and the known, bounded set of tastes we often construe as "identity," and his attempts to escape them: as those tastes are usurped by (and attributed to) "the one called Borges," the narrator must "imagine other things," until eventually his "life is a flight and [he] lose[s] everything and everything belongs to oblivion."

Our varied senses of cool engineer the willed construction of our public personae, personae in flight from what we see as mass tastes—because pop music belongs to everyone, and to oblivion, but we want to see ourselves as unique individuals. Cool can't suffer much competition in the form of widespread admiration—which leads the narrator of "Borges and I" to abandon such reasonable pleasures as "the taste of coffee and the prose of Stevenson" because Borges shares them "in a vain way that turns them into the attributes of an actor" (what a poseur!), and which leads my former students to pretend—or, who knows, to believe—that they like schlocky easy-listening pop. Cool derives from an emotional detachment, and we often need such a defense mechanism when even the farthest reaches of the pop-cultural multiverse have been colonized, when our tastes are data-mined and marketed back to us by corporations, and when asserting our individuality requires imaginative gyrations. Like cool, pop music cannot exist in a vacuum; endlessly referential, from the level of the riff to the level of the rip-off, pop depends on our familiarities with its basic forms, and our willingness to see the slightest distinctions as meaningful. That said, there *is* a meaningful distinction in the slight differences between Bohannon's groove ("The Groove I Feel," side one, *Dance Your Ass Off* LP) and Talking Heads' groove ("This ain't no party, this ain't no disco, this ain't no foolin' around"): I'd call it self-consciousness.

BAUHAUS: "All We Ever Wanted"
(*The Sky's Gone Out* LP, Beggars Banquet, 1982)

Bauhaus: a terrible band, but when I was fifteen they sounded dark, dangerous, deep. Daniel Ash's razoring guitars on *The Sky's Gone Out* dismantled me when a friend dubbed suicide anthem "In the Night" on a mixtape. I've long since sold most of my Bauhaus records—hopefully to misunderstood teens—but still own this LP. The only song I can now bear is the record's quietest: its lyrics, and its unassuming, inoffensive acoustic guitar and plucked bass—unlike the rest of the record, this song almost wants to be overlooked—typify the postindustrial "factorytown" where I was raised. "All we ever wanted was everything": sure, but we knew that asking rarely led to getting. We didn't ask because we were unwilling, or because we believed our requests excessive, or because we understood already that the favor wouldn't be granted, but because the only way to success, we'd been told, was work. Our working-class aspirations conflicted with vague, mostly unspoken desires to "shoot out of darkness": we were socialized to define ourselves according to occupation rather than what legitimately occupied us. I escaped in the pages of an outdated yard-sale *Encyclopedia Britannica World Atlas,* the leatherette spine of which finally disintegrated, and sustained myself with a secondhand stereo those years I hoped to elude the notice of others, while also secretly craving their acclaim more than I dared—and dare—admit: "Oh, to be the cream. . . ," Peter Murphy croons, and the song winds down to a sigh.

THE MINDERS: "Hand-Me-Downs"
("Black Balloon" 7″, Little Army / Elephant 6 Recording Co., 1998)

> The supply-side theory was not a new economic theory at all but only new language and argument to conceal a hoary old Republican doctrine: give the tax cuts to the top brackets, the wealthiest individuals and largest enterprises, and let the good effects "trickle down" through the economy to reach everyone else.
>
> —William Greider, "The Education of David Stockman," *The Atlantic Monthly*, December 1981

Reagan presided over the recovery, but Reaganomics as such did not work.... A restrictive monetary policy exacerbated the downturn in 1981, plunging the US economy into its worst recession since the 1930s.

Inflation was lowered, but only at the cost of very high unemployment, thousands of business failures, a decline in the wages of skilled labor, and a redistribution of income from the lower middle class to the upper middle class and the rich. Military spending was increased at the expense of education, welfare assistance, environmental protection, community development, and improved retirement payments.... The Reagan recovery of 1983 thus has little to do with the supply-side theories of 1981.

—Martin Carnoy and Manuel Castells, "After the Crisis?" *World Policy Journal* Vol. 1, No. 3 (1984)

In the spring of 1981, shortly before the onset of the painful recession, most Americans were optimistic about their economic future. A Gallup survey at the time found that 48% of the public believed the financial position of their household would be better in the next 12 months.... A year later, in September 1982, with the unemployment rate at 10.1%, most Americans were far from pleased with the state of the economy. A 54%-majority said Reagan's policies had made their personal financial situation worse; just 34% said the policies had made their situation better.

—Richard Auxier, "Reagan's Recession," Pew Research Center, December 14, 2010

▸

Just after John Hinckley, Jr., aimed his .22 caliber pistol at Ronald Reagan outside the Washington D.C. Hilton and fired six "Devastator" explosive bullets—one of which ricocheted off the president's limousine and hit Reagan under the arm—I'd come home from school and was shooting baskets in the rain with my father. He'd recently installed a hoop and backboard to a wood frame he'd fashioned and bolted to the rotting roof of our garage, not far from the hole raccoons would soon chew through mossy composition shingles to raid the garbage festering inside. I was supposed to drag the trash cans curbside every Thursday morning, but often forgot, and let trash pile up in the garage instead, since it was also my task to collect it from the kitchen and the rest of the house and carry it out to the garage. The hoop didn't stand a regulation ten feet, though that fact didn't matter to me then, only to my more serious basketball-playing friends who came over in later years, and whose blocked shots and errant passes broke the windowpanes in the garage door—all of which my father eventually replaced, one by one, with squares of plywood.

Like that solution, our game was hardly elegant, nothing any purist would've admired: all flagrant fouls, hip checks, goaltending, and traveling, instead of head fakes and crossover dribbles, it had little in common with the sport I sometimes watched on TV. Rain-soaked and giddy, my father and I elbowed each other, pulled sleeves, trash-talked, laughed at missed jumpers. As I dribbled the basketball along our frost-heaved driveway and tried to get off a shot against my six-foot two-inch father, I wore a navy blue hooded pullover sweatshirt, on the chest of which, in white block capitals, was printed the word ANDOVER.

I attended not Phillips Academy Andover but May Street School, a small brick public elementary school with an asphalt playground encircled by a chain-link fence. No one in my family had graduated from Phillips Andover. My mother, first in her family to earn a college degree, had matriculated at a good private university—where, years later, I taught undergraduates to write novels—until her father could no longer afford the tuition, and she'd finished her education at a state college. My father had enlisted in the Navy after high school, and then went to M.I.T., though he'd dropped out; on that rainy day in 1981, a few years remained before he'd complete his B.S. and M.B.A. degrees. The sweatshirt I wore had, until my father brought it home, gone unclaimed in a lost and found bin at the candlepin bowling alley my grandfather owned, where my father sometimes worked between other jobs, or when he'd been laid off. The bowling alley stood in a nineteenth-century brick industrial complex across the train tracks at the edge of town, and I wonder now whether whoever abandoned the sweatshirt there was even the garment's original owner. After I acquired it, someone explained Phillips Andover to me, though I had no understanding then of what the term prep school connoted, and even my active imagination could conjure only the barest version. I wore the sweatshirt the way I still wear most clothes—constantly—until I outgrew it, or lost it, or it fell apart in the wash. I liked that the single word it bore also held two words—and, over—but to me, Andover was just another place I'd never been, though it seemed only a quick drive up the highway when I scrutinized maps as a way of wishing myself elsewhere. The sweatshirt felt comfortable in a house where my parents didn't need a recently exiled president to tell them to turn down the thermostat and put on a sweater.

My mother opened the back door on its squeaky spring. "The president's been shot," she called out to us.

▶

The B-side to one of several 7″ singles the Minders released in quick succession during the late '90s, "Hand-Me-Downs" is a pop song that's anything but popular. It begins with a twangy four-note guitar riff, then jerks into the slapdash, fuzzy chords of some lost, post–British Invasion garage band. The song's breathy boy/girl harmonies, jaunty bassline, prominent tambourine, peppy drum fills, and backwards guitar solo—despite their apparent sloppiness—have a purity and inevitability. All the song's elements are handed down—its McCartney-esque sensibility, its unschooled Mamas and the Papas vocals, its crunchy *Nuggets* chords, its George Martin four-track experimentation, its AM-radio-friendly two-and-a-half-minute length: "I can't tell, they all seem so familiar," singer and guitarist Martyn Leaper admits in the first verse. If his voice sounded a little closer to Ray Davies', and if the late-'60s Kinks had had a female backup singer.... Still, the song is original in its filtered particulars, furious in its energies. You've probably never heard it, but you'll recognize it when you do.

Lyrically, it's ambiguous what is being handed down: "No, I won't talk about it, and I won't weep / Yes, I know all about it, everything indeed," Leaper and Rebecca Cole sing in the bridge; in the chorus, they say either "I was never clean" or "I was never free," before continuing: "flat broke at age nineteen—just behind, or so it seemed."

I've always understood the song—one of only a few written by bassist Marc Willhite—as describing the speaker's shame and sorrow about financial uncertainties he refuses to detail beyond a single, un-anteceded pronoun. That I read class into these vague lyrics says more about me than about the song. (And perhaps spending $800 on records in a month, as I've written about elsewhere, suggests no more than a vain attempt to catch up in my acquisition of cultural knowledge.) I wore many hand-me-down or otherwise inherited clothes as a kid, in part because of how quickly I outgrew them, in part because of family finances. Our cars were hand-me-downs, much of our furniture, most of my books. These facts were unexceptional: many of my friends wore hand-me-downs, too. We all benefitted from the barter economy our mothers had developed—exchanging tokens for hours watching each other's kids in the "babysitting co-op"; holiday cookie swaps; school carpools; rummage sales. Still, such mutual support couldn't mask the direction explicit in the phrase "hand-me-downs," which has always seemed imperative to how the locution reinforces class distinctions and underscores that we receive charity from some unknown benefactor above our own station—though in my case I often did know the slightly older kids whose pants I now wore. My pre-worn, faded, secondhand Levi's signified something different than they did when, years later, I sold similar jeans at a premium to the college students slumming, as part of their Saturday afternoon field trips into my hometown, at the vintage clothing store I managed.

▸

In my Massachusetts hometown: several liberal arts institutions, a technical university, a state college, a medical university, and various smaller and two-year colleges. A billboard on the interstate spur through our city once offered an insecure boast about the number of schools, as if drivers passing along that highway—which snakes through the city's less glorious, less picturesque neighborhoods—might fail to appreciate some obvious equivalency between education and civic stature. (Municipal boosters also promoted our city, without detectable irony, as "The Paris of the Eighties" on T-shirts in that decade.) Most of the colleges stand among blocks of three-deckers where laborers at the city's once-abundant factories lived in the nineteenth and early twentieth centuries; several of the colleges were founded by prominent local industrialists.

Despite a lifetime in—or at the fringes of—academia, I've always felt more town than gown. Even when, as a kid, I was made to understand that the colleges had been founded for my ostensible benefit, I couldn't conceive how to access those benefits except through the most basic means of territory-staking. My friends and I played football on the schools' vivid green fields, and then, when we splashed in a fountain to cool down, got kicked off campus by security guards who jotted down the fake names and addresses we provided them. I hopped a fence with a track teammate to run intervals on one institution's expensive, rubberized, four-hundred-meter oval instead of training on the knee-wrecking asphalt loop where we raced. Later, I watched bands play at university bars, attended art films at the college cinema, infiltrated student parties: a sad, familiar tale of awkward attempts at social climbing.

My hometown itself seemed a hand-me-down, mentioned, if ever, as a second sister to Boston. We all suffered from an abiding inferiority complex. Industry built our city, and in the decades since those industries' failures, departures, or buyouts, the city has displayed the anxiety and bitterness of the laid-off worker. We mythologize the "heroism" and "dignity" of hard work, and, despite years of evidence to the contrary, we still expect hard work to be rewarded. Our most popular forms of music have always been those that feature macho posturing (heavy metal, hip-hop) or that variety of mainstream rock that—lyrically, at least—asserts that luck or fate determines one's place in the world, and that hard work and perseverance (or a magical roll of the dice: losing scratch tickets litter our parking lots) present the means of escape. Bruce Springsteen, Bob Seger, and those who "told it like it is" were revered during my youth, and to reject this music in favor of something other was to reject such values as well as the local culture that sustained them.

The city keeps getting passed down to new owners—commuters to Boston or Boston's metro suburbs, these days—who try it on, realize it doesn't really fit or look particularly good, but who have no better options. All of us who grew up there understand the feelings of being discarded, of being reluctantly inherited.

▶

Hinckley's bullet, flattened after its impact with the limousine, had torn through Reagan's lung, surgeons at George Washington University Hospital discovered, and stopped an inch from the president's heart and aorta. Reagan lost half the blood in his body from the wound, but insisted on signing a bill (amending the Agricultural Act to prevent an increase in dairy price supports) during a breakfast meeting with his staff the next morning. "Despite some postoperative pain," the *New York Times* claimed, the president "was recuperating with remarkable speed."

"'I always heal fast,' Mr. Reagan told a nurse," the *Times* also reported.

▶

Pop music, divorced from the literal derivation of its name now that most media appeal to various niche demographics and very little achieves popularity on a mass scale, becomes ineffable. Though I'd prefer a more expansive, less prescriptive definition of the term, John Darnielle offers—in his 'zine *Last Plane to Jakarta*—the best explanation I've read:

> Real pop music should make you sick. It should make you regret that someone didn't kill you dead the moment you first experienced real yearning. It should make you willing to sell everything you own for one last taste of your youth. Its lyrics should overcome their own clunkiness by sheer force of weight; they should avoid any semblance of contemplation or studious-

> ness, and must rely heavily on the first-person present tense. The regret that its melodies instill in you should be so acutely painful as to make you want to double over, if you weren't too busy whistling along. It should come gunning directly for your heart where it's most vulnerable...

Darnielle defines pop as non-reflective, but I'd argue that the most affecting—the most yearning—pop songs, like "Hand-Me-Downs," involve some degree of nostalgia or backwards-glancing, and overlay the present with the past. Since pop music almost always arrives as a hand-me-down—we learn about songs or bands via friends' recommendations, radio, word-of-mouth, MP3 blogs, podcasts—it inevitably seems conjoined with a specific historical context: the moment a song somehow became intertwined with our life. We rarely encounter music—do we ever?—without some mediation, some intervention: it is never ours alone, as much as we want it to be; we do not own it, no matter how much a song may "mean" to us, and those facts have, for me, always made the yearning more intense.

▶

Ten years old, I didn't care about Reagan's physical recovery. (Several days after surgery, the president contracted a staph infection and suffered from a very high fever, though these facts were not reported at the time.) If I felt vulnerable, my concerns derived not from handguns but from trickle-down economics. My father was home the Monday afternoon Reagan was shot because he was unemployed or working nights: one of a series of moments we found him unexpectedly watching television when we returned from school, or absent when we sat down for supper: pancakes, maybe, since my sisters and I loved breakfast-for-dinner, though some part of us surely understood why our mother served them. My mother was home because, although she held various jobs and volunteer positions during my childhood, she too may have been unemployed—or because it was the year she slipped on some snow-covered steps, fell and hurt her back, and had to spend months in bed. I don't always remember verifiable facts from those years, both because my parents withheld information from my sisters and me—out of shame, financial anxiety, our ages, or whatever other reason—and because, in the absence of that information, I occupied a world in which cause and effect operated differently than they appeared to do for other people, even my friends.

That same spring, a friend invited me to his birthday party; we'd all go home from school with him, play games, and eat pizza and cake. Because our car was in the shop the week before the party, or because my parents had no extra money that week, or both, my mother couldn't take me to the toy store to pick out a birthday present. "Just be honest with him—tell him the car was getting fixed," my mother said the morning of the party, but I walked to school empty-handed and wishing I could stay home sick. At lunch, as we all sat a long folding table, I confessed to my friend that I'd have to bring him his present later in the week. "Car trouble," I explained. He didn't seem to care much. Another friend at the table admitted that his present would also be late. "Car trouble," he repeated, and I felt an irrational hope that I could share my shame.

We walked down Reed Street with our friend after school—and, just before we arrived at his house, the mother of the kid who'd also claimed car trouble drove up to meet us. "Here," she said, tossing what was clearly a gift-wrapped Nerf football out the window to her son, who caught it and handed it to the birthday boy. Then she drove off—the car was new; my friend's father owned a successful pizza shop; I should have known he'd borrowed my excuse so that the obviousness of his gift could remain a surprise for a few more hours during the school day. Though I know my mother did take me to buy a present for my friend a day or two after the party, I can't remember the gift: my entire memory of the party has been reduced to the vision of that five-dollar foam ball covered in wrapping paper—such a paltry thing, offered so easily.

▶

> Hinckley stated that he is currently unemployed...
>
> —Federal Bureau of Investigation transcript, April 1, 1981, Exhibit CR81–306, File No. WFO 175–311

▶

Even the phrase "hand-me-downs" is handed-down, a worn-out bequest from an era in which euphemisms protected one's pride.

"Vintage," as in the clothing store I worked at, connotes the benefits of careful aging, though garments are in no way like wine or whisky. "Gently worn," similar stores identified their wares a few years later, though the collar stains and missing buttons suggested otherwise: and if one can easily replace a garment, why wear it gently?

As soon as the current recessive era began undoing families' savings, house values, careers, and plans, the *New York Times,* reporting "the efforts of fashion and beauty publicists to spin the economic downturn as an attractive retail trend,""welcome[d] [us] to 'recession chic' and its personification, the 'recessionista,' the new name for the style maven on a budget." Further *Times* accounts noted the ways advertising acknowledged our diminished resources via a "sense that expensive purchases—even if consumers can afford them—have become gauche.""Watching a $13 DVD on the living room sofa is celebrated as 'the new movie night.' A $59.99 bicycle is presented as 'the new commute.' There are similar salutes to people who eat in rather than dine out, cut their children's hair and turn a backyard tent into 'the new family room.'"

But thriftiness is rarely a marker of cool when it doesn't involve choice, and the "trend toward frugality" or "austerity chic" the *Times* cited still ran in slender column inches surrounded by much larger advertisements for Cartier watches, AIG investments, Chanel handbags, Bloomingdales and Saks Fifth Avenue furs, and Balvenie twelve-year-old scotch. Most of these articles seemed less concerned about making do than about making sure that one's friends or co-workers didn't see one as insensitive to others' financial worries.

Most personal pop culture narratives—such as this one—elide the privilege encoded in loving descriptions of media-based memories: if I felt childhood shame from being unable to buy a friend a gift, then I grew up with far more than most. Of course the writer had the luxuries of money and time to acquire, accumulate, and ponder some consumer product: in my case, an LP not only costs me money, but demands some forty minutes of my life to listen to both sides. Americans almost always feel comfortable discussing the money we have spent or will spend—especially when we can discuss prices in terms of the good deals we've bargained for or lucked into. The hand-me-down garment ought to establish one's shrewd business savvy—the item of some value obtained for free—but whether because fashions in clothing change seasonally, and thus to attire oneself in the "wrong" sort of outfit marks one as outdated, or because of the physical intimacy between our bodies and our clothes, no one wants to shop at Goodwill except those who have to and college students seeking something cool amid the discards.

▸

I distrust my memory enough that I checked historical weather data to ensure that rain did indeed fall on my old ZIP code the day of Reagan's shooting—not out of some supposed essayistic obligation to objective truth, but simply to convince myself that my memories are accurate and real. "I" is always provisional and unstable, always invented as we go, always constructed from known and unknown influences, from our fantasies of whom we might be or become—as in the case of Hinckley, who, an hour before he left for the Washington Hilton, wrote to Jodie Foster: "At least you know that I'll always love you. Jodie, I would abandon the idea of getting Reagan in a second if I could only win your heart and live out the rest of my life with you, whether it be in total obscurity or whatever." Or, as in the case of the Minders, who with "Hand-Me-Downs" took something discarded—something apparently no longer usable or fashionable: guitar-based '60s pop, at a moment when many serious musicians and music fans were listening to the programmed wheezing and stuttering of machines—and transformed it. By recycling the primal riffs white British musicians recorded while trying to copy black American R&B musicians, and dousing it all in a literate, melancholic joy, they gave back to us something we'd almost forgotten.

The ways we clothe ourselves in what's handed down to us reveal much about our fantasy selves, whether we wish to be prince or pauper. My ANDOVER sweatshirt may have offered me access, had I felt like role-playing, but though even then I already enjoyed telling stories, I preferred to fantasize about various elsewheres than to pretend I'd lived in any of them: living my own life felt complicated enough.

▶

Reagan was released from the hospital eleven days after the shooting. That August, he signed the Economic Recovery Tax Act of 1981, which, according to the Ronald Reagan Presidential Foundation, "brought reductions in individual income tax rates, the expensing of depreciable property, incentives for small businesses and incentives for savings. So began the Reagan Recovery."

For another year, the economy sputtered on, but, prompted by massive increases in military spending as well as greater consumer debt prompted by lower unemployment and lower interest rates, it rebounded in 1983. Still, many economists doubted the vitality of this upswing: "The recovery since 1983 has been widely acclaimed," wrote Andre Gunder Frank in *Economic and Political Weekly*'s May 24, 1986 issue,

> not the least by President Reagan himself, as having overcome the economic problems of the previous decade through renewed growth. Yet this claim—or hope—rests on shaky foundations. Domestically, the recovery is weakly sustained in the US by consumer spending and debt finance; and internationally the spread of the recession has been slow and uneven.... There is always a next recession as there have been four in the present world economic crisis since 1967 and over forty since the rise of industrial capitalism around 1800.... There are many reasons to believe that the next recession may well be deeper again than the previous one.... None of the intervening recoveries overcame the accumulated legacies of the previous recessions, and the present recovery has substantially aggravated the structural and cyclical problems of the world economy.

Hand-me-downs, trickle-down: I don't recall much of the 1980s' national wealth reaching my family during that decade. My grandparents—living comfortably enough off the income from my grandfather's bowling alley—paid for a lot of the clothes and games and books my sisters and I owned, and probably many other things I had no knowledge of; we heated our home with wood that my father split and that I stacked and lugged inside; we went out to dinner or the movies only rarely; summer vacations, we camped in state parks or visited relatives. One weekend afternoon, my mother gone to the supermarket, I rummaged the kitchen cupboards, but found only bottles of salad dressing and soy sauce, foil-wrapped bouillon cubes, a tin of baking powder, dusty cans of California olives and condensed milk: my sisters and I had devoured the cookies, the crackers, the peanut butter, the Kraft Macaroni & Cheese. Before my mother could return with another week's worth of groceries, I shook most of a jar of imitation bacon bits into my palm and crunched mouthfuls of those salty crisps.

During Reagan's first term, I sensed that most of my friends lived lives like mine—lives in which money was an ongoing, ever-present concern; lives our parents might have characterized as "making do" or "getting by" though all of our needs and many of our wants were satisfied. Still, though I had no evidence beyond my sense of worry, our comfortable routines often felt precarious, our finances one step away from disaster, and anything might happen to disrupt them—like the wheel of our car falling off one night as we drove down the highway, my father hiking along the breakdown lane to call a tow truck, and hours passing while we waited in a

McDonald's for things to be sorted out so we could go home. At an early age, I learned not to count on much, especially things I wanted, and to recognize occasions for gratitude.

But by the time Reagan was re-elected, that shared experience of hardship seemed gone. Some families seemed to remain broke, while many others had somehow been elevated to a new standard of living: I watched ski lift tags accumulate on the zippers of kids' winter coats; other kids returned from February vacation with tans and T-shirts that read ST. CROIX or ST. MAARTEN; some kids left town all summer, gone to sports camps or beach houses. I didn't want any of these things: I wanted the sense of ease these kids all seemed to share, an ability to inhabit themselves and to negotiate the world with a self-confidence that I imagined came from a financial safety net.

When Martyn Leaper and Rebecca Cole harmonize on the crucial lines in "Hand-Me Downs"—"No, I won't talk about it, and I won't weep / Yes, I know all about it, everything indeed"—I inevitably hear the anguish of diminished circumstance. I've usually felt too embarrassed to ever complain about the things I wanted but couldn't afford, too ashamed to describe my guilt for wanting, too stupid for allowing myself to believe that buying something might bring me an otherwise unobtainable relief, too proud to talk about any of this. ("Feeling wonderful is better," Leaper and Cole deadpan, just before the song's final chord.) I didn't want anyone to feel sorry for me, in part because I often didn't feel sorry for myself—and though I've always known I was far luckier than most in my upbringing, I've still always felt myself struggling to catch up to economic standards I've never fully understood: "just behind, or so it seemed."

We've long since learned that the vast disparities in wealth that now exist in the United States began during the Reagan years; a few decades and a few economic recessions later, the idea of upward mobility appears a dream for many Americans. (Nicholas Kristof recently observed "three factoids" while discussing the Occupy Wall Street protests: "The 400 wealthiest Americans have a greater combined net worth than the bottom 150 million Americans"; "The top 1 percent of Americans possess more wealth than the entire bottom 90 percent"; "In the Bush expansion from 2002 to 2007, 65 percent of economic gains went to the richest 1 percent.")

While Reagan campaigned for and won a second term on the strength of his economic record, I graduated junior high, and my father finished earning his own degrees. In a family snapshot, the two of us stand on the deck he built behind our house—him, in cap and gown and sunglasses, clutching his diploma; me, in Duran Duran–inspired skinny electric blue tie, stuffing my hands in my pockets—following our near-concurrent graduations. Perhaps the billboard once enumerating our city's higher-learning opportunities was accurate: my father did seem home less often when I returned from school, and some weekday mornings, when I woke up before my mother and sisters, he'd already left the house—gone to the health club and then to his new job. In 1985, he bought the first new car our family had owned in ten years.

One dusky fall evening, some neighborhood kids and I, just uphill from my house, straddled our bikes or balanced on a fire hydrant's stubby arms as we talked. "Who's that man at your house?" one of them asked me, pointing. I looked: a tall man, dressed in suit and tie, and carrying a briefcase, mounted the steps to our front door. For a second I didn't recognize him myself.

"That's my father," I said.

NEW ORDER: "Blue Monday"
(b/w "The Beach" 12", Factory Records, 1983)

Ben and I were high school scientists. Though, like everyone else our age, we pursued old rail lines into tunnels, snapped photos inside abandoned state hospitals, and picnicked at midnight in a field glowing with the local airport's landing-strip lights, we also stole a centrifuge from our school chemistry lab so we could "separate drinks." (Ben's mom later sold it at a yard sale.) We picked random names we found interesting from our city's phonebook and mailed those people copies of our 'zine, *Sketch Fifty-Three*. (No one replied.) Ben endeavored to perfect the "cookie loaf," collecting, in a plastic bag in his fridge, a year's worth of leftover crumbs from every cookie he ate; when the bag was full, he mixed its contents with some cream cheese, spread it in a pan, and baked it. (Thin, hard, dense.) I sought to condition my body to require less sleep—an obvious waste—and stayed up weeknights until about one o'clock, then set my alarm for 5:24 A.M. exactly, at which point I'd rise, turn on the shower, and pass out on the bathmat for several more minutes until I was conscious enough to crawl under the water. ("So spiritual," a friend's mom remarked when I once explained this process.) Because of my increasingly low enthusiasm for school and my increasing sleep deficit, as well as my almost physical craving for music, I roused myself each day by blaring my stereo before I left the house at quarter past seven to walk the silent mile to school. One morning, I chose New Order's "Blue Monday" to test the power handling of my cheap-but-big Yamaha speakers. The volume control on the amplifier I used then did not go to ten but instead measured decibels from negative ∞ to 0, a scale I admired for its objective precision even if I didn't fully understand it. (My father had moved out months earlier, and we were all recalibrating our understandings.) That opening drum machine beat, already jackhammer-like, pounded through the house: my mother, still in bed trying to rally herself for her own day's efforts, howled, "Not yet!"

JOY DIVISION: "Love Will Tear Us Apart"
(b/w "These Days," "Love Will Tear Us Apart" 12″, Factory, 1980)

Ben, a cellist, sold copies of *Sketch Fifty-Three* for a quarter to the other kids in the Greater Boston Youth Symphony Orchestra—most of whom, though their moms drove them to rehearse Haydn or Mozart on weekend mornings, and though they toured Japan with Seiji Ozawa and Leonard Bernstein, seemed to know at least as much about punk and post-punk as Ben and I did. To try to stay ahead, we bought more records, wrote more reviews, wandered the brick factories past Institute Park taking more photos, published more issues. "One gets the impression that they are four college graduates who decided there are more important things to do than chase currency," Ben remarked about Mission of Burma. "Propelled by a soaring intro, 'Something Must Break' climaxes with Stephen Morris's cataclysmic drumming and [Ian] Curtis's despairing vocals," I observed about Joy Division. ("You're only seven years too late," complained an anonymous letter to the editors, written by someone who'd presumably discovered Joy Division the year before we had.) Ben's orchestra friends gave him buttons advertising Boston bands, and sent me mail—my address was printed on our 'zine's back page.

One girl—I'll call her S.—became my pen pal: our correspondence began with her questions about my review of Public Image Limited's *Paris au Printemps* LP, and my response, including a cassette with some songs from *First Issue* and *Second Edition.* I don't want to romanticize letter-writing, or compare it favorably to e-mail, instant messaging, texting, Skype. Still, the forty miles between S.'s house and mine meant that the post office delivered our letters—which we soon wrote each other almost daily—only a day or two later, and that slight but significant lull maximized whatever eloquence my sixteen-year-old self could muster. I ignored my homework, rummaged kitchen cupboards, scrawled in a spiral on a scavenged paper plate, then folded the plate in half, stapled the dimpled edge, inked S.'s address onto that crescent, and pressed a 25¢ stamp on it—about what AT&T then billed for a minute's long-distance conversation, yet another reason we wrote letters instead of, as with local friends, tying up the family phone all night in those pre-call waiting years. Or, I used a brown lunch bag as an envelope, and filled it with small handwritten notes and pictures I'd scissored from magazines. S. mailed bulging, half-sized stationery envelopes in pastel colors. She told me about her sister, her annoying neighbors, her appreciation for the music of Kitaro. I cataloged my complaints and chronicled my hometown ramblings. She drew cartoon sketches of herself. I sent more mixtapes. Within a few months, in the middle of a five- or six-page letter, she wrote that she loved me.

"She said she *loves* you but she's never even *met* you?" a friend said in the cafeteria the next day, when I bragged about it. "She's a psycho!"

I'd recently acquired my first car—a 1980 Mercury Bobcat station wagon, paneled in fake wood and adorned with three bumper stickers I'd affixed to the back window: the PiL logo, the radio pulses of the neutron star from the cover of Joy Division's *Unknown Pleasures* LP, and Newbury Comics' grinning idiot—and driving to S.'s house meant making my first solo trip on the Interstate. Bridge and overpass construction funneled the Mass Pike traffic into single lanes, and I sped through narrow corridors of Jersey barriers, chucked change into the basket at the Newton tolls, then took Route 128 to Route 2.

S. and I didn't call it a date: only parents used that word. But my hormonally electrified fantasies about our meeting were mostly the obvious ones. "Is she cute?" I'd asked Ben: it seemed information as crucial as the bits of our lives S. and I'd confessed to each other all that spring. Her family's house was a huge, shingled Victorian on a shady street that wound up a hill: my paper plates and postcards had gone *here?* I angled the tires against the curb, pulled up the parking brake, checked my mirrors one final time, and got out. S. already stood on the porch. She brushed blonde bangs from her eyes. "Hi," she called, looking at me and then away. I probably did the same. Was she cute? She wasn't not cute.

We walked through her neighborhood, looking at root-tilted squares of sidewalk and each other's scuffed sneakers, asking awkward questions and mumbling answers. Breezes swung new leaves, and ragged shadows shifted over the pavement: had I been walking alone, I would've mentioned it in a letter to her, omitting the guy pushing his lawnmower who seemed to stare at us as we passed. Then her mom gave us a ride to the Alewife T station and we took the train to Harvard Square.

A sunny, pollen-scented Saturday in May: even we were roused by the Square's finals-week energy to look at each other over sandwiches in a tiny café. S. slid vintage dresses along a rack at Oona's, but didn't buy any. We walked up the ramp at The Garage, wandered through displays of leather jackets, suede creepers, and Doc Martens at Allston Beat, and ended up at Newbury Comics. It's tough to talk when you're looking through so much vinyl, and impossible to make eye contact: I hunched over an imports bin. S. wandered away, maybe to the Kitaro section. I left the store with four or five new records, among them Joy Division's "Love Will Tear Us Apart."

The Red Line rattled us back to Alewife. There was no goodbye kiss, no damp hand shyly held. I have no idea whether my actual presence disappointed her, too. After that day our correspondence continued, for a little while, and we politely lied to each other about our meeting, but, in the absence of any sustaining fantasies, what else was there to say? S. and her family toured the northeast looking at colleges that summer, and she described these campus visits to me. I went door to door for the Massachusetts Public Interest Research Group, asking people for money and signatures to stop a planned solid-waste incinerator, but I didn't want to write about that experience to anyone. I got off work at ten each night, then hung out with friends at a late-night diner, or, if no one was around, listened to records. I already knew the Joy Division song, but now that I owned the single, it helped frame my summer: "And we're changing our ways / Taking different roads." I always preferred the B-side's tauter version of the song, without the guitar flourishes, which meant I listened to "These Days" a lot, too: "We'll drift through it all / It's the modern age." Like countless others before me, I both yearned for and cursed the affliction of modernity, and brooded over my mediated, irreconcilable, incomprehensible selves (incomprehensible to me, at least: my first day at MASSPIRG, a slightly elder co-worker took one look at me and said, "I bet you like Echo and the Bunnymen and the Jam"). Ian Curtis may have been singing about his failing marriage and the affair he'd been pursuing, but that didn't mean his lyrics couldn't dramatize my own teenaged disquiet about "touching from a distance, further all the time."

Sketch Fifty-Three's final number, published that fall, included—among illegally reproduced copies of Kevin Cummins's photographs of Joy Division looking serious among the concrete structures of Manchester, and Ben's and my photographs of ourselves looking serious among the concrete structures of our own post-industrial hometown—a poem by my new girlfriend. I'd met her over the summer: she stood outside a liquor store, cursing and shouting at the clerk who had refused her fake ID, and then she noticed—I swear—the *Unknown Pleasures* sticker on my car. In a last record review, in an act of unwitting self-awareness, I commented that Joy Division's 1979 single "Transmission" was a song "dealing with alienation, hypocrisy, and confusion." I can't remember if I ever mailed S. a copy of the issue.

R.E.M.: "Catapult"
(*Murmur* LP, I.R.S., 1983)

Michael Stipe's lyrical impenetrability marked R.E.M.'s sound and ethos so obviously in the early and mid-'80s that even my father—who, unlike the rest of his generation, seemed not to have experienced the 1960s musically—understood. As we drove beneath Mount Wachusett on our way to hike the nearby woods, a cassette copy of *Murmur* I'd dubbed from my LP playing on the car stereo, my father began yelping "Caterpillar!" during the choruses of the song "Catapult," knowing full well that what he heard, and sang, was wrong, but laughing as he did it anyway.

Our family had only recently acquired a car with a tapedeck, and we all bickered over what we'd listen to while driving: I was finally outnumbered when my parents reached a truce, which my sisters co-signed, on the Eagles' *Their Greatest Hits, 1971–1975* and Fleetwood Mac's self-titled record and *Rumours;* songs from these three albums still induce tremors and sweats when I hear them. Persuading my father to slide my cassette into the tapedeck seemed itself a kind of victory. Still, my consumption, circa 1984, of the first few R.E.M. records could best have been expressed by such verbs as "inhale" or "imbibe," so when he messed with the lyrics to one of their songs, I took it personally. I was thirteen, and took everything personally.

My father had, two years earlier, terrorized our household one week by playing Barbra Streisand's "Memory" over and over while transcribing its lyrics onto the dry-erase board stuck to the refrigerator. After the first day, his effort looked like a *Mad Lib;* he spent the rest of the week figuring those last few gaps. He didn't need Robert Christgau to tell him, about R.E.M.'s early records, that "physically incomprehensible lyrics make them harder to parse than somebody else's mystical experience," or that "by obscuring their lyrics so artfully they insist that their ('pop') music is good for meaning as well as pleasure." My father loved to sing—in the shower, while scrambling eggs on weekend mornings, walking to the kitchen for more root beer. Still, he treated most songs as occasions for goofy, ironic, *basso buffo* embellishments—jokes only he understood, though he'd throttle them well past the point of collapse trying to make us understand, too. He liked an inscrutable mix of bombastic classical music, standards, schmaltzy pop, and easy listening: Van Morrison, "Greensleeves," the Pointer Sisters, "Night on Bald Mountain," Cat Stevens. He invented lyrics of his own to accompany familiar tunes, like one called "Fried Clams" that he crooned to the melody of Henry Mancini's "Theme from *Peter Gunn*" (I can say no more—tremors, sweats, etc.).

During the brief weeks when R.E.M.'s "So. Central Rain (I'm Sorry)" was a minor hit, a DJ at one of the local rock stations asked listeners to call in and sing their take on the song's lyrics while he played the track in the background. We've become so accustomed to mumbled and obscure lyrics that what once sounded utterly strange and unknowable, so willfully other, now seems unremarkable and tame: how had we been so baffled by Stipe's maunderings? (And in terms of pretension, is Streisand's rendering of Andrew Lloyd Webber's lines "Every street lamp seems to beat a fatalistic warning / Someone mutters and the streetlamp sputters" any better than Stipe's "Eastern to Mountain, third party call / the lines are down, the wise man built his words upon the rocks / But I'm not bound to follow suit"?) The DJ's exercise was designed for cheap laughs, a group affirmation of the value of plain speech that made sense. Still, like my father with the dry-erase board, I was eager to learn even apparently nonsensical words—whose slurred vowels and phonemes I knew, though many of the phrases eluded me—but the versions my fellow listeners sang from home telephones to airwaves seemed as wrong as my father's rendition of "Catapult."

The urge to sing along with a pop song is the urge to participate, to lay private claim to a public thing, to turn a song's mystery into our mastery. My father sang along to Streisand until he hit a line he didn't know, then replayed the song from the start. When *Murmur* stirred me, I sang along mostly by imitating Stipe's vocal sounds, as if learning another language only by ear. It's rare for a pop song to offer much resistance—as Theodor Adorno has noted, "the composition hears for the listener," since popular music arrives "'predigested'": not only are pop songs easily consumed, they are easily condensed or excerpted, since they are mass-produced from essentially interchangeable parts. But Stipe's singing bewildered even R.E.M.'s drummer, Bill Berry: "At first I thought it was silly, kinda pretentious," Berry told *Musician* in 1985. "Then I realized it wasn't. The more I listened to it, the less I understood it, which was good."

R.E.M.'s songs frustrated my attempts at understanding them in the facile ways I then expected to understand pop songs, largely because of the aura of Stipe's mumbled and abstracted lyrics. *Murmur*'s title already warned that its contents would be spoken low, or heard only faintly, and the sepia-toned photograph of kudzu-covered shapes on its cover signified much the same. Not for the first—or last—time did it seem a band was playing and singing directly to me, and I was the only one who properly understood. ("I can hear you," as the chorus of *Murmur*'s "Sitting Still" has it.) In the backseat of our crappy Pontiac, I sulked against the window, my father's joyous "Caterpillar! Cat-er-pillar! Caterpillar!" slowly ruining that song for me, even though I too had no real idea what Michael Stipe meant.

Mitch Easter, who produced R.E.M.'s first three records—including *Murmur*—told an interviewer years later that Stipe "was an art school guy, and he wanted to sound like that. I didn't think it was a big deal. There's a grand tradition of rock and roll singers you can't understand.... I think it helped the mystique factor. They were all about mystique back then." Or, as Mick Jagger told a *Rolling Stone* interviewer who wondered whether mumbling his lyrics was "done purposely as a style," "I don't try to make them so obscure that nobody can understand, but on the other hand I don't try not to. I just do it as it comes."

Album cover, minor-chord jangle, song titles: everything connoted, nothing denoted. Maybe there was some profound meaning behind "Catapult," some insight I'd eventually attain if I listened enough times. In the meantime, I could invent whatever meaning I liked—one requiring no explanations, one unyielding to the common, boring desire for resolution.

COCTEAU TWINS: "The Itchy Glowbo Blow"
(*Blue Bell Knoll* LP, 4AD, 1988)

June 25, 1990

"I shouldn't be writing to someone I barely know," Rachel's postcard read, "when I'm this depressed + faithless. The smoke from my cigarette is even stinging my eyes."

I'd met Rachel a few years earlier, at Ben's house, during the brief time they were going out. She'd brought a VHS copy of David Lynch's *Blue Velvet,* then two years old, and the three of us, with Ben's younger brother, had gathered around the small television in his mother's sewing room to watch it. During the infamous scene where Kyle MacLachlan's character peeps from the closet while Dennis Hopper's character inhales nitrous oxide, then beats and dry-humps Isabella Rossellini's character, Ben's father walked into the room. A stern, quiet bookseller, Ben's father watched the movie for a minute, too, then shut off the television, ejected the videotape, and told us to go do something else.

When she sent me the postcard, Rachel and Ben had long since broken up, but I'd asked her to submit some writing to a one-off 'zine I planned to make. Rachel had given us some poems for *Sketch Fifty-Three,* and now took creative writing courses in college. I was nineteen, and wanted to produce a more serious, more literary 'zine than *Sketch,* filled with serious, literary stories—like the ones I'd just encountered by Carson McCullers, or like those my new girlfriend, Jen, told me she'd read in a literary journal called *Conjunctions.*

Rachel was a smart, glib, classically trained musician, and the first person I knew whose moods needed to be adjusted by psychoactive drugs. She wrote dark poems inspired by Sylvia Plath and Anne Sexton. But my planned literary 'zine did not impress her. "I'm apprehensive about sending you the completed 'sex piece' because of personal feelings + my changing attitudes about the person it's about," Rachel's postcard concluded. She'd addressed it only to "Josh," and a large, deliberate ink blot partially obscured the name of my street. Her handwriting looked like melted candlewax: the second "t" in "cigarette" descended two full lines. On the front of the postcard, Dylan Thomas cups a lit match to the tip of a cigarette hanging from his lips. The postmark has faded almost to invisibility—I'd discovered Dylan Thomas's earliest stories, such as "The Tree," that same year, and loved them, so tacked this postcard above my writing desk for years—but I can still, just barely, read the date.

August–October 1990

A month or so after I received Rachel's postcard, I moved into an illegal attic apartment up on Boston's Mission Hill, and that fall I began taking classes at UMass Boston, though I knew I'd transfer out: I'd been in Greece that spring, when I should've submitted my financial aid forms, and now I could only afford state tuition. My coursework was light. Home computers then still existed mostly in the homes of the wealthy, and our professors allowed us to handwrite our essays on lined pages if we owned no typewriter: I submitted my papers in neat block capitals. The other students sometimes groaned when our professors announced a reading assignment or reminded us of a due date. I rode the T forty-five minutes each way to and from campus, and worked twenty-five hours a week, but managed to squander a lot of afternoons looking through my apartment's skylights over rooftops, smokestacks, and church spires.

My roommate, a Mass Art student, spent entire days and a lot of late nights in the glassblowing studio. Otherwise, she was usually out with either an older guy who sometimes gave her money, or a long-haired artist boyfriend from school who said he'd tattoo my unimposing bicep with an ironic reproduction of one of Garth Williams's or E.H. Shepard's line drawings, though he never did. We had no lease on the apartment, which technically didn't exist. Every so often, home at the same time, we'd crank up Public Enemy, Queen Latifah, Elvis Costello, De La Soul, or Madonna on the stereo, but mostly we stayed out of each other's way.

Ben attended Boston University, though I didn't see him often. Sarazar also went to Mass Art, but after I'd confessed my more-than-friendly feelings for her, on the eve of our departure for Greece, I didn't see her often, either. Rachel went to college in the western end of the state. Jen had just started Bard, and that school's three-week intensive "Language and Thinking" workshop for incoming students interrupted our summer romance in early August.

1990

When I was nineteen, Cocteau Twins—the Scottish band I liked more than any other that year—seemed sophisticated: people didn't mosh to Cocteau Twins. They didn't—*couldn't*—even sing along to Cocteau Twins, since no one could really tell what Elizabeth Fraser, the band's singer, was saying. Instead, they had long, thoughtful conversations about art museums or overnight flights to Belgium while listening to Cocteau Twins, whose song titles included words such as "flagstones," "musette," and "hitherto"—words that might be spoken in such conversations. Cocteau Twins also seemed like good makeout music, but it would have to be serious making out, with occasional long looks into each other's eyes to indicate everything that could never be uttered, never be fully understood.

Jen, too, seemed sophisticated: she eschewed T-shirts and jeans for floral-print sundresses and delicate cardigans, wore her hair short, and worked at a bookstore where she read those early issues of *Conjunctions,* years before I'd heard of the writers in its pages.

She spoke softly. She knew way more about cinema than I ever would. She planned to major—and did major—in philosophy.

I wanted to be—or at least to appear—so sophisticated, but in my solitary moments I could acknowledge my posturing, if only to myself. All of my friends seemed—and were—more worldly than I was, but Jen's sophistication exceeded that of everyone else I knew. Most nineteen-year-olds, no matter how mature they feel, are, almost by definition, sophomoric: I certainly was. Around Jen, I often felt loud, clumsy, goofy. The fact that I rarely recognized my sophomorism probably made it especially awful.

The '80s

Few record labels have ever taken themselves as seriously as London's 4AD—the name, in true early '80s fashion, an artsy abbreviation of "forward." 4AD's aesthetic, in sound and visual design, initially followed the dour post-punk path blazed by Factory Records, but when, by the second half of the '80s, many of Factory's artists synthesized funk, New York hip-hop, Detroit and Chicago house, Ibiza's Balearic Beat, and Eurodisco into what became the "Madchester" rave scene, 4AD doubled down on its mist-shrouded, gold-filigreed aesthetic: the label's records featured cover photos of dressmaker's dummies and graveyard statuary, band names such as Throwing Muses and This Mortal Coil, typography that often looked like the handwriting on Rachel's postcard—all perfect for someone who took himself as seriously as I did.

No band on 4AD's roster defined the label as much as Cocteau Twins, who were themselves often defined by their vocalist. One critic named Fraser "the voice of God," while other critics and fans described her lyrics as anything from elvish to incomprehensible gibberish, and buried her singing beneath adjectives—angelic, operatic, cherubic, dramatic, etc.—as if to indicate only the inadequacies of descriptive language. In the 1980s, she sang like no other pop singer did. Her voice remains Cocteau Twins' most immediately striking feature, but it mattered to me mostly in how it contributed to the band's overall mood, since my moods were precisely why I loved to listen to their records, and since the band didn't offer much beyond mood, anyway: lots of processed guitar textures, arpeggios ringing like bells, the whooshes and hums of cathedral-sized ambience, drowsy basslines, and some of the least funky beats ever programmed on a Roland TR-808 Rhythm Composer. Most Cocteau Twins songs end in pretty much the same place they begin: the music's tension derives not from progression but from a lack of resolution.

I loved most the first two Cocteau Twins LPs, *Garlands* and *Head Over Heels,* recorded when the band members were nineteen themselves and making their most brooding and bummed-out music. *Head Over Heels* opens with the cannon-blast booms of a drum machine while an electronic high-hat rings like chimes in the background, and then, as what sounds like a lopsided Frisbee whizzes past, a treated guitar riff growls and dithers below a twinkling, tentative keyboard melody—and that's all before Fraser even begins singing in her weird, arresting voice. No other music sounded better when I drove down a dark, empty country road in the middle of the night, headlights flashing among tree trunks as I passed. No other music sounded better while snow accumulated over the city all afternoon. No other music sounded better when I lay atop my futon with headphones on, wondering why Jen no longer wanted to hang out with me.

November–December 1990

From the second-floor vintage shop in Kenmore Square where I worked for eight dollars an hour under the table, I watched the autumn sun set as B-line trolleys emerged from underground and rattled west on Comm Ave. Few customers found their way up the stairs the evenings I worked, and, as I'd now done for a few years, I sat by myself amid racks and racks of old discarded clothes that someone hoped still had value. Bored and lonely, I wrote Jen letters from the store, and one week mailed her a letter a day—long-distance calls were then billed by the minute—after which, feeling smothered, she decided to break up with me, though I didn't realize it yet.

I also didn't yet know that the entire block of old brick buildings where I worked—including famed rock club the Rat, into which my boss told me he'd watched David Byrne and Tina Weymouth carry their tiny amplifiers sometime in the '70s—would be razed, within a decade, to make way for a luxury hotel, but everything that season still felt provisional. After I closed the store, I'd sometimes walk through the T tunnel under the square where Mr. Butch sang to himself and asked me for a dollar, then up to the B.U. dorm where Ben lived, or I'd meet Ben at Planet Records to flip through the bins before we ate a couple of slices at Captain Nemo's Pizza, or sometimes I'd trek out to Somerville to visit a friend who lived with some activist womyn in a rental they called the Harambe House and who, because she knew I was broke, cooked me home fries with melted cheese and hot sauce, and brewed strong cinnamon coffee, and who yelled at me all fall for not wearing socks and warned me I'd get sick, but more often I'd walk home alone—down Brookline Ave., among groves of phragmites at the Fenway, past the Isabella Stewart Gardner Museum, and up the hill from Brigham Circle. Often one or two men slept in the scrubby bushes between Calumet Street and the parking lot of the sad shopping plaza I avoided except for the laundromat. I ate a lot of roasted acorn squash, for which I paid about nineteen cents a pound, and cornflakes from the corner bodega with soy milk from Star Market. In the first days of December, my bosses, citing slow sales, let me go. Jen came home for winter break and officially broke up with me. I caught a bad cold that turned into strep throat, and spent a week or so huddled on my futon, sleeping and waking, shivering and semi-hallucinating on Sudafed and a 103-degree fever. I lost my voice. All the local schools held their final exams, and for most of the month I saw no one. When I finally left my sickbed for a holiday party in a student apartment on the Riverway, I stepped in, swathed in a scarf and probably still contagious, and Ben greeted me, laughing: "Lazarus!" But I didn't feel quite alive.

1990

In Boston, the year began with the suicide of Charles Stuart. Several months earlier, Stuart had driven into my neighborhood, shot his pregnant wife in the head and himself in the stomach, then claimed they'd been carjacked, robbed, and shot by a pistol-wielding black man—an accusation which prompted a massive manhunt for the imaginary perp, including stop-and-frisk and public strip-searching of young African American men on Mission Hill, and which mangled the city's already-stressed race relations. When his brother finally revealed the truth to police, Stuart leaped from the Tobin Bridge. Two months later, in one of the world's largest, still-unsolved art heists, thieves dressed as cops stole a Vermeer and three Rembrandts, among other artworks, from the Gardner Museum. Iraq's August invasion of Kuwait, the resulting spike in oil prices, a housing slump, and the imminent collapse of the savings and loan industry all contributed to a recession beginning in July, and one in four Boston families with children lived at or below the federal poverty line. The city had more murders that year than any other in its history.

And then, two weeks into 1991, Operation Desert Storm, the United States–led coalition's aerial assault on Baghdad, began playing live on our television screens. We were not the civilians being bombed, our city was not transformed to night-vision spectacle, and, but for CNN's twenty-four-hour "breaking news" and the sudden proliferation of yellow ribbons, the war seemed distant. Still, a few friends and I—all of us had been required to register for the Selective Service a year or two earlier—felt anxious about being drafted, even as we marched to Government Center in an anti-war protest.

September 1990–January 1991

In the same notebooks where I wrote my essays for classes—Literature as an Art (B+); Introduction to Black Literature (A-); Twentieth Century Political Ideas (A-); Six American Writers (A-); Women, Culture, Identity (A)—I wrote short stories, in part to try to mitigate my increasing disappointment in the world, my friends, and myself, and in part to try to understand those disappointments. It felt easier to put my energies into imagined situations and characters than to reach out to my friends, easier to rewrite sentences and fuss over details than to make cold calls and find a new job. Being a writer had always seemed a serious and worthwhile ambition, and one I'd held for years, but now that I took mostly English courses—not caring about distribution requirements, given my plans to transfer—some of my professors valorized it. And if I fancied myself a writer, I could insulate myself from the world—turn the world into something to be observed, something to comment upon, something that affected other people more than it affected me, the detached observer.

But I've never been skilled at cultivating detachment. I'd convinced myself, in the short, dark winter days of my nineteenth year, that a woman I'd known for six months was key to my happiness, and in her abrupt, unexpected absence, my other friends and my social life no longer gave me much pleasure. I'd undergone other breakups before Jen—some I'd initiated, some I hadn't—but this one felt different, and there was no detaching myself from it. I took long, solitary, scowling walks through Boston and Brookline feeling sorry for myself, and for the world, and listening to tapes of Cocteau

Twins—whose music had sounded beautiful and mysterious when Jen and I listened to it that summer, but which now sounded doleful, forlorn, harrowed. As I muddled out of adolescence and into adulthood, little comforted me, and music that sounded as estranged from the world as I felt only underscored this fact.

June 1990

I met Jen around the time Rachel sent me her postcard declining to submit to my planned 'zine. Ben knew Jen from work, and for some reason he began plotting that the three of us have a midnight picnic. I proposed the wide, empty fields surrounding the regional airport on the hills west of town. On the misty night we chose, I drove us out to the suburb where Jen lived, then up behind the airport, and parked on the rutted roadside. We walked toward the runway and spread a blanket in the patchy grass. One of us had brought pita bread and tabouli—the kind made by pouring boiling water over a small box of bulgur wheat and a "spice sack" of dehydrated garlic and mint. Someone else had brought native strawberries. We'd either been unable to acquire wine or convinced we didn't need it. We sat in overgrown grass for a few hours, talking and listening to a Cocteau Twins cassette on a small boombox. Light winds blew scraps of fog around. The control tower spun a blinding white beam across us every thirty seconds, and blue-and-white landing strip lights glowed a quarter mile away. Ben's idea was cool and sophisticated, even if it was hard to feel cool and sophisticated while sitting in a dewy field with mint flakes and strawberry seeds in my teeth.

1982–1988

If I liked *Garlands* and *Head over Heels* because they sounded so bummed out, I also liked them because most of the songs on these records seem to concern love and sex, especially complicated, fraught, overwrought love and sex—i.e., a nineteen-year-old's take on love and sex—as suggested by songs titled "My Love Paramour," "The Tinderbox (Of a Heart)," "Blood Bitch," "Grail Overfloweth," "Dear Heart," "Wax and Wane." *Garlands* even included a few brief lyrics on the back of the sleeve, so I could read bits of what Fraser sings: "Grail overfloweth there is rain / And there's saliva and there's you," or "My mouthing at you / My tongue the stake / I should welt should I hold you / I should gash should I kiss you."

On the record that followed these two, the song titles referenced mythic figures—"Persephone," "Beatrix," "Pandora." A trio of EPs followed a year later, with songs titled after butterflies, colors, an elaborate art style, a bird, and archaic Scottish colloquialisms. The next record's titles appear to reference Antarctica. I could continue. Each passing LP seemed less earthy, less rooted in a mood of gloomy sex until, in 1993, discussing P.J. Harvey with *Melody Maker,* Fraser admitted that Harvey "goes on about sex a lot, which is another subject I don't particularly want to tackle."

Despite all the mentions of blood and saliva and things that "overfloweth" in those early songs, and despite an album title invoking a state of uncontrollable feelings, Cocteau Twins' music seemed chaste, a little repressed, their take on sex not entirely pleasurable. That is, their blurry songs made sex as muddled and raw as it sometimes felt for young people who—as was true of me—maybe weren't as sophisticated as they wanted to believe. Cocteau Twins' music deals with the head, not the body—or maybe with the head getting in the way of the body's urges.

August 24, 1990

After the midnight picnic, Jen and I saw each other as often as we could in the few weeks remaining before she left for Bard and I left for Boston. Our dates—though we would never have called them that: in fact, we disdained the "definitions" imposed by such words as "boyfriend" or "girlfriend" so much that even the shorthand of referring to her in that way here seems wrong—took place in other nighttime fields, or twenty-four-hour diners, or art cinemas.

At the very end of summer, on a day that felt like fall, I took the bus from Boston to my hometown, borrowed my mother's car, and drove to Bard, arriving in late afternoon. I was due back at work the next day. Jen and I ate dinner in Red Hook, then walked around Blithewood Mansion and its gardens, watched trains roll north along the causeway across Tivoli Bays as the sun slipped behind the Catskills, and went up to her dorm room and made out all night while her copy of *Blue Bell Knoll,* Cocteau Twins' 1988 album, played on repeat: the sad-but-bracing chord progression of "The Itchy Glowbo Blow" is forever bound up in my memories of this night.

Blue Bell Knoll was the first Cocteau Twins record released domestically in the US, the first one to appear here on a label other than 4AD. Since the term "import" in those days connoted far more than simply a record manufactured and released abroad, it didn't surprise me that this LP sounded poppier and more polished than previous Cocteau Twins records, nor that a video soon appeared on MTV. I hated a bunch of the songs on the LP, hated the preciousness of titles such as "For Phoebe Still a Baby" and "A Kissed-Out Red Floatboat," hated much of the record's kinder, gentler music. But in the tensions between Liz Fraser's multitracked vocals, Robin Guthrie's descending guitar chords, and Simon Raymonde's melodic bass, "The Itchy Glowbo Blow"—slick production and annoying title aside—contained all the plaintive, lonesome yearning I'd always associated with Cocteau Twins. I have no idea what Fraser is singing about, but the song sounds simultaneously breathless, exuberant, and devastated: pretty much how I felt by the end of that night I hadn't wanted to end.

September 19, 1917

Depressed, faithless, betrayed even by our own cigarette smoke: my friends and I had all mastered the self-dramatic literature of our own disappointments. Nothing ever went the way we hoped or desired—or, if it briefly did, we knew it wouldn't last, and had already resigned ourselves to inevitable failure. I cataloged my defeats in my journals—didn't every serious writer keep a journal?—and imagine many of my friends did as well. Kafka noted, in his own *Diaries,* "Have never understood how it is possible for almost everyone who writes to objectify his sufferings in the very midst of undergoing them"—but I certainly never shared his curiosity on this point. What was the point of writing if not to objectify—and amplify—my sufferings? To contemplate endlessly the sort of "personal feelings + changing attitudes" Rachel had mentioned on her postcard?

August 25, 1990

Jen and I hadn't slept. I left at dawn. My mother's house was nearly three hours away, and after I dropped her car in her driveway, I'd still have to walk a mile or two to the bus station, catch the 10:00 bus to Boston, and be at work by noon. The sun rose behind clouds as I drove along the Taconic State Parkway, and I cranked down the window for the unseasonably chilly air. Adrenaline kept me going for a while, but as I crossed the Connecticut River, the Mass Pike seemed to roll straight and nearly flat toward the horizon, and there were still few other cars on the road, and my addled brain decided that it'd be okay if I rested my eyes for just a second: I snapped awake to the sound of radials on rumble strip at sixty-some miles an hour, and stayed awake, hands white-knuckled on the wheel, the rest of the way.

At my mother's house, I ate some cereal, then shouldered my backpack and headed down Chandler Street. Rain began to fall. Waiting for a light to change, I saw a boy with a hand on one knee in a sprinter's stance across the intersection, then looked away for a second, heard a quick awful thump, and turned back to see the boy hopping back to the curb on one leg as blood poured from the other. I dropped my backpack and ran over to him. Another man already knelt at the boy's side. I dialed 911 on a payphone, told the operator to send an ambulance, then ran into the CVS at that corner and grabbed a pack of Huggies while shouting, "A boy's been hit!" Outside, I held diapers to the boy's skinny leg as they slowly filled with blood and rain. The man gripped the boy's shoulders. He asked the boy questions: how old he was, where he went to school. "Keep the pressure on," the man told me, "he's going into shock." Onlookers circled us. Blood blotched wet pavement. The boy's tibia and fibula poked through his skin. He screamed and screamed, but all I heard was the calm man: "Shhh," he said. "It's going to be all right. It's going to be all right."

October 4, 1840

A few weeks into the spring 1991 semester, after failing to find work, I left Boston and moved back to my mother's house—penniless, jobless, apartmentless, girlfriendless. I felt ready to begin a decade of seclusion upstairs in her house, as Nathaniel Hawthorne had done at his own mother's house. "Here I sit in my old accustomed chamber, where I used to sit in days gone by," he wrote in his *American Note-Books,* in a passage that, but for its elegance and self-awareness, might as well have come from the journal I kept, 1990-1991:

> If ever I should have a biographer, he ought to make great mention of this chamber in my memoirs, because so much of my lonely youth was wasted here, and here my mind and character were formed; and here I have been glad and hopeful, and here I have been despondent.

> And here I sat a long, long time, waiting patiently for the world to know me, and sometimes wondering why it did not know me sooner, or whether it would ever know me at all,—at least, till I were in my grave. And sometimes it seemed as if I were already in the grave, with only life enough to be chilled and benumbed.

I'd just read Hawthorne's short stories for an American literature course at UMass Boston. I now rode the Peter Pan bus an hour each way for my spring semester classes.

September 17, 1990

In their afterlife—or maybe even by 1990, when they'd essentially become their own cover band, their sound immediately recognizable and no longer challenging or changing—Cocteau Twins became a kind of shorthand. Most bands who stick around long enough, or who have a distinctive enough sound or ethos—as Cocteau Twins did—become shorthand for something, but to invoke the Cocteau Twins' name summoned would-be artsiness in its most pitiful forms: independent bookstore soundtrack; ponytailed serious guy who seems really sensitive but has repressed rage issues; film majors with Fisher-Price Pixlvision cameras and social anxieties; kids wearing all-black clothes and dyed black hair and black boots and black lipstick; candles and crystals and red wine new-agey foppery. The eventual accuracy with which the signifier "Cocteau Twins" identified such things reduced—for me, at least—an intriguing, original band to the sameness of its least intriguing, least original followers. I don't know that Cocteau Twins were ever interested in recording "ethereal," "otherworldly" soundscapes, though that was the easiest way to categorize the music they made, music that seemed previously unimaginable to most people I knew the first time we heard it. Is it Cocteau Twins' fault that by pursuing the specific sounds they imagined, their songs started to sound too much the same, to blend into one long aria?

Regardless, their music came to seem easy theatrics, manufactured atmosphere, willful obscurantism—so much so that, by the afternoon when I skipped Introduction to Cultural Anthropology (B-) with a friend from UMass Boston and took the T to Harvard Square to buy what would be my last Cocteau Twins record, *Heaven or Las Vegas,* on the day of its release, the album mostly sounded like a collection of learned, empty gestures. That title suggests some self-awareness that even their—our—spiritual ambitions were possibly just cheap glitz, and Fraser's lyrics became more discernibly English: phrases such as "a young girl's dreams," or "I only want to love you" were suddenly both tough to miss and seemingly aimed at giving listeners exactly what they expected from a Cocteau Twins record.

I failed to consider how my own struggles to at least learn the empty gestures of maturity before I rejected them had returned me to my mother's house, as if to try the lesson again. Rather than study, I kept dreaming along to my dreamy music. The world disappointed me because I wasn't mature enough to try to understand its intricacies and systems—or because it didn't exist in the precise forms I wished it would, or because I didn't understand what it expected of me—so I escaped between a pair of headphones and in the pages of my notebook, believing myself far more distinctive than the kids wearing all black when I, too, illustrated a set of clichés.

August 25, 1990

When the ambulance and the police came, one cop pulled aside the man who'd held the boy, and another cop put me into the cruiser. I sat in the back seat while he took notes. "Did it look like she was speeding?" he asked. Rain tapped the metal roof. I watched the paramedics kneeling beside the boy, and then the boy's mother arrived, jumping out of her car and leaving the door hanging open as she ran to him. I had to wait for the cop to let me out of the cruiser: the back door had no handle on the inside. Soon the ambulance pulled away, lights spinning across glass storefronts, and cleared traffic with a few short bursts of the siren. The crowd started to leave, and one of the cops picked up the sodden diapers. Traffic edged around the car that had hit the boy—one tire against the curb, blinker flashing, a dent in its fender.

I walked to where I had thrown my backpack, and saw for the first time that dried blood browned my palms and wrists, streaked my arms to my elbows. I lifted my bag to my shoulder and kept walking, holding my hands away from my body, wondering if I'd still catch my bus. Then I squatted on the sidewalk, tore wet leaves from some bushes that grew behind a chain-link fence, and wiped the boy's blood off my skin.

October 1990

My favorite story of this era, Carson McCullers's "A Tree • A Rock • A Cloud," describes a man who claims that after being "a man who had never loved," he's now made love a "science" and can feel immediate love for anything, and whose near-monologue to a boy he meets in an all-night diner, though apparently deep with feeling, offers such a performance that the owner of the diner kicks him out in disgust—presumably at having heard it before. My anxious personality, c. 1990-1991, consisted of a set of carefully curated experiences I'd happily share with anyone who'd listen. My connections with friends and girlfriends felt intense, but, too often, I'd have another confidant a few months later. McCullers's story spoke mostly to my fondness for diners and eccentrics—both of which filled my hometown—but, though I didn't realize it then, I too foolishly believed I could love anyone with minimal effort. I may have loved the idea of Jen more than the reality of Jen herself, and when I grieved her absence I may have been grieving the loss of a certain idea of myself: the serious, sophisticated, ambitious young writer who listened to serious, sophisticated music, and who had a serious, sophisticated, smart, lovely girlfriend.

November 17–18, 1990

Over October break, Jen and I took a train from Rhinecliff to Montreal, stayed in a pension, saw a Derek Jarman film, ate croissants, and wandered Mount Royal Park and the McGill ghetto for a few freezing days. Then I left her at Bard and headed back to

Boston—where, on consecutive days in mid-November, Cocteau Twins and their even darker, more dramatic 4AD label-mates Dead Can Dance were scheduled to play: I'd bought us tickets to both sold-out shows, and she would come stay with me that weekend.

She did come, and though that weekend should have been some sort of celebratory pinnacle of our relationship, it felt disordered, strained. Jen had never really written back to my week-long mail barrage, and I felt she'd arrived in Boston almost out of obligation. I retain only fragmentary memories of her visit: how disappointing Cocteau Twins were live, even with—or because of—a pair of additional guitarists as stage lights swirled through dry-ice fog inside the Orpheum; the solemn version of "I Am Stretched on Your Grave" that Brendan Perry of Dead Can Dance intoned in the Berklee Performance Center, and the furious medieval drumming encore the entire band performed; Jen closing her eyes and slumping her head against my shoulder as we rode the E-line back to Brigham Circle and I watched our reflections flicker in the smudged glass across the almost empty train.

March 1991

Back home, I found a part-time job at a small independent bookstore that managed decent sales figures moving children's books to suburban parents, but whose owners would soon, in a burst of early-1990s print culture optimism, move to a bigger space, expand, and then go out of business. Jen and I tried to maintain a friendship—she seemed depressed, too, and spent a fair number of weekends at home—but I was too wounded and she too withdrawn for anything more than the occasional awkward encounter. On the bus I took to and from Boston for classes, I sat near the back and steadily worked through the 555 pages of Flannery O'Connor's *Complete Stories,* which my friend Tia had given me as a birthday present. Amid so many uncomfortable stories about intelligent but unwise and emotionally immature or otherwise developmentally stunted adult children living at home with their mothers, I paused, in "The Comforts of Home," on the phrase "small tragic spearmint-flavored sighs." The name of my 'zine, I decided, would be *Tiny Spearmint Sighs*—maybe I borrowed the word "tiny" from the title of Cocteau Twins' *Tiny Dynamine* EP. According to my journal (March 7), "Ben said the name *Tiny Spearmint Sighs* is 'quirky + sad' + that that's how I always am, or at least how I always title things."

Despite my calls for submissions, *Tiny Spearmint Sighs* became a monograph, with an infrared photo of me my friend Jamie had shot as I waved a sparkler in the dark outside his mother's condominium: a curved streak of light not unlike that on the cover of *Heaven or Las Vegas,* though with my dumb face half-visible behind it. In one short story, three friends light a bonfire in a field, at which they burn various formerly prized possessions with unwelcome memories attached to them (one character burns her journal: "Rereading it all made her even sadder than she remembered being then so she just shut the book without reading anything else"). In another—a knockoff of McCullers's "A Tree • A Rock • A Cloud" set in the bus terminal at Boston's South Station instead of an all-night diner—a young woman lights "Marlboro Reds one after the other, not really inhaling but blowing a lot of smoke around," and receives instructions from a man waiting there on how she might make her dreams come true. In another, a young couple sharing an apartment has a tense conversation "punctuated occasionally by crackles of static" from the stereo in the silence after *Talking Heads: 77* has finished playing: "Why wouldn't he just go back to his fucking soup?" one character wonders as they argue. An artless, talky poem features an astonishing lack of enjambment. The titles of these pieces—"Reddish," "Cup Your Hands to Catch the Rain," "Wash My Face," "How to Melt the Sky"—might have been Cocteau Twins song titles, which I'm sure I intended: all of my near-plagiarisms, I probably hoped, would ally my writing, and myself, with something or someone already acclaimed, noteworthy, valued.

I photocopied and hand-numbered one hundred copies of *Tiny Spearmint Sighs,* most of which I never bothered to staple or give away.

January 21–22, 1991

Like O'Connor's character Thomas in "The Comforts of Home," who fancies himself a scholar because "he's president of the local Historical Society this year," my self-important literary ambitions far outstripped my efforts—still another fact I did not yet realize. Maybe Cocteau Twins and the rest of the music 4AD released in the '80s encouraged such self-importance, because of how seriously it all seemed to take itself. Or maybe self-important people gravitated to such music because it confirmed our ideas of ourselves. Rereading my old journal now, I cannot answer such conjectures. Nor can I recognize much of myself in the young man who felt the need to chronicle so minutely his ever-changing moods, and who had such a misunderstanding of the word "surreal," and who apparently listened to the blown-apart cover version of Van Morrison's "Come Here My Love" recorded by This Mortal Coil before writing—un-self-consciously? entirely self-consciously? impossible, now, to tell—the following:

> 21 January 1991. 2:09 PM. It snowed again last night. The blankets were all over the place when I woke up. Last night I went with Joanna, Meredyth, and Francesca to Denny's where I also saw Jamie. Jen hadn't wanted to go. What a surprise. I keep almost-but-not-quite crying. My insides are churning. And now I'm listening to This Mortal Coil and all I can think of is Jennifer M.'s long-ago comment that she doesn't like this music because of fifteen-year-old death rockers from the suburbs who listen to it and feel depressed. ("This melancholy feeling just don't do no good.")
>
> 22 Jan—early hrs. After the last entry I spoke with Jen and then lay on the couch for several hours as it grew dark. Then I agonized over whether to call her again or just end everything with us or go out walking or what. Eventually I did call + ended up going out with her. We went to a 24-hour Dunkin' Donuts where one man was reading the *Boston Herald* + one nice but bored-looking woman was working. We got chocolate croissants

> and coffee and sat in the corner and talked about "us" (how cheesy). The radio was playing "Lovesongs after Dark" (and I quote) which included Fleetwood Mac, Julee Cruise, George Michael, Donna Summer, et. al. Jen did reassure me though and I feel much happier. It was such a cool scene too—truckers and creepy-looking men kept coming in for coffee and sandwiches, the woman at the counter was looking so bored reading, us sitting talking, sugar flakes on Jen's lip + us asking each other if we had chocolate on our teeth. It was so surreal; sometime I'll have to work it into a story. Jen hugged me goodbye. After I left I drove to the field of the by-now-legendary midnight picnic, listened to Cocteaus, "Kookaburra."

April 3, 1991

I suppose taking oneself seriously constitutes necessary training for becoming a writer—and certainly no one else would take my work seriously until I'd improved it. The reassurance I sought from Jen—that she still liked me, even if we could barely manage to endure each other's company?—was no different than the reassurance I sought in writing: I wanted to know that my thoughts, my ideas, my imagination weren't worthless. During those months, they felt about all I could claim—so even as I recalled my sadness, I contemplated its literary value; even after a relationship had ended, I wanted to believe I could control that ending.

Meanwhile, I finished every one of O'Connor's short stories

on the bus, then began *Light in August*. I listed writers' names in my journal, planning to read them, although twenty-some years later I still have read very little Yukio Mishima, Doris Lessing, and Thomas Mann. I bought *Lolita, Mrs. Dalloway,* and the *Collected Stories* of both Dylan Thomas and Carson McCullers at the bookstore with my employee discount. I first read "Wakefield" and "Bartleby, the Scrivener," and I can still hear my professor laughing while he read to us the sentence about Nippers putting blotting paper beneath the legs of his desk to level it. I wrote unintentional imitations of the writers I encountered in my classes—Faulkner, Delmore Schwartz, Conrad Aiken, Katherine Anne Porter, Ernest J. Gaines. But the imitations soon ceased to satisfy: I wanted my sentences and my stories to sound distinctive.

In my journal, I noted how "hurt" (January 15) and "excruciatingly depressed" (January 19) and "completely drained" (February 8) and "betrayed" (February 23) and "heartbroken" (March 4) I felt, even as I recorded my flirtations with another friend I'd soon start seeing. I also noted my transfer application to a small college in Vermont: in August, I'd show up there with way too many LPs, too big a stereo, and a box of books, and gain admission to the fiction workshop by submitting yet another story set in a twenty-four-hour diner: the beginning of writing seriously, and having my writing taken seriously.

On an early spring night, I drove my old Subaru to Boston and parked just off Comm Ave., a mile west of Kenmore Square. Cocteau Twins were playing at Boston University's Walter Brown Arena, and Ben had gotten us tickets. The B.U. hockey team's season had just ended with a triple-overtime loss in the national championship, and the arena was still refrigerator-cold, the ice covered with lumpy layers of heavy gym mats so we could walk on it. By the end of the show my feet felt frozen. As they'd done in November, Cocteau Twins shrouded themselves in chemical smoke and dazzled the crowd with colored lights to compensate for their boring performance: framed by tall racks of blinking electronic gear, they stood in place, swaying from foot to foot and cradling guitars and bass with serious, intense effort. Maybe they felt tired, or hungover—their tour ended here—but in any case I already had more interest in Galaxie 500. (Galaxie 500 broke up the next night.)

I no longer wrote in my journal—instead of documenting my complaints, I'd started writing a novella. On May 2, beginning with *Light in August,* I listed the books I'd been reading: *Their Eyes Were Watching God, The Ballad of the Sad Café, The Optimist's Daughter, Dubliners, The Prime of Miss Jean Brodie, The Book of Laughter and Forgetting*—a record I kept for several more years, filling many pages in tiny handwriting. The next entry (June 26) consists of another long list, headed "books to get," and then, after a few blank pages, I wrote down some further ideas for revising the novella (August 3), and the tracklists for a few mixtapes I gave to friends that summer. Cocteau Twins did not appear on any of these tapes: I still listened to their LPs, if not nearly as often as previously, until my interest in all the intense drama of 4AD's seriousness soon faded.

As I left the hockey arena that cool spring night amid a swarm of students, in what would have been, had I not taken a year off after high school, the end of my sophomore year of college, I could not have told you that the word sophistication derives from the Greek *sophos,* wisdom. Nor could I have told you that the Greek sophists were originally considered truth-seekers and lovers of wisdom, before that term acquired pejorative connotations. And though I could have told you that wisdom is often linked to age and experience, I remained the same awkward kid—neither worldly nor refined, though at least I'd been working on my cultural knowledge, in classes and outside of them, as my earnest lists demonstrate. Music and literature—the obscurer the better—might at least lend me the appearance of sophistication to those who didn't really know me yet, even if I still knew the truth. How much of sophistication is always an elaborate show of fog and light to disguise our vulnerable, sophomoric selves?

BIG STAR: "Big Black Car"
(*Third / Sister Lovers* CD, Rykodisc, 1992 [1978])
BLACK TAMBOURINE: "Black Car"
(c/w "By Tomorrow," "Pack You Up," "Drown" 7″, Slumberland Records, 1991)

Like many of us with a passion for our own corners of pop music, I'd guess, I often daydream sequences of songs to appear on imaginary mixtapes I never end up recording. It's an idle but enjoyable pursuit, not unlike that of bands that record film scores to movies that do not exist. One of my hypothetical cassettes would include a segue between Big Star's "Big Black Car" and Black Tambourine's "Black Car"—a tremendous stylistic collision, from reverbed strings and hushed singing to overloaded feedback buzz, from the echoes of some wide and desolate space to the crowded basement hiss of saturated tape. (Recent circumstances have also brought these two bands together; Big Star's Alex Chilton died on March 17, 2010, two weeks before the twentieth-anniversary reissue of Black Tambourine's recordings; in the press accounts of these occurrences, writers noted that both bands were initially overlooked, but hugely influential in their afterlives.) But maybe such transitions—and the opportunities they offer for displaying one's music-nerd cleverness, for reading a narrative in the stacks of one's records—suggest one reason I contemplate this sort of mix.

According to Jim Dickinson, who produced the album known variously as *3rd, The Third Album, Sister Lovers,* or *Beale St. Green* (Big Star's third and final album—recorded late in 1974, abandoned, released posthumously in 1978, and reissued under different titles and tracklists ever since), Big Star's singer and guitarist Alex Chilton "used a basketball for a snare drum" at one point during the recordings, and, for the album's high point, "Kangaroo," "recorded the vocal and the twelve-string guitar on the same track" (thus rendering them inseparable during mixing) to annoy Dickinson. Still, no matter how much Chilton sabotaged these recordings, no matter how rough and unfinished many listeners find these songs ("will seem completely beyond the pale to those who already find his regular stuff weird," wrote Robert Christgau in his review; "A shambling wreck of an album," claims Allmusic.com; "I can't listen to it," says a friend who loves Big Star's much cleaner first album), the songs maintain, to my ears, the multi-tracked sheen of studio production. (Have there ever been more pristine recordings of the strummed acoustic guitar than those that fill Big Star's three records, including this one? See "Give Me Another Chance," "What's Going Ahn," or, indeed, "Big Black Car" should you require proof.)

By comparison, the deliberately distorted, budget recordings of Black Tambourine, descended from punk's DIY ethos (and, according to band member Archie Moore, captured in "a home basement studio" on "a very modest set-up: 8-track reel-to-reel analog tape…, which we thought was a whole lot of tracks at the time"), shun such aural niceties in favor of conveying mood. In "Black Car," they reduce Phil Spector's wall of sound from tidal wave to tinny squalls, and I mean that in a good way.

Rick Clark, in his liner notes to the Rykodisc version of *Third/ Sister Lovers,* writes that Chilton—disgusted with his band's lack of commercial success despite its superb reputation among critics—"performs…as if he had nothing to lose." Freedom from failure was a foregone conclusion for Black Tambourine, four college-age kids who had little to gain, at least by the usual terms of musical success, from their performances—performances which, despite the meager circumstances of their recordings and the band's minimal output, have become revered in certain circles of independent music fans. (The two 7″ singles and handful of compilation tracks they released during, and just after, their brief 1989–1991 lifetime have now twice been reissued: first, in 1999 on a ten-track album titled *Complete Recordings,* and again—this time the world was ready—in 2010 on a sixteen-track album titled *Black Tambourine,* which adds four newly recorded songs and two early demos.) "If there's any justice, Black Tambourine will see their name inserted into revisionist histories of American independent rock," Chris Ott wrote for *Pitchfork* in his review of *Complete Recordings,* but the members of Black Tambourine didn't realize the influence their music would someday have: "I didn't have any [expectations] for Black Tambourine except to put out records and play as much as we could because being in a band with your friends and putting out records on your own label sounded like *nada* but fun," singer Pam

Berry recently told me. "I've always loved recording better than playing live because you can do things a few times till you get it right. But with Black Tambourine it wasn't so much about getting it right as being pleasantly surprised to get it at all."

▸

Early in my last year of college, only a few months after I'd sold my Subaru to a junk dealer for $125, I met a woman at a party in Cambridge, Massachusetts, who told me that her husband bought and fixed vintage VW Beetles, and then offered me one of his current projects—a black '70-something Beetle that he'd just restored—for some absurd sum: one or two hundred dollars. I felt certain that her husband would value the car more highly than she did, and that I'd be lucky ever to see her again, since she lived on Cape Cod and I in Vermont.

But for a few hours, under the fluster of vodka and party, I allowed myself to dream a dream in which I drove through the autumnal foothills of the Green Mountains in my unheated VW bug, the blackness of which was a large measure of its essential charm. (For years I coveted a Karmann Ghia, and an old Beetle seemed the next best thing.) I was humming up Route 9, its hairpin turn halfway up from Brattleboro not yet blasted away and straightened out, wipers clearing the windshield of a light rain, listening to—it was a specific dream—Moonshake's then-new song "Little Thing," though I'm tempted now to claim I was listening to Kraftwerk's "Autobahn"—is there a more perfect song for a 1970s German auto? (The Minimoog synthesizer that Kraftwerk played in this track was "known to cost as much as a Volkswagen at that time," claims the Wikipedia entry on this LP.) Somehow this black car made me infinitely, ineffably cooler than I liked to think I already was. In my mind, I could hear the distinctive lawnmower rattle that those VW engines made as they accelerated; I was, as Alex Chilton suggests in "Big Black Car," "going and I [didn't] know how far," but on my way to meet someone, if only some fantasy version of myself.

I never did see this woman again, never spoke to her husband; not long after, I lost touch even with the mutual friend who'd thrown the party. I have never owned a big black car, nor a small one.

▶

Many of the songs from Big Star's first two albums, *#1 Record* and *Radio City,* illustrate suburban teen experiences from a male perspective, particularly as these experiences involve cars. (And in nearly all of the ten songs that comprise Black Tambourine's oeuvre, Berry's lyrics describe teen experiences from a female perspective; her lyrics offer a counterpoint to the same melodramas Chilton rehearses, and project the same mixture of vulnerability and self-determination: "I was wrong to count on you" and "By tomorrow, if you don't leave her, I'm a ghost" and "You'll never change 'cause you don't know / don't want to hear your tales of woe" and "You can deny your jealousy / but that's just a lie that I'm not buying // Please don't cry / I'd like to die / Just turn around and say goodbye.")

"In the Street," from Big Star's first LP (a song made widely known by Cheap Trick's cover of it as the theme for *That '70s Show*), offers an imagistic narrative as simple and familiar as the song's repeating guitar line and basic drum patterns, and Chilton sings it in the strained, high-pitched voice of an adolescent:

> Hanging out
> down the street
> the same old thing
> we did last week
>
> Not a thing to do
> but talk to you
>
> Steal your car
> and bring it down
> pick me up
> we'll drive around
>
> Wish we had
> a joint so bad
>
> Past the streetlight
> out past midnight

The facts that the car needs to be stolen (from parents, presumably), and that this narrator finds it important to note the late hour, contradict the faux-worldliness of his other lines: there may be nowhere to go and nothing to do, but at least the car represents the fantasy of escape, the possibility of some slight rupture of the routine—even though the more likely scenario is, as Kristen Hersh put it in Throwing Muses' song "Saving Grace," "So we drive, and we've driven ten thousand miles in our hometown."

The sound of *Radio City* (recorded after founding member and songwriter Chris Bell quit the band late in 1972, after the commercial failure of *#1 Record;* Bell died in a 1978 car crash) essays a tough rock edge while outgrowing most of the first record's acoustic delicacy. Two back-to-back songs on side two chart an evolving relationship between a boy and his car, with a love interest playing a cameo role. "Back of a Car" offers a moment of anxious hesitation between a young couple—"Sitting in the back of a car / music so loud / can't tell a thing / thinking 'bout what to say / I can't find the lines." By the time we reach "Daisy Glaze," the love interest has gone, and the boy, bereft, turns to his car for solace: "I'm driving alone / sad about you / not going home / What's to do?" As both songs make more than obvious, the car is now less escape than meager refuge, the sole private space available.

"Big Black Car," however, has little to do with the teenage experience. Chilton sheds the strained highs and airy harmonies of the first two records in favor of a weary half-sung, half-spoken delivery in this Novocained narrative of anywhere-but-here, who-cares unease: "Nothing can hurt me / nothing can touch me," he claims, but his tone and delivery betray his wounds, and perhaps the only reason he doesn't hurt is that he can no longer feel much of anything. It is nearly impossible to imagine this voice as the same which sang "Won't you let me walk you home from school? /

Won't you let me meet you at the pool?" a mere three years earlier. The acoustic guitar rings and shimmers, as it does on the first two Big Star albums, but given the sparseness of this arrangement, each reverbed strum hangs in the air a moment before Chilton's voice breathes it away—before the tremoloed electric guitar slides in, or one of the slow drumbeats. Nothing about this song communicates speed, motion, transport:

> Why should I care?
> Driving's a gas
> It ain't gonna last
>
> Sunny day highway
> If it rains it's all the same
> I can't feel nothing
> I can't feel a thing
>
> I've got a big black car

It's tempting to see this song ("I'm going and I don't know how far / So, so long": an expression of distance, a careless goodbye) as a metaphor for Chilton's career trajectory, but I prefer to imagine it as a plaintive hymn to the insular moment. Chilton's drawn-out and over-enunciated sibilants and plosives seem touching, a failing attempt to recreate some of the energy or passion from the first two Big Star records, to prolong a passing time, to make himself understood.

▶

A year or two after my dream of owning a black car, I recorded (on an actual mixtape) Black Tambourine's "Black Car" for a girlfriend with whom I'd been living, and who was now on a summer internship in North Carolina. It was a time in my life of frequent changes-of-address, when I felt wistful over objects and events only six months old—never mind those a few years old, as this 7″ single was then—so, as I transferred the song to cassette, it seemed a bit of ancient history I'd recovered. The foldover sleeve—a messily crayon-colored line drawing of a bob-haired girl stomping in a puddle, rainhat in one hand, umbrella in the other—furthered the record's aura of nostalgia.

The songs are fuzzed-out, unpolished pastels-in-pop influenced by everything from doo-wop to '60s garage rock to the late '80s UK *C86* bands. "Black Car," a bittersweet three-chord lament, conveys some aspect of what I was feeling those months, its prettiness nearly—but, crucially, not quite—obliterated by pink-noised guitars and abrasive warbles of feedback. Pam Berry's vocals are untrained but sweet and melancholic ("a wavering, off-key batch of dodgy lyrics," in her own words), and reverbed even more heavily than Alex Chilton's. Archie Moore's "all-on-one-string" bassline climbs beside Berry's voice in the chorus and then subsides; a ticking ride cymbal floats above the din, but the drums (Moore: "just an overturned kick drum resting on cinder blocks, a snare, and an all-purpose cymbal") sound as though they're being pounded from within some deep cavern. The sonic palette differs from Big

Star's, but the mood is similar. The lyrics manage both to describe and embody the same teen awkwardness of the early Big Star records:

> Your black car and your front seat
> To touch your hair and feel your heat
> Try to get the courage up to tell you that I think you're
> neat
>
> I watch you
> But you don't see me
> I'll touch you
> But it's in my dreams

Until Berry recently corrected me, I'd always heard the first verse as "Your black car and your front seat / Do you touch your hair and think of me? / I try to think of her name / Try to tell you that I think of you." (While deciphering lyrics has never been among my skills, my mistranslation here is perhaps a testament to the density of Black Tambourine's feedback. When I asked for help with the lyrics, Berry responded, "It was probably for the good of the public that the lyrics were buried under all that ace guitar noise, so...don't have hopes for anything life-affirming once they're on paper!") My version, I think, suggests, rather than a crush, a complicated separation—which the distance between my girlfriend and me would, soon enough, become—though my mixtape-as-missive intended to convey only some of the song's yearning. The feedback that I heard as a welcome trespass on the song's plaintive melody, elevating it from pretty guitar-pop into something darker, more somber, more vital—in 1991, guitar feedback hadn't yet become entirely clichéd—my girlfriend heard as screechy and annoying, and it rendered the song unlistenable for her.

▸

Another version of the narrative we might trace:

The Rolling Stones: "Paint It Black," *Aftermath* (1966):

I see a line of cars and they're all painted black,
with flowers and my love both never to come back

Big Star: "Thirteen," *#1 Record* (1972):

Won't you tell your dad "Get off my back,"
tell him what we said 'bout "Paint It Black"?

Big Star: "Big Black Car," *Third/Sister Lovers* (1975):

Driving in my big black car,
nothing can go wrong.
I'm going and I don't know how far—
so, so long.

> Black Tambourine: "Black Car," "By Tomorrow" 7″ (1991):
>
> Your front seat of your black car,
> I'll take the wheel and drive us far
>
> Alexander Theroux, "Black," *Conjunctions: 30* (1998):
>
> In this sharp dichotomy along the lines of "us" versus "them," black is—legendarily, has always been—precisely that wickedness. If white is known, safe, open and visible, black[,] unknown, hostile, closed and opaque, is the masked and unmediated alternative.... It has an unholiness all about it, does black.... Black suggests grief, loss, melancholy, and chic.... Mystery doesn't so much surround the color black as it defines it.

Well before Mick Jagger sang about wanting to blot out the sun and paint everything black, rock music was the established province of the misunderstood outsider (or at least the insider who wanted to believe he or she was still an outsider), and both "Big Black Car" and "Black Car" are written from the perspectives of such outsiders—people whose feelings are somehow different (one who feels too little, one who feels too much), people whose tastes are different. But as the endlessly replicable digital file has become the primary format in which most of us listen to music, the computer or smartphone the primary means of playback, and vinyl increasingly an artifact rather than a consumable, it seems nearly impossible to differentiate oneself according to one's tastes or feelings about music. The newest, most minor band possesses at least hundreds of online friends and well-wishers; the earned expertise of the pop-culture scholar has been replaced by the hyperlink; the most obscure information is accessible, every digital track accompanied by metadata, and, online, everyone is invited to contribute ratings, opinions, and lyrics—often as laughably incorrect as my rendition of "Black Car." Black may be unknowable, mysterious, the "unmediated alternative," but our music is now mediated and knowable in ways unimaginable only a few years ago.

▶

"Driving's a gas," Chilton sings in "Big Black Car," and this poor pun has, perhaps—despite the song's near-concurrence with the 1973–1974 oil shock—never achieved the resonance it now possesses. In the past decade alone, American car preference has evolved from ever-bigger SUVs to the Toyota Prius; a Republican president with a century-long family history in the oil industry used the State of the Union address to warn that "America is addicted to oil"; the price of gasoline in the United States reached, in July 2008, four and a half dollars per gallon; that fall, crowds at political rallies chanted "Drill, baby, drill!" In 2010, we watched the slow-motion disaster of the British Petroleum Deepwater Horizon oil rig explosion, one of the worst environmental disasters in our history: oil-drenched pelicans on the coast of Louisiana, dead sea turtles and dolphins, "tar balls" and gobs of rust-colored oil, plumes of oil drifting through the waters of the Gulf of Mexico. Oil, as ever, shapes our habits, our politics, our beliefs, our shifting global climate, our country's decade-long war, our frail world economy.

The black car is not meant to be flashy, is not meant to draw attention to itself except in comparison to other, brighter colors: the black car is not a muscle car, a hot rod, or any other phallus-by-proxy, but rather the color of the hearse, and similarly attuned to memory, loss, nostalgia, an unrecoverable past. (It is thus unsurprising that both "Big Black Car" and "Black Car" depend so heavily on the device of reverb.) Still, whatever iconographies we might assign to the color black—and the passage I've quoted from Theroux's meditation more than implies the idea of racial otherness and appropriation that has been a profound tension in rock music since its beginnings—lately I can see in these songs and my memories of them only the blackness of oil: both the car and the vinyl record are products of the petrochemical age now passing from an extended era of decadence into its final agonies. Not so long ago it was utterly natural for me to purchase music stamped into the molten discs of dead dinosaur bones and to pump more of the same into the tank of my car so that I could drive endless loops around the city in which I grew up, mainly as an excuse to commune with the music I'd recorded from LPs onto cassettes for the car: such were the luxuries of my life, the limits of my teenage imagination, and the price and plenitude of oil, that I could happily waste the proceeds from my job on refined crude in several of its many guises. Nor did I have much sense that I was rehearsing the teen narratives that Chilton had sung about inheriting over a decade earlier.

I'm not certain how—or if—those narratives have been revised. With gasoline so expensive, and the LP, for most consumers, just another dinosaur to leave behind, what teen is going to drive in circles to listen to her iPod? What private spaces are left for teenagers now that they transcribe their melodramas on Facebook, revise them hourly on Twitter, and upload them to YouTube? And do they daydream themselves into black cars? Does a black car still connote danger, otherness, any of the atmosphere I ascribe to it? (Consider that, in 1975, Chilton's big black car would almost certainly have been an old car; a new car would have been compact, fuel-efficient, and painted safety orange.)

When, lonely for my girlfriend in North Carolina, I listened to the tape I was making for her (I'd record a few songs, then drive around town for an hour; record a few more the next night, and repeat—all mixtapes are, after all, constantly evolving daydreams), it never occurred to me to accumulate those miles driving south down I–95 rather than retracing endlessly the concentric grooves of Park Ave and Salisbury Street, Chandler Street and Mill Street; gasoline cost, that summer, probably under a dollar a gallon, and few of us worried about the size of our carbon footprints, but I am a Massachusetts boy, and any drive over an hour or two still seems unbearably long. "Black Car" was perhaps a song better suited to accompany a teenager mooning over an unattainable crush than a circumstantially and temporarily single college graduate, but at that moment North Carolina seemed a long way from New

England, and, in my nostalgic self-pity, I felt fourteen again. Quite often, I still do. It's taken years for me to feel old enough to fathom any of the exhaustion Alex Chilton voices in "Big Black Car," though I'm beginning to understand it better every day.

RUSH: "Fly by Night"
(*Fly by Night* LP, Mercury, 1975)

The plan required snow, a snow beginning overnight: snow heavy enough to help hide my escape, not so heavy that dispatchers would have sent plows out ahead of it. Those overnight hours would be all the time I'd have. From the cupboards, I'd steal peanut butter, Ritz crackers, a big jar of applesauce, a box of granola bars, packets of hot chocolate. I would already have stashed my other supplies—flannel shirts and wool socks, waterproof matches in a metal container from the brief weeks I was a boy scout, the *Boy Scout Handbook* itself, Swiss Army knife, flashlight, sleeping bag—in the mess of my bedroom closet. My father's fiberglass canoe didn't weigh much, and he'd shown me how to heft it from foot to hip to shoulder and portage it: but I wouldn't need to carry it, since, I assumed, its patched belly would glide through new snow, my provisions and its paddles weighting the back end as I pulled it by the length of clothesline tied to the bow. I was pretty sure I could cover the distance, dragging little more than an eighteen-foot sled, overnight: and, come morning, snowplows would have erased my tracks completely....

That summer my parents had taken my sisters and me to a small state park in the town next to ours: a pond spilled over a dam and downhill through a fieldstone channel to what had once been a gristmill. Now woods and overgrown fields surrounded the place, and, rambling among the azaleas and mountain laurel above the pond while my boring family lingered at the shore, I found granite ledges I was sure sheltered some small caves, though my mother called me back to the car before I could explore them. A runaway boy, I realized on the drive home, could paddle around the pond, catch fish, disguise a canoe (which quickly became "mine," not "my father's," in this fantasy) under sticks and leaves at nightfall, huddle in the cave in a sleeping bag—or light a fire at its mouth if there were no people around. I assumed someone would eventually see me, paddling the edges of the pond, or bathing in it, but, in a state park, who would find the presence of a boy with a canoe remarkable? Before long, some other family with a girl my age, as estranged from her family as I sometimes felt from mine, would arrive for a hike, and she would wander off from them. "Do you want to see my cave?" would be a pretty cool line.

And though the fury at my family—the desire to quit them and flee in the night—came often enough during those preadolescent years, I never did find the correct alignment of snowy night, rage, and gumption to put my plan into action. Nor did I ever quite forget it, no matter how ridiculous I knew it was.

▸

Along with so many kids in the late '70s and early '80s, I liked the band Rush and owned a handful of their records, though I saw them play live only once, on their *Grace Under Pressure* tour. I attended the show amid the unlikeliest cross-section of friends: a future varsity basketball player, a musician-turned-jock, a road bike freak, a future "best dressed" prep, a skate punk. My self-understanding that year evaded me so reliably I have no idea how my friends might have described me, or how I might have hoped they'd describe me, or even how I might have described myself.

"Rush pulled off a triumph," one review of that concert read, "...proving that lingering rumors and the band's worst fears were groundless: rumors that the Canadian trio was fragmenting after years of almost non-stop touring; fears that their fans...were beginning to drift." Still, the affections my friends and I may once have shared for earnest virtuosity, epic drum solos, "profound" lyrics, and a bass player who—as one elder kid once assured me—"played keyboards with his feet" were maybe the last forces keeping us together. We could no longer agree on long hair in back vs. long hair in front, *Saturday Night Live* vs. *Night Flight,* Nike vs. Converse, smoking vs. not smoking, but we all air-drummed Neil Peart's fills and solos in the privacy of our bedrooms when "Subdivisions" or "Limelight" came on the radio. Before long, we'd all moved on to mostly mutually exclusive cliques, and, as we each contended with how we'd "be cool or be cast out," even passing each other "in the high school halls" felt awkward.

Embarrassed I'd ever liked Rush, I hid the band's records amid my mother's old LPs in the living room cabinet. That October night I saw them, the band didn't play "Fly by Night," one of my boyhood favorites, which was just as well: "This feeling inside me says it's time I was gone.... / Enough with the reasons: I want to get away."

RACCOO-OO-OON: "Antler Mask"
(*Behold Secret Kingdom* LP, Not Not Fun, 2007)
FUCK: "Shotgun (H)ours"
(*Pretty...Slow* CD, Walt / Esther / Rhesus, 1996)

Jake asked to interview me on my "vinyl listening habits" for his media studies project: "I'm interested in your relationship with records," he wrote in an e-mail.

"Well, that's kind of personal..." I responded.

A skinny, spectacled undergrad, Jake had introduced himself to me a year earlier, after he'd read an essay I'd written about record collecting. He DJ'd a soul show on the college radio station, appreciated '70s-era Brian Eno at least as much as I did, and ran a noise-punk record label out of his attic apartment, where his burgeoning vinyl collection consumed most of the floor space. He wore a scruffy beard and always-mismatched socks. Our conversation about records rapidly became an excuse for him to spin a bunch of the LPs scattered all over.

Jake was eager to play me stuff I'd never heard, including a record called *Mythos Folkways, Vol. III* by a band with the exceptionally stupid name Raccoo-oo-oon: I recall it as a bunch of improvised stoner drone skronk. That said, Jake's excitement about the record must have influenced my judgment (or maybe I felt the first anxiety that my students were starting to know more about obscure vinyl than I did): the next day I ordered one of Raccoo-oo-oon's LPs. In grad school, a friend had complained that coming to my own attic apartment invariably involved listening to tuneless, beatless music that sounded like broken vacuum cleaners—and he was probably right—so improvised stoner drone skronk was a genre with which I had some familiarity.

Before the Raccoo-oo-oon LP had even arrived in the mail, Jake e-mailed me a link to a blog post about the band written by Tom Lax, sole proprietor of Siltbreeze Records, a label that's always "specialized in putting out music you either got or you didn't; music you absolutely adored or really fucking hated," per Philadelphia's *City Paper.* "I dunno about you," Lax wrote on his blog, "but I never cottoned to this band on account of the name.... My loss? Perhaps, but that's the chance I took.... It's easier to be a judgmental asshoo-ooo-ole. Feel better? Me too-oo-ooo!"

I've always shared Lax's bias against bands with dumb names—by which I mean names that don't jive with my aesthetic, itself of course finely tuned: I'm surprised I even bought the Raccoo-oo-oon record. I find it difficult to get over this prejudice, I told Jake, maybe because I remember being fourteen and facing the question, "What's that you're listening to?"—whether from parent or peer—and looking away while muttering, "Echo and the Bunnymen" or "The Psychedelic Furs."

"Try telling your mom that your record label is called Lovepump," Jake replied, "and that it features bands like AIDS Wolf, the USA Is a Monster, and Child Abuse."

▶

Ye Olde Buttfuck, Anal Cunt, Butt Trumpet, Prick Decay—even writing these names in the privacy of my home, accompanied by no one except the dog, nearly makes me blush: I'm embarrassed for the immature dorks who thought these names would scandalize anyone except their own grandmothers. If the aim of a punk or noise band is to wreck me—and, by extension, culture, social life, decent churchgoing folk, etc.—through testing the limits of unlistenability and whatever else will shock my sensibilities, well, I'm sorry, but bands called Dying Fetus or Assück or Slicing Grandpa are going to have to try harder, at least name-wise. When so many actual atrocities go underreported and unnoticed, and when so much outrage seems manufactured for political ends, music—like profanity—retains only a much-diminished capacity to shock us. My pubescent jaw may have dropped the first time I heard Deborah Iyall sing "I might like you better if we slept together" in Romeo Void's "Never Say Never," or Gordon Gano wonder "Why can't I get just one fuck?" in the Violent Femmes' "Add It Up," but what teenager has ever been able to identify indecency?

Still, pretentious names trying to slip the tropes of pop music nomenclature often seem far less decent than the trying-to-offend: I similarly blush, or have blushed, for Oneohtrix Point Never, Toad the Wet Sprocket, Fear Falls Burning, and Gene Loves Jezebel.

In the mid and late '80s, Strange Fruit Records began releasing on vinyl some of the studio performances bands had recorded for broadcast on John Peel's famed Radio One show. The sleeves of these records were all exactly the same: a monochrome border, the name of the band across the top, and, in tiny type covering the rest of the sleeve, a roster of bands that Peel had invited into his studio. This list offered me, pre-Internet, another way I might locate interesting music, and I scrutinized these names. So many seemed like goofs: Strawberry Switchblade, Half Man Half Biscuit, We've Got a Fuzzbox and We're Gonna Use It, Yip Yip Coyote, So You Think You're a Cowboy, Dawn Chorus and the Blue Tits, Trixie's Big Red Motorbike, Little Red Duffle Coats. That these names were interspersed among those more readily recognizable—AC/DC, Yes, Duane Eddy, Leonard Cohen, David Bowie, Pink Floyd, Donovan, Elvis Costello and the Attractions, Fairport Convention, Fleetwood Mac—evidenced not only Peel's longevity and catholic tastes, but also the fact that all these bands, regardless of vast differences in sounds or sales or notoriety, still shared some essential condition: I was stupid to think otherwise. These *Peel Sessions* sleeves furthered my education in the arcane—and formed part of a legitimizing process for me, before I realized that the music I listened to needed no legitimization other than my own.

▸

Circa 1993—not long after commercial radio and MTV re-christened the Butthole Surfers the B.H. Surfers to play their songs or videos—naming your band Fuck might have seemed like a good idea: the name suggested a who-cares attitude, a willed obscurity, a mild confrontation, a refusal to entertain anyone else's values. The name might be understood as noun or verb, obscene or tedious, exclamation or muttered disappointment. It must have been clear to the members of Fuck that few megastores would stock their records, that few mainstream publications would print the band's name without some sanitization. And, because Fuck's music was often gentle and pretty (at least by '90s indie-rock standards: even when their acoustic guitars build to some song's obligatory noisy part, the music's still restrained), the crude name offered listeners a cognitive dissonance the band must have found amusing.

Fuck's Timothy Prudhomme told *Exclaim!* magazine—for a feature on bands whose names include the F-word—that the band

> figured that anyone who had a problem with the name would not be the kind of music fan, club, or label we were hoping to catch.... Our songs are a bit too esoteric for most majors... On our first US tours, more clubs booked us because of our name. They knew what we knew—curiosity seekers would come out to see what kind of band would call themselves "Fuck."

Google did not yet exist when Fuck began playing; not until the cusp of the millennium would Google eclipse all other early search engines—remember Infoseek, Altavista, Lycos?—and eventually become our brains' primary reference and instruction manual. Fuck released their last record in 2003, a year before Google's long-anticipated initial public offer, and then seem to have quietly faded away: it's now difficult to imagine a single less Googleable word, a word that will produce more irrelevant hits, than the band's name. Entering the term "Fuck" into Google—"SafeSearch" off, of course—produced 2.1 billion results for me this morning, none of which I wanted to click. Atop the second page of results, I found the catalog for the "Supermegacorporation" website, which "began as a way of handling mail-order for the band Fuck," and the fourth page offered me Wikipedia's "Fuck (band)" entry, but I can't imagine that the band's name has helped many people remember or discover them—except in lists such as *Exclaim!*'s, or a similar one the *Guardian* ran a year later.

That's too bad, because Fuck wrote some interesting songs, most of them filled with defeat, more than occasional self-loathing, and lonesome, empty spaces between a shaky-voiced, literate singer and a minimalist ensemble. (The band originally met while spending the weekend in an Oakland holding cell after a rambunctious house party ended in a police roundup.) The half-whispered lyrics to "Shotgun (H)ours" may describe the aftermath of a shotgun wedding's unwanted pregnancy, or may describe the moments before suicide-by-shotgun, or both—or they may be simply a series of evocative phrases stitched together in slippery, noncommittal style. But the song's also nearly a campfire sing-a-long, with strummed acoustic guitars and a mournful lead and, by the ending, a bunch of vocal harmonies.

Fuck seemed, technologically, a band of its era: the dying era of photocopied fanzines, payphones, records purchased from print catalogs with money orders sent via US mail. During a 1996 interview with *Cool Beans!* magazine, the interviewer told the band that he'd "listened to [their new album] on the Internet.... it's this web thing called Sonicnet." The band's responses ranged from "Really? What?" to "The whole thing? See, I just thought it was going to be one track, or a sample of a song."

"You should see the looks on your faces right now," the interviewer continued. "You're all freaked out that people could get copies of your new album for free, right?"

I too am a product of that moment when material culture lost out to digital culture, and—perhaps freaked out that I can get copies of new albums for free—I still judge bands' names far too severely, at a time when these names might bear less burden of signification than they once did. Before I could stream songs on Bandcamp or listen to a band's own YouTube channel, a name suggested a band's sound as much as anything else. Standing in a record store, holding several shrinkwrapped LPs, how was I to know what Algebra Suicide or Pylon or Cabaret Voltaire sounded like, beyond what their names and their records' cover art evoked? What differences might exist between the June Brides and Death in June? Death in June and Dead Can Dance? Dead Can Dance and Dislocation Dance? There was only one way to be certain, so I'd head for the cash register.

Alas, the curiosity seeker who'd like to hear Fuck now will have to make do with the song samples—one or two per album, as the band expected in 1996—that the band continues to maintain online at their "Fuck World Headquarters." I doubted whether a website more than fifteen years old still existed, and when I typed www.sonicnet.com into my browser window, I landed on the home page of VH1, which presumably purchased Sonicnet many years ago. Still, like an eleven-year-old boy, I entered the word "Fuck" into the VH1 website's search function, and returned 601 results, the forty-fifth of which was a link to the first of Fuck's two 1996 albums: "Listen to *Pretty ... Slow* by F*ck for free at VH1.com. Check out more albums by F*ck," the link prompted me. But once I clicked through to the record, there were no links beneath the "Audio," "Video," and "Lyrics" headers: even where we might search the band out, it eludes us. Fuck released records (and a number of compilation tracks) on a grab-bag of independent labels, including their own, over the years—each label no more than a temporary home. The humility of the band's enterprise—and the confrontational name that obscured that humility—seems best marked not by the Internet's effortlessness, but by the labor-intensive facts of their two 1996 albums: one packaged in a matchbook-style sleeve, the other in a tiny white box stuffed with candy and trinkets, its artwork pasted on by hand. Dead links and 404 errors are a bleak way for things to disappear: better to leave the traces of a former presence in physical remains than in the invisible impulses of electrons.

WAVVES: "Weed Demon"
(c/w "Beach Demon" 7″, Tic Tac Totally, 2008)

On Thursday, December 11, 2008, as the *New York Times* reported, the "legendary" and "consummate trader, Bernard L. Madoff, was arrested at his Manhattan home by federal agents who accused him of running a multibillion-dollar fraud scheme—perhaps the largest in Wall Street's history." Within days, of course, everyone in the country knew the name of "New York's most hated man" (as a *Times* blogger soon referred to him), Bernie Madoff, and at least some of the details of the elaborate Ponzi scheme his firm had operated for decades.

Five days later, on the Terminal Boredom web forums—which have for years offered a smart and rowdy clearinghouse for record reviews, want lists, for-sale ads, and what-are-you-listening-to-now threads about music that fits both narrow and generous understandings of the term "punk"—a poster with the handle

WOLFGUTSSS offered a pre-order sale for an upcoming 7″ record, titled "In Here," by a then-still-somewhat-mysterious band called Blank Dogs, in the caps-locked typography of the online-inept and the conciseness of the initiated-only:

> TWO GREAT BD SONGS. 700 COPIES. 100YELLOW (PRE-ORDER ONLY), 200 CLEAR BLUE AND 400 ON BLACK. ORDERING INFO ONTHE PAGE.

WOLFGUTSSS included a link to the spare website of his brand-new label, Down in the Ground. "ALSO PUT UP A SECTION FOR USED/SECOND HAND STUFF," he noted. His post was time-stamped 9:15:27 A.M., December 16, 2008.

Within twenty minutes, another poster had already replied: "money sent. psyched, etc." Blank Dogs had, in 2007 and 2008, released a series of well-received and highly collectible singles on various micro-labels while remaining anonymous—though Blank Dogs was soon revealed as the solo project of a guy named Mike who worked at Brooklyn's Academy Records and previously played bass in the band D.C. Snipers—so such a reaction was foreseeable. Three minutes after that, WOLFGUTSSS followed with a warning to anyone else reading the thread: "Fuck[,] these are already going fast." By midday, a number of other posters who had "Paypal'd" funds for the record wondered if they had paid their seven dollars too late to have acquired one of the hundred copies of the record pressed on yellow vinyl. Just after 1:00 P.M., on the second page of the thread, WOLFGUTSSS reassured these anxious posters: "First 100 are yellow, second 200 are blue, the rest (400) are black, so if you want to view it from an eBay standpoint, the first 300 are eBay gold haha. Or you could keep it and listen to it."

There followed some complaints over the price of the record, and rebuttals to those complaining—"$7 is pricey it's true / however; I don't know if you guys have noticed but the economy is, in a word, fucked / ...it just means I take less [*sic*] gambles on records for now" one poster noted; another suggested that the complainers weren't "considering the PayPal fees [WOLFGUTSSS's] gotta pay too." WOLFGUTSSS himself responded with this explanation of his economics:

> I'm not cutting any costs with these releases and each record is coming out to about a buck or so less than the wholesale price I'm charging for it. Every dollar I get goes into the next record being released, period. If I was pressing 1000+ of each record it'd be much easier for me to charge a lot less and still get records out but I'm kind of stuck doing it this way or else it'd be a failing endeavor.

Only hours after the initial post, the point was clear, even from the person releasing the record presumably for the love of the music: this record was a commodity, understood in its particulars entirely in the language of the market. A few pages into the thread, only two posters had casually noted that they liked the music on this record; no one had even bothered to describe it.

▶

In the mid-2000s, around the same time the housing bubble peaked, many retail record stores went out of business. The last Tower Records stores—some of them large enough to occupy former grocery stores, or, like the one I frequented in Boston as a teenager, several floors of a Frank Gehry office building—closed days before Christmas in 2006, but countless smaller, independent shops had already shut their doors. It's a commonplace to blame such closures on file-sharing and other changes in listening habits, or preferences for digital rather than physical media, and no one needs me to rehearse the ways the Internet has forever changed commerce. (As my friend Hua has noted, in his eulogy for Manhattan's Fat Beats, "a good record store can be a theater of dreams, but I've never expected anyone beyond this community of finicky consumers to understand this, or care about all the record stores hanging on for dear life. Their ranks are dwindling, and, given the free movement of MP3s across the Internet, there's really no reason this shouldn't be the case.")

Still, it is perhaps worth considering some ways that the Internet has affected (and enabled) the movement of collectible media. If inventories are now largely online, if prices paid at auction are indexed and searchable, if everyone has far greater access not only to price and stock information but also to the same desire-manufacturing blogs and online fanzines, then knowledge of what is or isn't valuable—always highly volatile where musical tastes and fashions are concerned—becomes democratized: geography, age, and lack of expertise are no longer handicaps. Seeing records "from an eBay standpoint" becomes habitual. The Securities and Exchange Commission's description of day trading—"Day traders sit in front of computer screens and look for a stock that is either moving up or down in value. They want to ride the momentum of the stock and get out of the stock before it changes course. They do not know for certain how the stock will move..."—also applies pretty well to contemporary record collecting, where one needs to check in regularly, if not obsessively, with trusted forums or blogs to keep up with even a portion of what's being released.

Most vinyl sellers moved their auctions from Usenet newsgroups like rec.music.marketplace.vinyl to eBay around 1997 or 1998, and with eBay's explosive growth and corresponding exposure, the competition for truly rare and/or desirable records increased wildly, as did prices; common records lost value; perceptions of supply and demand fueled turbulent market fluctuations and swift corrections (a supposedly rare record that sold for a high price on eBay was inevitably followed by a flood of additional copies for sale—all with opening bids near the first record's final price). Crate-digging no longer required rising at 4:00 A.M. to hit garage sales and thrift stores, but only some good bid-sniper software, or the willingness to click through thirty-six pages of Google results. There exists a finite number of every record, but it began to seem possible to find absolutely anything online, given a little time and an understanding that one would likely pay a premium.

Independent hobbyist labels—often run out of someone's bedroom (or parents' house), as opposed to the few independent record labels with paid staffs—tend to press vinyl in small quantities for reasons of both capital and demand, especially since so many of the bands on such labels are new and unknown. So the pre-order—an inversion of Wimpy's "I'll gladly pay you Tuesday for a hamburger today"—allows the young entrepreneur to fund the manufacture of five hundred 7″s, and by issuing different quantities of the record on different-colored vinyl, or housing some of them in different sleeves—and, crucially, publicizing such quantities—he or she can help ensure their desirability.

Our Band Could Be Your Life, Michael Azerrad's engaging history of 1980s American independent music, details the lessons famed Seattle indie label Sub Pop Records learned about producing and marketing their singles:

> Limiting supply...would increase demand; that and their customized inner labels, colored vinyl, and bold artwork would automatically make Sub Pop releases collectible fetish objects. Lo and behold, the pressings sold out and then shops would put the records on display for exorbitant prices.... When the first pressing of [a record] sold out almost immediately, Sub Pop did a reissue..., getting around the limited edition tag by using a different shade of vinyl, also ensuring that a certain percentage of collectors would buy the single again just for the new color. The scam would be copied by countless other indie labels in the years to come.

Shortly thereafter, Azerrad notes,

> Sub Pop...started to get letters complaining that their limited-edition singles (a) were hard to find and (b) sold

> out too quickly. "We put the two conditions together," says [Sub Pop partner Jonathan] Poneman, "and realized we had a great marketing tool." The Sub Pop Singles Club was born. For $35 a year, subscribers got a single a month—a pretty good deal, but the brilliant part was that Singles Club subscribers paid before they got their records, which gave the label a significant financial boost. "On a limited budget, if you have the desire to sell a lot of records," [Sub Pop founder Bruce] Pavitt says, "you have to figure out ways to scam and manipulate the public."

For the collector, especially one who buys several copies in order to later flip some of them, the vinyl pre-order offers a futures market. The entire fragile enterprise is maintained by various levels of speculation and trust. No record pressed in minuscule quantities is designed for sale in a shop, anyway: given the low number of units, the label won't be able to sell it wholesale much more cheaply than retail, and distributors have little incentive to carry a record that will go out of stock instantly. You'll find these records in a few shops—in Brooklyn, Providence, Chicago, Los Angeles—but otherwise you can only acquire them online.

To "sleep" on a record—that is, to fail to "PayPal" it immediately, the minute someone announces its availability—is to potentially risk paying twenty, thirty, forty dollars or more for a record that last month—last week—was offered at five or six bucks postpaid. And of course everyone who *did* buy it then will proudly describe that record's face-melting qualities on blogs and online message boards—if for no reason other than to protect their own investments—so that as you search for a record and find these various descriptions, its apparent desirability only increases. Demand for some records—the recent reissue of Dolly Mixture's *Demonstration Tapes* LP in an edition of 300, for example—can be so high that the records sell out within a day of the initial public offer, even when, as is often now the case, labels and distributors limit purchases to a single copy to prevent speculators from buying in bulk. In the era of Internet commerce, when everyone knows of the existence of pretty much everything, artificial limits on quantity are the only way to ensure a product's exclusivity and desirability: the fear of missing out becomes the engine powering the market. One can't deliberate about such purchases, or one will quickly find oneself unable to make them: the clickable PayPal button will disappear, replaced by the words "SOLD OUT."

If nothing else, the Internet has made us all expert consumers. Jean-François Lyotard predicted as much, in 1979's *The Postmodern Condition: A Report on Knowledge:* "The miniaturization and commercialization of machines is already changing the way learning is acquired, classified, made available, and exploited," Lyotard wrote then; his report concludes with the observation that "the computerization of society…could become the 'dream' instrument for controlling and regulating the market system." When I first learned of the iPhone, my immediate thought about how I might use it involved Googling LPs while I was standing in the record store—and trying to establish a market value of the pieces of vinyl I could potentially buy more cheaply on the spot. Like all traders, I imagined how the machine could offer me an edge. Of course, some of the most popular smartphone apps enable exactly such price comparisons via barcode scanning.

The Internet's effect on trading in markets where real money is at stake has been even more profound: the subprime crisis, short-selling, credit-default swaps, and especially the so-called "Flash Crash" of May 6, 2010, in which the Dow Jones plummeted nine hundred points and then recovered most of these losses within a matter of minutes—as a result of computerized high-frequency trading and flash orders, executed in microseconds—all offer evidence of such market manipulation. Or, as the *New York Times* quoted Joseph M. Mecane of NYSE Euronext, "which operates the New York Stock Exchange," trading has "become a technological arms race, and what separates winners and losers is how fast they can move.... Markets need liquidity, and high-frequency traders provide opportunities for other investors to buy and sell."

Still, to pre-order a bunch of 7″s based on pre-release hype or expected demand is to build a record collection filled with assets as troubled as those on Lehman Brothers' balance sheets in 2008. For every five-dollar record that turns into a forty-dollar record, there are scores—hundreds—of five-dollar records that turn into one-dollar records, as a quick look through the floor-level bins in most of those now-long-gone record stores would have shown.

▸

The first record by Wavves—originally the one-man-band home recordings of Nathan Williams, a twenty-something from San Diego—was the sort of 7″ that sold out on pre-orders within two days in November 2008. Almost immediately, those who missed out questioned the decision by label Tic Tac Totally to release the record in a "one-time limited pressing of only 300 copies gloriously packaged with '80s cool-kid nostalgia via spray-painted fucking grip-tape sleeve and shamelessly self-promoted regular printed sleeve" when descriptions of this unheard band's sound—"Beach Boys-meet-Siltbreeze," per the label—gave record nerds the shakes. But within weeks, posters on Terminal Boredom were simultaneously mocking the already overwhelming hype about Wavves and whining that their pre-ordered records hadn't yet arrived—to which Matt, the owner of Tic Tac Totally, joked that he was "ripping everyone off. There is no Wavves 7″. Never was one." Since a nonexistent record by an unknown band could inspire such lust, another poster instantly responded: "Quit stealing my 'making up fake records to make money' idea."

Wavves has always seemed more than a little absurd: the goofy name, lyrics such as "I'm getting high / to pass the time / no reason why...," the either deeply cynical or obliviously naïve pastiche of failsafe Hipster 101 musical reference points and retro-slacker vibe, Williams's statement in an interview that his passion, "if it can't be masturbating or smoking weed[,]... is playing video games." And this debut record—two songs, titled "Beach Demon" and "Weed Demon," in a sleeve sheathed in skateboard grip tape—invoked the clichés of Southern California so unambiguously it had to be a joke (right?—but the songs often seemed earnest in their delivery). The beach, surf, weed, skateboarding, boredom, sunshine: Jeff Spicoli seemed to have arrived intact from 1982, surveyed the scene, and decided to cut a record that suited 2008 the same way Van Halen had suited his era.

"Beach Demon" is a simple rocker: quickly strummed, distorted guitar chords and semi-shouted vocals with drum-machine beats, the whole thing level-maxed for an overblown-speakers effect. It sounds like countless other independent records released since 2007. "Weed Demon" is a simple ballad: slowly strummed and sloppily fretted guitar chords with sweeter, multi-tracked vocals that rise to a falsetto in the chorus. Neither song provides anything particularly special, but for whatever reason—the wistful chord progression; the fact that I've always liked B-sides—I thought "Weed Demon" sounded pretty good. I didn't know then that it would reappear on Wavves's second LP, so I wanted to track down the 7″ to have the song—and thought I'd also try to pick up an extra copy.

Through strategic acumen, good timing, connections, a bit of luck, and an understanding of how to exploit the inefficiencies of the independent record market—valuable skills that evade me entirely in the more important financial dealings of my life, such as jobs and mortgages and refinances and mutual funds—I acquired, at the regular retail price of $5.50, three copies of the "Beach Demon" single at the height of its value, in January 2009. Had I listed the duplicates on eBay upon receiving them, I might have sold them for something like $90–$100—as several copies did fetch in that initial period: a nice 1,700 percent profit, which one imagines even Bernie Madoff would have admired. Instead, I gave one copy to Hua, and let the other two sit on the floor next to my stereo as the demand—apparently, everyone who'd ordered a copy quickly flipped it, or else the listening public had realized that Wavves' music was not nearly as extraordinary as his sense of the musical Zeitgeist—approached equilibrium with supply. Copies were trading at $40 a week or two later, at $30 a few months later, and have now settled around $20.

▶

In late January 2009, a few posters revived the Blank Dogs preorder thread: "I forgot all about this record…good thing these threads exist or I'd never know where my money's mysteriously disappearing to via PayPal." Several others chimed in, wondering whether the records had been shipped yet. WOLFGUTSSS reassured everyone with the explanation that the "Blank Dogs vinyl is being picked up at the plant on Friday." A week later, he claimed that "the Blank Dogs vinyl was supposed to be done Friday but they called and said Tuesday or Thursday." Days later, he posted a photo of another record he was releasing—a split 7″ with songs by three bands, including his own—on his label atop a pile of sealed cardboard mailers, and then he added that the "first 100 Blank Dogs records (yellow wax) go out on Monday. Thanks again!" All seemed well; the posters variously urging patience, quoting Media Mail transit times, or defending WOLFGUTSSS seemed vindicated.

But those contributing to the thread grew restless. "One Blank Dogs 7″ sold on eBay = about 10 pop records I'll actually listen to more than once," one poster noted: "There's a lot of money to be made in garbage." Another wondered if he could "make more money flipping burgers or flipping records." Others griped that they had paid individual shipping rates for three of WOLFGUTSSS's records, but that he would ship them in a single package and collect the profit. Still others noted that because more than forty-five days had passed since the initial transactions, PayPal would no longer allow them to file claims for missing records. And when WOLFGUTSSS admitted that the "dude who cuts my lacquers fucked up and had 880 copies pressed instead of 700[,] so the first 100 on yellow have an alternate sleeve," there was mock outrage about records that weren't as limited as advertised (and paid for: "25% more records = 25% less speculative value!!! You should PayPal us a 25% discount!!!").

A number of posters—all of them suspiciously new to the forum—also began offering innuendoes about WOLFGUTSSS:

> A little bird told me that the shit-stain that does Down in the Ground is a few days from getting knifed due to eBaying a copy of the 3-way split before giving [copies] to the other 2 bands. And then lying about it. Over and over.

> Is this the same douche who ran away from Portland? Do things ever change? ... To anyone who doesn't know well enough not to deal with [him], be cautious.

> I believe in second chances but this kid is a permanent fuck-up. He's an internet troll parading around collecting hyped bands for his label and people are foolish

> enough to fall for it, to no fault of their own, but hopefully time will prove all the wiser. You know he's read all these threads where people are asking the status of their orders but doesn't reply.
>
> This is the biggest scam since Watergate.

WOLFGUTSSS responded to his critics with a simple rejoinder: "All I do is package and send out records every day." He then posted a photograph of three copies of the Blank Dogs 7″—with yellow, blue, and black vinyl records peeping from the sleeves—and offered refunds to anyone who wanted one. "No one has been ripped off," he wrote on March 2, 2009.

Ten days later, in a Manhattan courtroom, Bernard Madoff declared his mind clear and, in response to the eleven charges he faced, pleaded guilty. "I operated a Ponzi scheme through the investment advisory side of my business," he told Judge Denny Chin. "When I began the Ponzi scheme I believed it would end shortly and I would be able to extricate myself and my clients from the scheme. However, this proved difficult, and ultimately impossible, and as the years went by I realized that my arrest and this day would inevitably come." Among several victims of Madoff's scheme who spoke, Ronnie Sue Ambrosino asked Judge Chin to reject Madoff's plea in order to "find out information as to where the money is."

I hadn't placed a pre-order for the Blank Dogs record, but found the escalating drama (and comedy) over its production as gripping as the various recessionary dramas unfolding in the national media. Like everyone who's ever mail-ordered vinyl, I've had two or three records go missing over the last twenty years, and I've signed up for a few twelve-month subscriptions that took well over twenty-four months to fulfill, but have generally found my trust in the system, such as it is, well-placed. I doubt that Internet anonymity has made record-for-sale scams much easier than ones perpetrated via mail, but I can easily imagine the potential for abuse when a would-be impresario types a brief description of a record in an online forum and suddenly finds a few thousand dollars in his PayPal account. ("When it took me over a year to get the [Last Sons of Krypton] LP done after pre-orders it was due to a combination of laziness and lack of funds to pay for postage. Sure everyone paid for postage, but I spent all that $$$ right away, and postage is expensive!" someone admitted on Terminal Boredom, by way of potentially explaining WOLFGUTSSS's behavior.)

Michael Azerrad's *Our Band Could Be Your Life* also reports that Washington, D.C. punk band the Teen Idles had, "in their one-year existence,...amassed $900, all of which went into a band kitty kept in a cigar box. When the band dissolved, they had to decide whether to split the money four ways or press up the recordings they'd done.... The choice was obvious." But in the easy-credit era, there may not be cigar boxes filled with cash funding the indie records, so the pre-order, like crowd-sourcing and micro-lending, allows instant access with minimal personal investment, just as subprime mortgages allowed many borrowers without good credit or sufficient income to overspend on houses, or leverage one property to acquire others they could refurbish and flip at a profit. But this notion of something-for-nothing runs counter to the fundamental ethos of punk and independent music, which has always been summed up by the acronym DIY—do it yourself—even after all the home-improvement reality TV shows spawned by the housing bubble appropriated that term. The 7″ pre-order speculators were—like those who put down 3 percent on a $450,000 house financed with an adjustable-rate mortgage—gambling that the 7″ would be worth something after the sale; they were also gambling that it would exist at all.

▶

The first year I owned a home, I bought very few records. A mortgage payment—never mind a new hot water heater—felt as daunting as the hours I spent cosigning documents to acquire it suggested, as did the total figure to which thirty years of those monthly payments would amount.

Sarah and I began house-hunting—though we wouldn't have called it that—in the winter of 2001–2002. We'd recently moved to coastal Rhode Island, and hoped to make that move permanent. Decided amateurs and academic itinerants, we weren't yet paying close attention to market trends or the post-9/11 housing boom, though we quickly became experts. Still, our motivations were old-fashioned: we wanted a house as a home, and for the feelings of permanence and stability we fantasized it would offer us, not as an exercise in speculation. George W. Bush had yet to deliver his October 2002 speech in which he stated: "You see, we want everybody in America to own their own home. That's what we want. This is—an ownership society is a compassionate society."

Houses in one nearby town jumped something like \$100,000 in asking price one year while we dithered. Interest rates were low, our credit scores were high, and lenders preapproved us for preposterous sums, but we never found a place that we desired and felt we could afford; like many buyers, we had little cash to put down, but, risk-averse, we also couldn't stomach the gamble of an adjustable-rate mortgage. We made an offer on a Sears house with cathedral ceilings, a fireplace, and too many rooms, though the deal fell apart when our home inspector discovered an actively leaking roof and asbestos-wrapped ductwork. By 2004 we gave up our rented beach house and relocated again, this time to a dingy apartment in Poughkeepsie, New York: in that town, for parts of three years, we looked at overpriced and poorly maintained bungalows desecrated by aluminum siding, dropped ceilings, wall-to-wall shag, and fake wood paneling, and we despaired. Walking the dog a day after we'd decided to stop looking, we found the house we eventually bought.

And soon I began buying records again: we were able to pay extra on each month's mortgage payment and still have enough money to replace the broken dishwasher, install a bluestone patio, and even, doing much of the work ourselves, gut the bathroom to studs and joists and renovate it—and to buy records, too. I rewired two-prong electrical outlets (stereo components need to be grounded properly). We knew we'd bought at the peak of the market, but reasoned that we'd be in our house for some years—long enough for the market to recover, we thought.

"It's a good thing our jobs are secure," I said to Sarah, standing in the kitchen of our house some night in the fall of 2008.

By the fall of 2009, we'd listed our house for sale: when an institution loses several hundred million dollars from its endowment, we learned, no jobs are secure, and all promises are revocable. A few months later, we'd moved. In April 2010, we closed on the sale of our house, writing a check for about $100 to make sure the mortgage we'd paid down early was now fully paid off.

My market timing has always been terrible. Though I'm skilled at buying records low, rarely do I profit from my shrewdness. I've bought and then held various records that I had no real interest in keeping, or that I even possessed duplicates of (duplicates often purchased for the express purpose of reselling), so long that they lost whatever demand or collectiblility they once had. The vinyl market is far more fickle, and far more prone to irrational exuberance and profound crashes, than even the housing markets of Las Vegas or Phoenix—people need houses to live in, but very few feel they need obscure 7″s. (I will leave unanswered questions concerning why someone with a mortgage and the means to pay it purchased punk 7″s, and which particular failures of maturation these purchases might indicate.) Rare 7″s, if the songs are good, inevitably get reissued on compilations shortly after the 7″ goes out of print; if the songs aren't particularly good, the 7″ becomes one of those dollar-bin specials. At a certain point, the only real value in a 7″ is in having the thing itself—since most of them are available digitally these days—and in being able to impress one's friends with it. These records are a form of financial and physical self-burdening—as anyone who's moved as often as I have can attest.

▸

Twelve pages into the Terminal Boredom thread chronicling the Blank Dogs pre-order debacle, Mike of Blank Dogs chimed in:

> I'm still in "benefit of the doubt" territory and hope the records arrive before tour. Despite what others have said, [WOLFGUTSSS]'s been fine in emails and the 1st batch should be in transit here....
>
> Again, sorry about this record in particular; from now on there will be a "no pre-order" clause if I do a record with a smaller label again.

Still, calling this situation a debacle on page twelve, after the thread has—as of December 16, 2010, exactly two years after it began—grown to 108 pages, and been viewed nearly 89,000 times, may have been premature: like the recession, the commentary on this one record has endured longer than some experts predicted, even after it was declared over. We might now read this thread as a registry of all the stages of grief at our collective foolishness with our money, and our subsequent attempts to laugh off that foolishness. A seven-dollar 7″ is just one among innumerable useless things we bought amid the seemingly unending growth of the 1990s and 2000s.

"At this point everyone should just consider [it] a poor investment and get on with their lives, we're not going to see them."

"First I lose money on the Stanford Bank scam and now this?" "Does this record even exist?" "Man does anything really 'exist,' it's all a dream b'rah." Someone Photoshopped an image of a fake LP sleeve titled *Pre-orders Across the Internet: 18 Essential Punk Rock Scams* (riffing on an actual series of compilation LPs—*Bloodstains Across the UK: 16 Essential Punk Rock Blasts*, *Bloodstains Across Texas: 18 Essential Punk Rock Blasts*, and countless others), and it was collectively decided that it should become an actual LP. WOLFGUTSSS disappeared from the thread for almost four months and did not, apparently, answer e-mails; his silence helped inflame a lynch mob mentality developing among posters to the thread—not unlike that around Madoff after his release on bond and house arrest. Finally, Mike said that he would release the record, under new title and artwork, on his own label, Captured Tracks, and sell it at wholesale price, as a way of trying to accommodate the fans and would-be profiteers who'd pre-ordered it from WOLFGUTSSS: "If I could make it free, I would," he wrote.

While much of the outrage expressed on Terminal Boredom stemmed from record freaks feeling swindled out of cash, some part of it came from the apparent betrayal by someone those same freaks felt was part of a community they'd all built—a community whose members were supposed to be treated fairly, according to its own unspoken codes. Madoff and his advisors also enlisted their own communities—especially southern Florida Jewish communities—whose members trusted him to deliver the returns an investment with Madoff promised. Those whom Madoff defrauded "know him socially, through the Palm Beach Country Club or the Glen Oaks Country Club," a lawyer representing some of these victims told the Associated Press in December 2008. "They played golf with him." That same month, the *New York Times* noted the anguish of "Jews all over the country": "Here is a Jew accused of cheating Jewish organizations trying to help other Jews, they say, and of betraying the trust of Jews and violating the basic tenets of Jewish law. A Jew, they say, who seemed to exemplify the worst anti-Semitic stereotypes of the thieving Jewish banker." And Laurence Leamer, Palm Beach resident and author of *Madness Under the Royal Palms*—in which, according to *Publisher's Weekly*, he "reveals the secrets of the Palm Beach elite who reside behind the high walls and manicured hedges of this exclusive enclave"—told the *Times* that "anyone can get robbed. Madoff's scam was so much worse because he was one of their own."

▸

When I started collecting records, in the 1980s, a 7″ single cost about $2.50, maybe more if it was an import. From the early 1990s and through the dot-com bubble and bust, 7″s regained currency as a medium for independent bands and labels—occupying some middle ground between the single as a promotional loss leader and its current status as quasi-artifact—and the pricing reflected it: most of these records cost $3 or $4; again, a dollar or two more for imports, especially when the dollar was weak. By about 2000, a price of $5 seemed to be the benchmark; during the just-concluded decade, 7″ prices remained flat, though more recently labels have taken advantage of vinyl's continuing renaissance, arbitrarily limited editions, and the speed and fury of Internet hype, and have begun charging $8, $10, or more for a single. Still, if we accept $6 as average for a 7″ record today, then prices have climbed about 140 percent since the 1980s. According to United States Census data, the average sale price of a new house in 1985 was $100,800; in 2010—the most recent year for which data is available, and even taking into account the slump in housing prices—that figure was $272,900, for an increase of about 170 percent.

These rates of increase seem relatively comparable, though the jump in record prices—given that the cost remains, twenty-five years later, in single digits—*feels* smaller. But are vinyl records and houses, as commodities, pursuing opposing trajectories? The 45 RPM 7″ record, introduced to the public by RCA Victor in 1949, was first touted as a technological triumph (better-sounding than a 33 ⅓ RPM disc), but because of its short playing time and consumers' reluctance to abandon the convenience of LPs, quickly became something of a disposable, intended for pop singles, and, as the November 14, 1949, issue of the *RCA Distributor's Record Bulletin* noted, the teenage market:

> And—from coast to coast—teen-agers are lining up for bargain player attachments. The whole thing's on key with their allowances—neat little records they can slip in their pockets, with a first-class band playing their favorite hit—for 49 cents.... They go for...the lowest priced at the new speed, they go for the little disc that fits on the shelf beside their paper-backed novels,

> is unbreakable, and has quality of tone that can't be matched. Sell 'em, sell 'em "45."

In the popular imagination, the 7″ single is iconic for being stacked on record-changers at sleepovers or being plucked from carousels by the whirring machinery inside jukeboxes. ("The 45 rpm record once provided the basis for something like a religion," Geoffrey O'Brien remarks in *Sonata for Jukebox.*) The value was promotional; sleeves were often generic, company-issued. Now invisible to mass culture, 7″ records have evolved into significant documents of various musical subcultures, and their production reflects this status.

Records once accumulated value because the passage of time proved how popular or musically important a given record was, and either because few copies were originally produced or few people got rid of their copies, thus making originals hard to find. Today, records accumulate value because calculated scarcity manufactures high demand. Houses were once regarded not as investments but simply as domiciles, structures that required constant vigilance and upkeep; before the 2008 recession, artificially low interest rates, loose lending practices, the repackaging and trading of mortgage-backed securities, and government-fueled anxiety about safety and security combined to change the referent of "investment property" from a four-family unit in a poor urban neighborhood to a suburban raised ranch a buyer never intended to inhabit.

The custom-designed home, built by experienced craftspeople using quality materials and construction techniques, has for decades been an anomaly among houses fabricated from whatever shoddy, inexpensive, and readily available industrial products—asbestos, plywood, drywall, vinyl siding, T-111, PVC pipes, asphalt shingles—were not yet deemed toxic by consumers or regulatory agencies. In his book *The Geography of Nowhere*, James Howard Kunstler describes the innovation of "balloon frame" wooden house construction—which is how my former house was built, c. 1930:

> A house could be whacked together out of two-by-four inch "studs" nailed at sixteen-inch intervals. A couple of "framers" could do what used to take a dozen carpenters under skilled supervision in the old post-and-beam days.... [An] enduring legacy of the balloon frame was that it transformed the craft of house building into an industry. In so doing it turned houses into commodities, things made above all to be sold at a profit, so that those who ended up living in them were not the same ones who built them, meaning that they were houses built without affection—merely products whacked together for a mass market. These became the first speculative subdivisions of identical houses, built for a growing industrial middle class.

By skimping on materials and cutting corners during construction, a homebuilder can easily increase profit margin. One source of real bitterness among the vinyl fetishists on Terminal Boredom was that

WOLFGUTSSS's seven-dollar records had no printed labels and only photocopied sleeves.

▸

I haven't listened to that Wavves song in years, and even then heard it only via iTunes; those two grip-taped 7″s are filed somewhere among too many other 7″s. Hua arrived at my house one night with a copy of the first Wavves LP for me shortly after I gave him the 7″, but I'm not sure I've ever played it. Bernie Madoff, as everyone knows, was sentenced to 150 years in a medium-security federal prison in Butner, North Carolina. Madoff's son, Mark Madoff, hanged himself on the second anniversary of his father's arrest; days later, Barbara Picower, widow of Madoff insider Jeffrey Picower, created a $7.2 billion trust for victims of Madoff's investment scams: "We will be returning every penny received from almost 35 years of investing with Bernard Madoff," Picower said. "I believe the Madoff Ponzi scheme was deplorable and I am deeply saddened by the tragic impact it continues to have on the lives of its victims." And in *Rolling Stone*, writer Matt Taibi claimed, in an article on the foreclosure crisis, that "the great American mortgage bubble of the 2000s [is] perhaps the most complex Ponzi scheme in human history."

On Terminal Boredom, in true Google-vengeance fashion, WOLFGUTSSS was outed as Toby Francis, his father discovered to be ZZ Top's live sound engineer, his telephone number and home address posted and hyperlinked, and many threats made;

one poster said he'd heard that WOLFGUTSSS did nothing with his ill-gotten gains but eat Subway sandwiches every day (Madoff's infamous collection of Rolex, Cartier, and Patek Phillippe watches was sold at auction, along with his golf clubs and yachts); another, that he'd been beaten up outside a show his band played ("Madoff was treated for a broken nose, fractured ribs and cuts to his head and face" after being assaulted by a fellow inmate, according to the *Wall Street Journal*); still another, that he'd asked for help breaking into a high school to steal P.A. equipment. Others linked to a different web forum where, in December 2010—as I wrote this essay—Francis purportedly scammed other people by promising to sell various expensive and sought-after vintage Fender and Gretsch guitars, collected hundreds of dollars while sending empty envelopes for tracking confirmation, and, when he was finally flushed from Internet anonymity, bounced the refund check he sent to PayPal.

Some posters to Terminal Boredom received their records from WOLFGUTSSS during 2009; others apparently never did. Mike Sniper released the Blank Dogs 7″; now out of print, it's still easily found for under ten bucks. Copies are also, allegedly, still available at the 2008 price via WOLFGUTSSS's label, Down in the Ground...

Since Sarah and I sold our house, we've moved into another rental in another state, and have begun looking for a new house we might purchase, but without any of our former ardor for unpainted oak trim and crown moldings, brick fireplaces and pocket doors, remodeled kitchens and mature trees; I'm not sure how she sees the loss of money we spent on our former house, since talking about it usually causes us more grief than seems worthwhile or healthy, but, when I look back at that house, I sometimes imagine it as stacks of vinyl records I could've purchased.

I used to think—as much as I contemplated such things at all—of the ever-increasing bulk of my vinyl collection as a kind of nest egg, or long-term savings plan: something I could sell, probably at a profit, if circumstance ever forced me to. I imagine that all the homeowners who, in the past decade, refinanced their houses and cashed out the equity to fund other purchases saw their houses similarly. These were assets we developed and tended over years. By using my credit card to buy doubles of new 7″s, I participated in short-term speculation: higher potential gain, higher risk of complete loss. In so doing, we collectors viewed records purely for their exchange values, only as abstract vehicles by which we might profit. Whether we liked a record by Blank Dogs or Wavves didn't matter, as long as someone else out there liked it—or maybe thought they could make a buck off *our* prices. But my record collection is unlikely ever to be an instrument for wealth-building—indeed, my addiction to music has cost me tens of thousands—and, given my sorry history of wheeling-and-dealing as a seller, I no longer expect it to be. That said, if you pulled any record from the racks in my living room, I could recall something about it, and memory, at least, offers its own kind of wealth.

THE VINYL COMMUNITY

Sarah has, quite possibly, never displayed the depth of her commitment to me as clearly as on a frigid February morning early in our marriage: that Saturday, she woke in the 6:00 A.M. darkness to accompany me to the Rhode Island Rock 'n' Roll Collector's Convention. Squinting against low sun, we drove along the nearly deserted highway to North Providence, following directions I'd scrawled on a slip of paper the night before to a white cinderblock Knights of Columbus Lodge, its parking lot edged with frozen piles of gritty week-old snow and filled already with dozens of cars.

For the several years we lived in Ithaca, New York, I'd dragged Sarah at an even earlier hour to stand in line for that town's famous Friends of the Library Book Sale—for which people routinely line up two days in advance, pitching tents along the sidewalk half a block from busy Route 13 and disregarding the vagaries of

Upstate October weather in the hopes of being among the first two hundred let into the huge warehouse filled with a year's worth of donated books. We always managed to arrive in time to make that cut: those who don't must wait for someone to come out of the building, due to the fire code's maximum occupancy, and in bibliophilic Ithaca—where among the discarded books are often rare first editions, or scholarly texts with some Cornell luminary's marginalia—this is a long wait.

But on those morning trips to sift someone else's junk, Sarah had a personal interest in the sifting, and often came away with armfuls of books. She's indulged my obsession for record-hunting many times during our marriage, either by seeking solace in a nearby shoe store or boutique while I spend hours in some basement, or by following me inside the shop for some patient but aimless browsing, or even, sometimes, by waiting in the car or a café while I binge on rows of LPs—just one more row, I think, just one more row and I'll go find her. (One of her colleagues, himself a record collector, upon finding out that I sometimes dragged her along to record shops, exclaimed, "That's spousal abuse! You can get help for that, you know!") This time, however, even I had reservations: I'd previously been to only one other record fair, where most of the records were overpriced and uninteresting, and had decided to try this one more as an excuse to get out of the house during a bitterly cold winter than with the hopes of filling any of the holes in my collection. For years, I considered the record fair an excuse for people too lazy to do real crate-digging to pay stiff finder's fees for albums someone else has plucked from yard sales and Salvation Army stores. I withdrew only $50 from an

ATM—let's be honest: a pittance, given the circumstances—and even this enforced spending limit turned out to be optimistic.

As I steered the car into a parking space, I doubted that Sarah would find much to occupy her inside, and noted the same nagging guilt I feel when we're in a record store and she says, "I'll just go wait outside," or when, at home, I pause to notice the shelves of records that require an entire wall; the LPs leaning, dozens deep, against the couch and the coffee table; the CDs stacked unevenly on the floor beside the vacuum record-cleaning machine and bottles of cleaning solution. My archive overflows our living room—which we recently rearranged, in part, to place my stereo's speakers more optimally. Sarah's passion for music differs from mine mostly in that she feels much less need to own it: when we met, her music collection consisted of about six dozen CDs and a shoebox of old cassettes, including those mixtapes with which I wooed her. At times she'll ask me a question or two about something I'm listening to, and I'll believe that I've roused some interest, but when I ask her what I should put on the stereo while we cook dinner, she usually replies, "I don't know—whatever you want." On a long car trip, Sarah once asked me about Beat Happening, whose first CD I was playing as we drove, and my extemporaneous dissertation about that band, K Records (the band's homegrown label), and their shared importance to rock music—"Kurt Cobain had a K Records tattoo," I probably pointed out—may have required several dozen miles of the New York State Thruway, as well as whatever was left of Sarah's patience and curiosity.

More recently, I put the Clash's first album (UK pressing, of course) on the turntable, and a moment later Sarah walked into the room, singing along with Joe Strummer on "Career Opportunities."

"Did you like the Clash back in high school?" I asked, surprised that she knew the words.

She paused to consider. "Yeah," she said, "but mostly I liked the boys who liked the Clash."

At the Knights of Columbus Lodge's smudged plate-glass door, a man clenching a cigarette in his teeth collected our $2 admittance fees and stamped our hands. Inside the hall—dark and smoky after the glare of early sun on snow—dealers stood behind folding tables on which they'd set cardboard boxes of LPs. More such boxes were shoved underneath the tables. A few dealers had hung framed posters or old concert bills behind them in a vague gesture toward giving the musty interior a rock-and-roll vibe, but the prevailing mood was suggested by the faux wood paneling, the dropped ceiling, the haze of smoke.

Like the displayed LPs themselves—out-of-date, worn, their jackets frayed, castoffs rescued from attics and basements and yard sales: not overpriced gems, as it turned out, but mostly commonplace junk—the gathering seemed both eccentric and behind the times. At thirty-two, I was one of the younger attendees. I heard little conversation; almost everyone in the room had bowed his head to flip through the albums. I've used the male pronoun here intentionally.

"Am I the only woman here?" Sarah whispered to me.

One man wore a colorful vintage Hawaiian shirt and jaunty tweed cap ("Are you a fan of Astrud Gilberto?" he inquired, when I paused over *The Shadow of Your Smile* at his booth); a few were outfitted in studded and safety-pinned leather jackets; some, in khakis and wool cardigans, evoked off-duty librarians or schoolteachers; some wore muddy workboots, faded Carhartt coats, and baseball caps pulled low; some wore—unironically—hockey haircuts and heavy metal concert T-shirts printed with tour dates from 1987; others appeared to be grandfathers, their watery eyes magnified behind thick glasses. Several carried tiny portable record players—I can't use the word turntables—beige or avocado relics of the 1970s: these men squatted on the floor and, as if they were at a seventh-grade sleepover, played 45s from which they'd just shucked the dealer's protective polyethylene sleeves. The expressions on their faces, as they held the plastic monaural speakers to their ears, suggested neither transport nor the excitement of discovery so much as a fierce, calculating focus. Some of the men might have been taking their first ventures outside in weeks. Like the members of twelve-step meetings one sometimes sees assembled for a cigarette break outside a church's back door, the common denominator among these people—among us—was, except for context, invisible.

As reluctant as I was to admit it, I felt perfectly at home in this crowd, though I was made to feel immediately like an interloper: Sarah and I walked to one of the nearest tables, and even before I could begin to dig through this dealer's boxes, he smiled at us. He wore a coonskin cap over unwashed, untrimmed hair, and his glasses reflected the overhead fluorescent light. "Is this your first show?" he asked. "I don't remember seeing you before." Were the people who came to these conventions so few, I wondered, so consistent in their habits?

Bringing your wife to a record fair is both a blessing and an indignity, like having your mom drop you off at school on a rainy morning just as a group of your drenched classmates walks past. In some ways, Sarah's presence instantly marked me—and certainly her—as other, even to those dealers who do not keep attendance records. I attempted a casual posture by which I meant to indicate that yes, I was married, and Sarah and I had better things to do than pick through salvaged LPs all morning—that this was simply the first stop in our busy Saturday schedule, that we were not really part of this gathering—though my attendance here belied that attitude, and though this posture transformed into the familiar crate-digger's hunched slouch as soon as I saw the records. Still, I refused to elbow my way in at the crowded tables, and strolled the aisles rather than methodically, obsessively flicking through every record in the hall.

Sarah discovered almost immediately a pristine mono copy of Donovan's *Sunshine Superman* LP, priced at $3, which I bought (nothing special, but a nice addition to the library); she'd pulled it from one of the bins on the floor, through which she'd rooted with abandon. "What else should I look for?" she, flushed and smiling, wanted to know.

But a few tables later—after we'd split up for a bit—we were searching side-by-side boxes when she pulled out a copy of Cyndi Lauper's *She's So Unusual* LP and held it toward me. "What about this?" she asked.

By this point, among the show's attendees I could count perhaps two more women, one of whom stood on Sarah's other side. I blushed. Cyndi Lauper? This from the woman to whom I'd pledged my life? Even as the example of cheesy 1980s nostalgia she intended, this LP was indefensible. I shook my head in what I hoped was a dismissive way—in case any of the record dealers might be looking—and continued finger-flipping the albums, trying not to sneeze with each puff of dust. But the woman next to Sarah suddenly spoke.

"Oh, I love Cyndi Lauper," she offered. "I went to see her in concert with Cher."

In half a lifetime of record shopping, I've come to see such unsolicited conversational gambits as an inevitability—one record store owner once proclaimed, when I bought John Phillips's solo album, "John Phillips! John the Wolf King! Ah, to have had Michelle Phillips when she was young!" It often seems that simply stepping into the dim confines of a used record store invites the proprietor to regale you with his—again, with a few happy exceptions, I'm using the pronoun deliberately—theories on any topic from music to politics to sex, from shoplifters to social media to fashion. Sometimes record shopping feels like waiting at the bus stop, listening to the man standing beside you and hoping that the No. 6 arrives quickly.

Guessing where this conversation was headed, I patted Sarah on the hand and left for another dealer's table. As I walked away, I heard the woman saying something about how good Cyndi Lauper still looks, "probably because of her positive attitude."

A few minutes later, examining an overpriced Chi-Lites LP that I decided not to buy, I tried to tune out another conversation next to me. A man dressed in baggy corduroys, a sweater I imagined his mother had given him on some long-past Christmas, and duct-taped running shoes—he looked like the former editor of his high school newspaper, who ten years later was now publishing, from his parents' attic, a Xeroxed fanzine—stood talking to a dealer and jotting notes in a steno pad, when I quite clearly heard the dealer say, "That's not my area of expertise. You should talk to Big Al or Peck." At this point, I flipped open my mental steno pad, trying to determine what sort of information the questioner wanted, who Big Al and Peck were, and what their area of expertise might be, while continuing to leaf through the LPs, if less attentively. The conversation appeared at first to concern local musicians who'd found national success, and I was tempted to name a few Rhode Island musicians whom these two hadn't mentioned, but it quickly became clear that the part of the conversation I'd ignored was the key to understanding it, and I moved on.

Perhaps overlong association with me has led Sarah to believe that music is best purchased excessively and often, and in multiple formats as needed: when I next saw her, she had bought the LP *Blue* by Joni Mitchell, even though she already owned the CD. To my raised eyebrows Sarah replied, "You always say vinyl sounds better than digital." (At a recent dinner party, I turned from my conversation to hear her arguing this same opinion at the other end of the table, though I'm unsure if the conviction was her own or if she was simply defending her crackpot husband.) She stood at my elbow for a moment before saying she wanted to go outside for some air. I twisted my wrist from my sleeve to look at my watch, calculating how much patience she had left.

At the next dealer's table, another young man and I worked our way through the LPs: as if he were one of my old running partners on the high school track team, we assumed a silent and steady rhythm that neither of us seemed willing to break—concentrating on our every physical movement, yet always monitoring each other in our peripheral vision; secretly sizing each other up, the way my old training partners and I kept precise mental account of the hierarchy of our race times. And, just as on an eight- or ten-mile training run, I began to note the smallest details. Crammed into Ernest & Julio Gallo wine boxes, the LPs moved stiffly; the remnants of brittle shrinkwrap still stuck to some of them rustled. My fingertips felt dry and dirty. I smelled mildew. My shoulders ached from stooping over the tables, trying to reach the back of a box. Somewhere in the near-silent hall, a gruff voice burst into laughter.

I've often considered crate-digging a competitive pursuit, with its own tacit code of conduct—a code outwardly governed by issues of propriety, nuance, and status, yet covertly cutthroat. If you believe, as I sometimes do, that should you pass on buying a certain LP now, you may never have the opportunity again, then every other shopper is a potential competitor. Call me paranoid, but every time I find some rare piece of vinyl I've been hunting for years, it seems the only extant copy: I feel "a version," as Greil Marcus writes in *Lipstick Traces,* "of what Ulrike Meinhof called Konsumterror—the terrorism of consumption, the fear of not being able to get what is on the market, the agony of being last in line, or of lacking the money to join the line: to be a part of social life." But such anxieties drive nearly every record collector I've met. In a crowded record store, I flip through the bins as quickly as possible, not only to increase my viewing rate, or to ensure that no one sees me studying the sleeve of some musical guilty pleasure, but also to signal my sagacity and experience with used LPs—i.e., I've already seen so many of these stupid records in other stores that now I recognize them with the merest glance, and am frustrated that here, again, they impede my progress toward uncovering something I want. I pull anything remotely of interest, even if I don't think I'll buy it, and carry it around with me as long as I stay in the store: someone else might snatch it up, otherwise. I do not subscribe to the school that dictates one should hide such interesting-but-not-immediately-purchased records in the back of innocuous sections such as "Folk Singers: Male" or "Soundtracks: W–Z" so that no one else will find them, including the store's clerks, though I do understand this impulse.

The young man stayed ahead of me, but when I got to the last box at that table—nothing worth competing over here—he moved to my other side and began hunting through some of the LPs he'd already seen. Then he turned to the dealer: "Is there still a Tom Petty twelve-inch in here? Did somebody buy it?" I guessed he'd been at this table earlier, hadn't bought the record then, and had returned for it now.

"Don't know," the dealer said. "I don't remember selling any Tom Petty."

"I think it's in this box," I said, pointing. The man had simply overlooked the record; I'd flicked past it moments ago. I'd spoken even before deciding to do so. Perhaps I should have added something along the lines of "Man, Tom Petty, how stoned is that dude?" or "All his albums since *Hard Promises* have sucked." But irony failed me; I'm too well-acquainted with the momentary desperation this guy was feeling to have wanted to tease him.

I tucked the few LPs I'd bought under my arm, gave the room a parting glance, and, blinking, walked out into the morning. Two men passed me on their way inside. Sarah stood on the walkway to the parking lot.

"They just asked if I was a British girl," she said.

"What?"

"Those two guys just asked me if I was a British girl. Maybe because of my eyeliner."

"Your eyeliner?" Her eyes looked normal to me. "Were they trying to pick you up?"

"No, I think they thought I was a musician, maybe."

We got into the car and headed down the road in search of a diner for breakfast. About a mile or two from the Knights of Columbus hall I spotted, in a small strip mall, a fluorescent piece of posterboard on which someone had scrawled "GOING OUT OF BUSINESS! ALL VINYL & CD'S 20% OFF!!"

"Just for a minute?" I begged, turning into the strip mall's parking lot before Sarah could answer.

▸

A few weeks later, driving home from work, I noticed—it's like a bird-watcher's skill, I guess—a hand-painted sandwich-board sign standing in front of a Congregational church at a rural crossroads in Tiverton, Rhode Island. It read, simply,

Record Sale
33–45–78
Saturday 10–2

With another bribe of brunch to lure her, I brought Sarah to join me for this service. (The crossroads where the church stands is named Bliss Corners—a good omen, I hoped, for what I would find in the record crates.) We filed along a wooden wheelchair ramp and into the church basement among a crowd attired, apparently a day early, for the ceremony upstairs: they wore windbreakers over soft cardigan sweaters, polyester slacks, eyeglasses on thin chains, and hairdos from the 1950s. Not a one of them looked to be on the hunt for garage rock, post-punk, or soul 45s, or obscure psychedelic LPs. We were, by twenty to forty years, the youngest in this congregation.

Except for the setting, the formularies here were essentially the same as in our observance in North Providence: I paid a dollar for each of us to a pair of white-haired women guarding a petty cash lockbox and we entered a long, low-ceilinged room next to the church kitchen. Again, LPs slumped in mildewed boxes atop folding tables, and people milled about, though many of these folks appeared more interested in their styrofoam cups of coffee and the big-band oldies playing from a radio in the corner than the vinyl. I saw no dealers, no leather jackets, no one whose name might be Big Al or Peck, and assumed the records were parish donations that the pastor had decided, finally, to clear out of some closet to make room for the Christmas pageant costumes. I leaned over a table and began to work through a box. All of the LPs were shabby and worthless, the sort I'd expect to find at thrift stores: Herb Alpert & the Tijuana Brass, Connie Francis, Percy Faith, Johnny Mathis, Barry Manilow, the Baja Marimba Band, Mantovani, Harry Belafonte, André Kostelanetz, the soundtracks to *The Sound of Music* and *The King and I*. On the sleeves of most of them, someone named Lloyd had inked his name in big block letters. His presence, mysterious and diffuse (since his taste in music did not help to differentiate him from anyone else buying LPs in the 1950s and '60s), inhabited the room, and I wondered if he had recently died and now his estate occupied the boxes before me. The event took on some of the feel of a combined open-casket funeral and its subsequent reception.

As I flipped, I felt another nearby presence; this one occupied the space just behind my right shoulder, like someone on the subway spying on my smartphone screen—or, maybe, like my conscience. I turned to see a woman in a Western-style shirt with faux mother-of-pearl snaps. She wore a heavy perfume with the fragrance of some tropical flower. Old enough to be my grandmother, she winked at me. "It's easy for me if I just watch while you flip," she confessed.

I saw that her fingernails were long and painted. "Okay," I said, turning back to the albums and moving from one to the next far more slowly than usual. "Anything you're hoping to find?"

"Not really," she said. "I'm just looking."

Together we studied, in a reverent silence, the sleeves of Lloyd's LPs. There was absolutely nothing for me here, I realized immediately, but I felt some not unwelcome obligation to continue guiding my companion through the box at a sacramental pace. The

LPs themselves possessed the enduring familiarity of ritual: André Previn. Dionne Warwick. The 101 Strings Orchestra. I may as well have been turning the well-worn onionskin pages of a hymnal. "Hmm," the woman said at the sight of one LP, but, when I turned to see if she wanted me to pull it for her, she added, "You can keep going." For a moment, crate-digging suggested—in its tedium and monotony, its apparent endlessness—a form of devotion or penance: perhaps murmuring the rosary to absolve some venial sin. We lingered over the last LP a moment, and then, since there was another browser on either side of me, I turned around. Except for a few weddings and this record sale, over three decades have passed since I have gone to any church, but now I felt something akin to the moment, in the occasional Catholic masses I attended as a child, when I would turn to my neighboring parishioners, extend my hand, and shyly whisper "Peace be with you" as they did the same to me.

"Well, thank you," the old woman said. "Good luck."

Sarah was amusing herself looking at the cheesecake photos on old records—the buxom 1950s models posed atop pianos or in leis and bikinis on sunset beaches—and that seemed as good a way as any to buy a few. I chose *Hawaiian Percussion in Ping-Pong Stereo,* mostly because of its op-art sleeve, and the *All in the Family* LP with Archie and Edith on the sleeve, paying another dollar apiece, and then ducked my head at the low lintel and followed Sarah out into the sunshine. Four dollars, I calculated, was about what each member of the laity might drop in the collection basket passed down the pew tomorrow.

▸

As much as I enjoy the process of buying LPs—especially used LPs in a well-curated store, where the stock has the potential to surprise me—I've long thought that the real pleasure in hunting for vinyl comes in the moment when I carry my prizes home, unwrap them, and—in the seclusion of my living room, perhaps with the added layer of insulation my headphones afford—set them on my turntable and drop the stylus. For years, music has been my private pursuit, something not everyone else understands, something I don't always want to—or need to—share. As with my toys when I was younger, I've often sought some controllable combination of the joy of seeing another person appreciate my records, and the joy of appreciating them alone myself; freed from any admonitions to "play nice," I've allowed myself to be as selfish a listener as I've wished, to chase the sublime through the medium of a stamped vinyl platter.

But music, of course, is foremost an act of communication, and most of the music I treasure—no matter that it was first recorded in someone's bedroom or basement—arises from small, self-defined, intersecting communities; to overlook this aspect of my taste seems the truest denial of the pleasures of record-collecting and of listening. If I try to act as sole architect of my experience, I am reminded of the towns I used to construct on the kitchen floor, and the famous family photos of my younger twin sisters, like Godzilla and Mothra, crawling through my careful arrangements of wooden blocks or Legos and laying waste to my creations. In these photos, the countenance on my four-year-old face is, as I reach to repair my tumbled bridges and towers, some immeasurable combination of frustration and delight.

Though we who collect records are commodity fetishists and idolaters (forgoing music's dialogic communion between artist and audience, at times, in our selfish zeal to commune instead with an original pressing, a limited-edition fanclub release, or a recalled sleeve), at least the record fair allows us some sense of community—as do, for their own members, the fraternal society hall and church in which these two record fairs were held. The *Oxford English Dictionary*'s definitions for "community" include "members of a civil community, who have certain circumstances of nativity, religion, or pursuit, common to them," and "social intercourse; fellowship, communion," as well as "joint or common ownership." Of course, all record freaks want to practice private rather than joint ownership, but collectively we possess an abiding respect less for the popular than for the shunned and the undervalued; a passion for redemption (I treat my recent rescues with a two-step process of Record Research Lab's "Super Deep Cleaner" and "Super Vinyl Wash"); and a hand, however small, in the writing, rewriting, and declaiming of various musicological gospels. In these custodies, despite our often mutually exclusive tastes, we can find fellowship as we pursue our purchases—a fact that, until recently, I did not fathom.

The dealer in North Providence who asked if I was attending my first show probably wanted only to get a handle on what I was hunting so that he could help me find it—and, along the way, brag about his own collection and inquire about mine. The old woman in Tiverton wanted to protect her manicure, yes—but also, I like to think, wanted someone to notice these songs and artists that formed the soundtrack to the dances and car rides of her younger years, rather than to watch me negate both music and memory with impatient flicks of my fingers as I mindlessly chased my own narrow nostalgia.

But there are practical considerations in such fellowship as well. Among today's e-mail messages has come a note from Sarah's record-collecting colleague—who, a month or two back, introduced me to a semi-secret used LP shop, and has since hinted about others that are larger, better, and also little-known. "Record run on Wed.?" he asks.